Abstracts of Loudoun County Virginia

Register of Free Negroes

1844–1861

Patricia B. Duncan

HERITAGE BOOKS
2010

HERITAGE BOOKS
AN IMPRINT OF HERITAGE BOOKS, INC.

Books, CDs, and more—Worldwide

For our listing of thousands of titles see our website
at
www.HeritageBooks.com

Published 2010 by
HERITAGE BOOKS, INC.
Publishing Division
100 Railroad Ave. #104
Westminster, Maryland 21157

Copyright © 2000 Patricia B. Duncan

All rights reserved. No part of this book may be reproduced or transmitted in any form or by any means, electronic or mechanical, including photocopying, recording or by any information storage and retrieval system without written permission from the author, except for the inclusion of brief quotations in a review.

International Standard Book Numbers
Paperbound: 978-1-58549-616-7
Clothbound: 978-0-7884-8522-0

Introduction

The following are abstracts from the Loudoun County, Virginia Register of Free Negroes, 1844-1861. Loudoun County Microfilm No. 135, available through Interlibrary Loan from The Library of Virginia, 800 East Broad Street, Richmond, VA 23219-1905, was used for this project.

The entries in this register were recorded in compliance with Virginia Laws, which were passed 10 December, 1793.

Chapter 22 – An Act for regulating the police of towns in this commonwealth, and to restrain the practice of negroes going at large.
   1. Whereas great inconveniences have arisen in many, if not all the towns within this commonwealth, from the practice of hiring negroes and mulattoes, who pretend to be free, but are in fact slaves; for remedy whereof,
   2. Be it enacted by the general assembly, that from and after the passing of this act, every free negro or mulatto, who resides in, or is employed to labour within the limits of any city, borough or town, shall be registered and numbered in a book to be kept for that purpose by the clerk of the said city, borough or town, which register shall specify his or her age, name, colour and stature, by whom and in what court the said negro or mulatto was emancipated; or that such negro or mulatto was born free. A copy of the said register, signed by the clerk, and attested by one alderman or town magistrate, shall be annually delivered to the said negro or mulatto, for which copy the clerk shall receive twenty-five cents, to be paid by the person receiving the same.
   3. Any person harbouring or employing any negro or mulatto, who has not a certified copy of the said register, shall forfeit and pay for each offence five dollars to the owner of such negro or mulatto, and if there be no owner, to the informer, to be recovered by warrant before any alderman or magistrate, and shall be moreover liable to an action for damages at the suit of the party grieved.
   4. And be it further enacted, that in case any negro or mulatto, who resides in or is employed to labour, in any city, borough or town, shall neglect to procure such certificate, it shall be lawful for any alderman or magistrate, to commit to jail such negro or mulatto, there to remain till such copy is produced and the jailor's fees paid.
   5. And for the prevention of free negroes and mulattoes going at large in the several counties of this commonwealth, Be it further enacted, that no free negro or mulatto shall be allowed to go at large or hire himself or herself to labour in any county, without having his or her certificate registered in the clerk's office of the county wherein he or she resides, and have a certified copy of the said certificate. For registering and granting such certificate, the clerk shall be allowed twenty-five cents.
   6. Any person employing or harbouring any negro or mulatto, coming within the purview of this act, shall forfeit and pay for each offence five

dollars, to the use of the informer, to be recovered by a warrant before a justice of the peace; and shall be moreover liable to an action for damages at the suit of the party grieve.

7. Every such free negro or mulatto, shall once in every three years, obtain a new certificate, under the same rules and regulations, as are prescribed for obtaining the first.

8. And in case a negro or mulatto, who resides in or is employed to labour in any county, shall neglect to procure such certificate, it shall be lawful for any magistrate in the said county to commit to jail such negro or mulatto, there to remain till such certificate is produced and the jailor's fees paid.

9. This act shall commence and be in force from and after the first day of January next.

Chapter 23 – An Act to prevent the migration of free negroes and mulattoes into this commonwealth.

1. Be it enacted, that it shall not be lawful for any free negro or mulatto to migrate into this commonwealth, and every free negro or mulatto who shall come into this commonwealth, contrary to this act, shall and may be apprehended and carried by any citizen before some justice of the peace of the county where he shall be taken; which justice is hereby authorized to examine, send and removed every such negro or mulatto out of this commonwealth, into that state or island from whence it shall appear he or she last came; and for this purpose, the sheriff or other officer, and other persons, may be such justice be employed within the commonwealth, upon the same terms as are by law directed in the removal of criminals from one county to another. And every free negro or mulatto who shall come or be brought into this commonwealth by water from any country, state or island, may and shall be exported to the place from whence he or she came, or was brought, and the charges attending the same shall be paid by the importer; to be recovered by motion in the name of the commonwealth, upon 10 days previous notice thereof in any court of record.

2. Every master of a vessel, or other person who shall bring into this commonwealth by water or by land, in any vessel, boat, land carriage or otherwise, any free negro or mulatto, shall forfeit and pay for every such person so brought, the penalty of one hundred pounds lawful money; one half to the commonwealth, and the other half to the person who shall inform thereof; to be recovered by action of debt or information in any court of record, and the defendant in every such case shall be ruled to give special bail.

3. This act shall not extend to masters of vessels bringing into this state or any free negro or mulatto employed on board and belonging to such vessel, and who shall therewith depart, nor to any person travelling into this state, having any free negro or mulatto as a servant.

4. And be it further enacted, that in case any slave shall be brought or come into this state from Africa or the West India islands, directly or indirectly, upon information thereof given to any justice of the peace, it shall be his

duty to cause such slave to be apprehended immediately and transported out of this commonwealth, and the expense attending such transportation, shall be paid by the person importing such slave, recoverable in the name of the justice directing such slave to be transported, by warrant before a single magistrate.

   5. This act shall commence and be in force from and after the first day of January next.

Included in these abstracts are the name of the free negro, proof of freedom, description of the individual, date of registration in Loudoun County Court, record number, and the register page.

Be aware that the use of the term "mulatto" refers to the color of the skin and not as reference to a mixed parentage.

Special thanks to the Albuquerque Special Collections Library and The Library of Virginia.

No. 1407

Virginia To wit

I Charles G. Eskridge Clerk of the County Court of Rockbridge do hereby certify that Delia Thompson a free woman of Colour as proved by the Oath of John Poh said woman is about 29 years of age 5 feet 1½ inches high, no scars or particular marks was this day registered in my Office according to law Deed

Given &c 9th 1844

Dec 9th 1844 C. G. Eskridge

Example of Register Entry

Loudoun County, Virginia Register of Free Negroes 1844-1861

Register of Free Negroes 1844-1861

NAME	FURR, Catharine
PROOF	free woman as proved by oath of George HEAD
DESCRIPTION	abt 58y old, black colour, 5'4" tall, scar in the breast by a burn some 6" long across the breast, a scar on top of her head from a burn & a large flesh mole on the left side of her neck just below the hair
DATE	11 Jun 1844
RECORD #	1378
PAGE	1

NAME	FURR, Mary Ann (daughter of Catharine FURR)
PROOF	born free as proved by oath of Susan SHIPMAN
DESCRIPTION	abt 17y old, black colour, 5' ½" tall, small scar in the forehead above the right eye & two other small scars in her forehead
DATE	11 Jun 1844
RECORD #	1379
PAGE	1

NAME	MYERS, Emily Ann
PROOF	free by oath of [___]
DESCRIPTION	abt 18y old, bright mulatto woman
DATE	[Jun 1844]
RECORD #	[___]
PAGE	1

NAME	JACKSON, George (child of Sarah JACKSON)
PROOF	free born as proved by oath of Miriam HOLD
DESCRIPTION	abt 8y old, round scar above the left eye brow caused by a burn & a long scar abt 1" in length below the right eye
DATE	8 Jul 1844
RECORD #	1380
PAGE	2

NAME	JACKSON, Isabella (child of Sarah JACKSON)
PROOF	free born as proved by oath of Miriam HOLD
DESCRIPTION	abt 6y old, large dark flesh mark on the right shoulder
DATE	8 Jul 1844
RECORD #	1380
PAGE	2

Loudoun County, Virginia Register of Free Negroes 1844-1861

NAME	JACKSON, Hester Ann (child of Sarah JACKSON)
PROOF	free born as proved by oath of Miriam HOLD
DESCRIPTION	abt 2y old, no mark
DATE	8 Jul 1844
RECORD #	1380
PAGE	2

NAME	WINTERS, William (son of Sarah WINTERS)
PROOF	free born as proved by oath of Miriam HOLE
DESCRIPTION	abt 6y old, dark mulatto
DATE	8 Jul 1844
RECORD #	1381
PAGE	2

NAME	JACKSON, Henry (child of Mary Ellen JACKSON)
PROOF	free born as proved by oath of Miriam HOLE
DESCRIPTION	abt 5y old, bright mulatto with light straight hair, a small mole on the left side of his neck and another on his right shoulder
DATE	8 Jul 1844
RECORD #	1382
PAGE	2

NAME	JACKSON, Charles William (child of Mary Ellen JACKSON)
PROOF	free born as proved by oath of Miriam HOLE
DESCRIPTION	going on 2y old, mulatto with no marks
DATE	8 Jul 1844
RECORD #	1382
PAGE	2

NAME	DUVAL, Orpha
PROOF	free woman of colour as proved by oath of Duana WATT
DESCRIPTION	abt 37y old, 5' 6 3/8" tall, bright brown colour with a white spot on her forehead & something of the same appearance in her left eye brow
DATE	23 Jul 1844
RECORD #	1383
PAGE	3

NAME	WILLIAMS, Amanda
PROOF	free woman as proved by oath of Duana WATT
DESCRIPTION	abt 31y old, bright brown, 5' 2" tall, quite fleshy, with a scar in forehead, one on left hand just above thumb, several small moles on left arm & above right wrist a scar from a burn
DATE	23 Jul 1844
RECORD #	1384
PAGE	3

Loudoun County, Virginia Register of Free Negroes 1844-1861

NAME	DUVAL, Sarah Elizabeth (child of Orpha DUVAL)
PROOF	free born as proved by oath of Duana WATT
DESCRIPTION	abt 10y old, light complexion, two small scars on the back of the right arm midway between the elbow and wrist, a small black scar in the same location on the left arm, a scar of a white cast abt 1½" long on the left side of the neck, say between the side
DATE	23 Jul 1844
RECORD #	1385
PAGE	3

NAME	DUVAL, Duana Jane (child of Orpha DUVAL)
PROOF	free born as proved by oath of Duana WATT
DESCRIPTION	abt 8y old, light complexion, a small black mole on the wrist of the left hand abt 3" above the upper joint of the thumb, two small scars on the back over the shoulder blade, 2 or 3 small scars on the right arm above the wrist
DATE	23 Jul 1844
RECORD #	1385
PAGE	3

NAME	DUVAL, Melvina (child of Orpha DUVAL)
PROOF	free born as proved by oath of Duana WATT
DESCRIPTION	abt 2y old, light complexion, a small scar just at the burr of the right ear, no other scars or marks visible
DATE	23 Jul 1844
RECORD #	1385
PAGE	3

NAME	WILLIAMS, Francis Ann (daughter of Amanda WILLIAMS)
PROOF	free born as proved by oath of Duana WATT
DESCRIPTION	abt 3y old, light complexion, a large scar on the inside of the left arm caused by a burn, just below the arm pits, a natural mark of an eruptive character on the throat immediately under that chinn
DATE	23 Jul 1844
RECORD #	1386
PAGE	4

NAME	WRIGHT, Betty (formerly Betty GREEN)
PROOF	emancipated by her husband Alfred WRIGHT, a free man, having purchased her from Samuel CLENDENING by bill of sale dated 27 Sep 1837
DESCRIPTION	abt 28y old, light complexion with a scar abt ½" long in the right eye brow, a small scar abt ¼" long at the right ? of the left eye brow, a flesh mark on the side of the face abt 1¼" from the corner of the right eye, the lower extremity of the left ear separated by being torn by a ring, the palm of the left hand almost entirely covered with scar caused by a burn, 4' 11" tall
DATE	23 Jul 1844
RECORD #	[___]
PAGE	4

NAME	BUSH, Alsy Ann
PROOF	free person as proved by oath of Duana WATT
DESCRIPTION	abt 20y old, light brown complexion, has a small black mole on the inside of the left arm immediately on the joint, 5' 7" tall
DATE	25 Jul 1844
RECORD #	1387
PAGE	5

NAME	BUSH, Nelson W.
PROOF	free person as proved by oath of Duana WATT
DESCRIPTION	abt 18y old, light brown complexion, a scar on the right side of the left foot about midway, 5' 6½" tall
DATE	25 Jul 1844
RECORD #	1387
PAGE	5

NAME	BUSH, Amy Eleanor
PROOF	free person as proved by oath of Duana WATT
DESCRIPTION	abt 16y old, light brown complexion, two small round scars on the face immediately under the left eye, no other scar or marks visible, 5' 4¼" tall
DATE	25 Jul 1844
RECORD #	1387
PAGE	5

NAME	BUSH, Duana
PROOF	free person as proved by oath of Duana WATT
DESCRIPTION	abt 14y old, light complexion, a small mole on the front of the neck, no other scars or marks visible, 5' 1" tall
DATE	25 Jul 1844
RECORD #	1387
PAGE	5

NAME	SHAFER, Sally (now calling herself CONTEE)
PROOF	free woman who has heretofore been registered as free & has a certified copy of her r[eg]ister of freedom with the County seal affixed
DESCRIPTION	abt 38y old
DATE	13 Aug 1844
RECORD #	1388
PAGE	6

NAME	CONTEE, Amanda Elizabeth (daughter of Sally SHAFER, now CONTEE)
PROOF	free born as proved by oath of Jonathan WENNER
DESCRIPTION	abt 22y old, bright mulatto, 5' tall, with five small black moles scattered about her neck, no other scar or mark
DATE	13 Aug 1844
RECORD #	1388
PAGE	6

NAME	CONTEE, George (son of Sally SHAFER, now CONTEE)
PROOF	free born as proved by oath of Jonathan WENNER
DESCRIPTION	abt 14y old, dark mulatto has a large scar above his left eye brow, three small scars nearly in the center of his forehead & a small scar on his left thumb
DATE	[13 Aug 1844]
RECORD #	1389
PAGE	6

NAME	CONTEE, Mason (son of Sally SHAFER, now CONTEE)
PROOF	free born as proved by oath of Jonathan WENNER
DESCRIPTION	abt 3y old, darker mulatto than brother George, no scars
DATE	[13 Aug 1844]
RECORD #	1389
PAGE	6

NAME	DAVIS, Thomas
PROOF	free born as proved by oath of Joseph S. HOUGH
DESCRIPTION	abt 21y old, brown colour, 5' 10" tall, a mole on the right cheek, a scar supposed to be caused by Kine? Pox, on the left and a large scar on his right wrist on the inside, a few inches above the hand
DATE	13 Aug 1844
RECORD #	1390
PAGE	7

NAME	McPHERSON, Armistead
PROOF	free born as proved by oath of Joseph S. HOUGH
DESCRIPTION	abt 23y old, brown colour, 5' 6" tall, small scar in the center of the forehead, a larger one over the left eye brow, a scar 2" long above the right thumb, several scars on his left hand and a scar 8 or 10" long on his right leg on the outside & a scar near the knee (a small one)
DATE	13 Aug 1844
RECORD #	1391
PAGE	7

NAME	STEWARD, Maria
PROOF	free born, proved to be the daughter of Bella JACKSON who was a free woman by the affirmation of Usher SKINNER
DESCRIPTION	abt 21y old, 5' 3" tall, scar on left arm about 3" below the elbow & quite a small scar abt 3" above the wrist joint and another on the back of her right hand
DATE	13 Aug 1844
RECORD #	1392
PAGE	7

NAME	WINTERS, John
PROOF	free man as appeared by oath of Michael MORALLEE, stated in a former register in this Court, made on 16 Mar 1836
DESCRIPTION	abt 27y old, light mulatto with dark eyes and eye brows, 4 scars caused by burn on his neck and breast, a scar abt ¾" long on the back of the left hand near thumb, a scar abt 1" long on the inside of the left arm abt 1½" below the joint, 5' 4½" tall
DATE	13 Aug 1844
RECORD #	1393
PAGE	8

NAME	BARNES, Samuel (alias Dyer)
PROOF	free born as proved by oath of James ALEXANDER
DESCRIPTION	abt 24y old, very light mulatto, scar above the thumb rather on the inside of the left hand & another on the forefinger of the same hand crosswise near the upper joint & a small scar on the upper joint of the thumb on the right hand, and a large scar on the heel of the right foot & several small black moles on the face and neck & a deep scar in the forehead just below the edge of the hair, 5' 7 3/8" tall
DATE	13 Aug 1844
RECORD #	1394
PAGE	8

Loudoun County, Virginia Register of Free Negroes 1844-1861

NAME	JACKSON, Thomas Henry (son of Teressa JACKSON a free woman of colour)
PROOF	free born as proved by oath of Miriam HOLE
DESCRIPTION	4y old, dark mulatto
DATE	9 Sep 1844
RECORD #	1395
PAGE	9

NAME	JACKSON, James William (son of Teressa JACKSON a free woman of colour)
PROOF	free born as proved by oath of Miriam HOLE
DESCRIPTION	1y old the 10th of June last, dark mulatto
DATE	9 Sep 1844
RECORD #	1395
PAGE	9

NAME	STAUNTON, Ann
PROOF	free born mulatto woman as proved by oath of Sarah McCORMICK
DESCRIPTION	going on 22y old, 5' 3½" tall, no scars, a large black mole on the right side of her neck & a very small one further back her right shoulder being some lower than the left which is discoverable by close examination
DATE	9 Sep 1844
RECORD #	1396
PAGE	9

NAME	WRIGHT, Maria
PROOF	emancipated by the will of Susan G. DAGG dec'd
DESCRIPTION	abt 40y old, dark complexion, a cluster of small moles immediately under the left eye, two small scars on the right side of the right arm just below the joint, a scar abt 1½" long on the same arm, also below the elbow a scar abt 1" long on the back of the left arm abt 3" below the elbow, also a scar on the right side of the right knee caused by a burn, 5' 1¾" tall
DATE	10 Sep 1844
RECORD #	1397
PAGE	9

NAME	WILLIAMS, Kitty (alias Kitty FIELDS)
PROOF	free woman as proved by oath of Presly SAUNDERS & Thomas W. EDWARDS
DESCRIPTION	abt 45y old, bright mulatto, 5' 2¾" tall, the nail on middle finger of right hand shows that it has been injured, a small scar on right arm & just below the elbow & two spots of a light appearance on the left arm just below the elbow which she says was produced by inoculation, with several specks scattered over her face, her hair pretty straight
DATE	14 Oct 1844
RECORD #	1398
PAGE	10

NAME	McGEE, Meranda (daughter of Sophia McGEE)
PROOF	formerly registered as free by reference to No 495 of May Court 1824 when abt 3y old, proved to be the same by affirmation of Jonah STEER
DESCRIPTION	abt 23y old, 5' 4 3/8" tall, bright mulatto, somewhat freckled with 3 small moles one on the breast, one on right side & on middle finger of right hand on the inside abt the middle something like a wart which she says was produced by a cut
DATE	14 Oct 1844
RECORD #	1399
PAGE	10

NAME	CARTWRIGHT, Zacchariah
PROOF	free man as proved by oath of Newton KEENE
DESCRIPTION	abt 25y old, 6' 2" tall, brown colour, 2 scars on the right wrist, on the inside of the wrist near the hand of the right side, one of them an inch long, the other much smaller and nearest to the hand, no other apparent scars or marks
DATE	11 Nov 1844
RECORD #	1400
PAGE	11

NAME	TAYLOR, Ann
PROOF	emancipated by will of late Margaret FRYE, as proved by the oath of George K. FOX
DESCRIPTION	abt 22y old, 5' 4½" tall, black, 2 scars on her left arm below the elbow on the thick part of the arm, and a scar on the forefinger of the left hand, and 2 scars just below the right eye near each other the upward scar nearly an in[ch] length the other not so long crosswise of the face
DATE	11 Nov 1844
RECORD #	1401
PAGE	11

Loudoun County, Virginia Register of Free Negroes 1844-1861

NAME	BRADY, Peyton
PROOF	free born as proved by the affirmation of John SMITH
DESCRIPTION	abt 21y old the 10th of March next
DATE	12 Nov 1844
RECORD #	1402
PAGE	11

NAME	CARTWRIGHT, Warren
PROOF	emancipated by his father Philip CARTWRIGHT
DESCRIPTION	abt 23y old, dark complexion, 6' 2¾" tall, scar abt 2½" long on the middle of the thick part of the right thigh, no other scars or marks visible
DATE	10 Dec 1844
RECORD #	1403
PAGE	12

NAME	GORDAN, Harry
PROOF	free man as proved by oath of David CARR
DESCRIPTION	abt 46y old, nearly black somewhat gray haired, 5' 7" tall, has lost a toe on the right foot, the one next to the big toe with several large scars on the same leg, also the forefinger on the right hand crooked at the last joint, and the thumb on the left hand scarred and somewhat crooked about the centre, and the little finger on the same hand crooked at the last joint, and a scar nearly 1" long across the nose
DATE	9 Dec 1844
RECORD #	1404
PAGE	12

NAME	JOHNSON, Samuel
PROOF	free man as proved by oath of David CARR
DESCRIPTION	abt 36y old, 6'½" tall, nearly black, a scar in the forehead, a scar on the arm, and a scar on the forefinger of the right hand the middle joint
DATE	9 Dec 1844
RECORD #	1405
PAGE	13

NAME	THOMPSON, James Eskridge
PROOF	free man as proved by oath of John ISH
DESCRIPTION	24y old, 5' 9½" tall, black colour, has a kind of scar or spot on the right side of the nose & a long scar on the left cheek bone
DATE	9 Dec 1844
RECORD #	1406
PAGE	13

NAME	THOMPSON, Delia
PROOF	free woman of black colour as proved by oath of John ISH
DESCRIPTION	abt 29y old, 5' 4½" tall, no scars or particular marks
DATE	9 Dec 1844
RECORD #	1407
PAGE	13

NAME	CARTWRIGHT, Ann Mahala
PROOF	emancipated by her father Philip CARTWRIGHT as appears in Liber 4U folio 123
DESCRIPTION	abt 22y old, 5' 7¼" tall, brown colour, with a crooked scar just above the first joint of the forefinger of the right hand, and above the scar a small mole
DATE	14 Jan 1845
RECORD #	1408
PAGE	14

NAME	CARTWRIGHT, Letitia
PROOF	free woman as will appear by a deed of emancipation from her father Philip CARTWRIGHT recorded Liber 4U folio 123
DESCRIPTION	going on 20y old, black, 5' 9¾" tall, no scars or marks
DATE	14 Jan 1845
RECORD #	1409
PAGE	14

NAME	AMBROSE, Sinah
PROOF	free woman as proved by Charles F. FADELEY who delivered a deed of emancipation
DESCRIPTION	abt 45y old, very dark mulatto, 5" 3" tall, she has a dull or faint scar on the right cheek, a small black mole on the left side of her neck and two scars on the back of her right hand
DATE	14 Jan 1845
RECORD #	1410
PAGE	14

NAME	SELVEY, Martha Ann (daughter of Esther SELVEY)
PROOF	free born as proved by oath of Landon W. WORTHINGTON
DESCRIPTION	abt 28y old, 5' tall, light complexion, a large scar on the inside of the right arm just above the elbow caused by a burn, another scar of the same kind about midway between the wrist and elbow of the same arm, no other scars or marks visible
DATE	13 Mar 1845
RECORD #	1411
PAGE	15

NAME	SELVEY, Francis (child of Esther SELVEY)
PROOF	free born as proved by oath of Landon W. WORTHINGTON
DESCRIPTION	abt 20y old, 4' 11½" tall, dark complexion, a very large scar on back of right arm immediately above the wrist, forefinger of right hand, crooked at end and a small black mole on middle joint of the left forefinger, no other scars or marks visible
DATE	13 Mar 1845
RECORD #	1411
PAGE	15

NAME	SELVEY, Margaret (daughter of Esther SELVEY)
PROOF	free born as proved by oath of Landon W. WORTHINGTON
DESCRIPTION	abt 15y old, 5' 6¼" tall, light complexion, a scar about ½" long just above the right corner of the left eye brow, a small scar on the back of the middle finger of the left hand between the middle & upper joint, no other scars or marks visible
DATE	13 Mar 1845
RECORD #	1411
PAGE	15

NAME	SELVEY, Harriett (daughter of Esther SELVEY)
PROOF	free born as proved by oath of Landon W. WORTHINGTON
DESCRIPTION	abt 11y old, 4' 5" tall, very light complexion, with a small scar on the right arm just below the shoulder, no other distinguishing marks
DATE	13 Mar 1845
RECORD #	1411
PAGE	15

NAME	WHEELER, Anna (daughter of Mary WHEELER)
PROOF	free born as proved by oath of Landon W. WORTHINGTON
DESCRIPTION	abt 11y old, 4' 4" tall, very light complexion, a very small scar above the left corner of the mouth & a small mole near the left nostril, no other scars or marks visible
DATE	13 Mar 1845
RECORD #	1412
PAGE	16

NAME	SELVEY, John (son of Martha SELVEY)
PROOF	free born as proved by oath of Landon W. Worthington
DESCRIPTION	abt 7y old, light complexion with a scar on the right breast in front, about the size of a ten cent piece, caused by a burn, no other distinguishing marks
DATE	13 Mar 1845
RECORD #	1413
PAGE	16

NAME	JOHNSON, George
PROOF	free born, some of his time with John SWART as an apprentice, as proved by John SWART
DESCRIPTION	abt 21y old, very dark brown colour, 5" 9¾" tall, two faint scars on his left hand, one above the middle finger upwards an inch long, the other abt the same length between the forefinger and thumb running somewhat lengthwise with the forefinger, a small scar on the right cheek & one above the right eye brow, also a round scar on the outside of his left leg nearly half way between the foot and knee, and a scar on the back produced by the bite of a dog near the joint of the right shoulder blade
DATE	22 Apr 1845
RECORD #	1414
PAGE	16

NAME	MANDLEY, William (alias for Bill)
PROOF	free born who was bound to Robert BAYLEY
DESCRIPTION	21y old & upwards, 5' 7½" tall, brown colour, a small scar about ½" above the left eye brow & another just behind that running into the wool, about 1½" long, running upwards & a round scar on the breast and one on the middle finger of the right hand near the end & also a scar over the right eye near the hair
DATE	12 May 1845
RECORD #	1415
PAGE	17

NAME	CLAGETT, Fanny
PROOF	emancipated by Wm. CARR
DESCRIPTION	abt 43y old, brown colour, 5' 4½" tall, small scar on right cheek & two long scars on her right arm some 5" or 6" above the hand & on the back of the same hand several small scars
DATE	9 Jun 1845
RECORD #	1416
PAGE	17

NAME	HUGHS, Willis
PROOF	emancipated by William CARR
DESCRIPTION	abt 44y old, 5' 8 1/3" tall, mulatto, scar on the middle finger of the right hand on the inside across the ball between the first and second joint, and also a large round scar on the left leg nearly halfway between the knees and ankle & near shin bone
DATE	9 Jun 1845
RECORD #	1417
PAGE	17

NAME	JACKSON, Isaiah
PROOF	freedom proved by affirmation of Burr PIGGOT
DESCRIPTION	abt 24y old, 5' 8¼" tall, scar just above the wrist of the right arm, another on the left, the one on the right is lengthwise about an inch long, the one of the left crosswise about ¾" long & one on the left arm just below the elbow about the size of half dollar, some small scars on the forehead & a small mole on the left cheek
DATE	10 Jun 1845
RECORD #	1418
PAGE	18

NAME	FIELDS, James
PROOF	free man as proved by oath of John BEAVERS
DESCRIPTION	nearly 29y old, 5' 9½" tall, black colour, two scars in the forehead, a small & a large one & one on the back of his left hand very plain just above his forefinger about 1" long
DATE	10 Jun 1845
RECORD #	1419
PAGE	18

NAME	WILLIAMS, Eliza
PROOF	free woman proved by oath of John BEAVERS
DESCRIPTION	abt 37y old, 5' 1½" tall, very plain scar in the forehead just above the left eye, a small scar on the left arm and two others on the left hand above and near the thumb on the same side
DATE	10 Jun 1845
RECORD #	1420
PAGE	19

NAME	MAHONEY, Mary
PROOF	free born as proved by affirmation of Joshua PUSEY
DESCRIPTION	abt 18y old, 5' 3" tall, light complexion with a scar about ¾" long in the palm of the left hand, a small scar on the inside of the right arm about 3" above the wrist, a small scar on the back of the right forefinger between the upper and middle joint, a small scar on the right thumb near the wrist, no other scars or marks visible of any importance
DATE	15 Jul 1845
RECORD #	1421
PAGE	19

NAME	GANT, William (son of Ann GANT)
PROOF	free born as proved by John SINCLAIR
DESCRIPTION	going on 16y old, brown colour, two scars on the back of his right hand one a round scar and the other about 1" long across the upper joints of his fingers & a scar on the inside of the wrist of the same hand lengthwise about ¾" long & on the inside of his left ear the appearance of a hole
DATE	11 Aug 1845
RECORD #	1422
PAGE	20

NAME	PIERCE, Margaret
PROOF	free born as proved by oath of James THOMPSON
DESCRIPTION	abt 22y old, bright mulatto, scar on her breast about the size of a quarter of a dollar, has a mole in the palm of her left hand & a mole on the little finger of the same hand, also a scar in the right eye brow
DATE	11 Aug 1845
RECORD #	1823 [misnumbered]
PAGE	20

NAME	THORNTON, Cariann
PROOF	registered in office 11 Sep 1835 when 13y old & freedom proved by affirmation of Joshua PUSEY
DESCRIPTION	abt 23y old, 5' 9½" tall, quite black, with a small scar in the forehead, two small scars on the right arm near the elbow, her left hand & wrist deformed by a burn
DATE	12 Aug 1845
RECORD #	1824
PAGE	20

NAME	PAINE, William Jefferson
PROOF	free man proved by affirmation of Seth SMITH
DESCRIPTION	abt 23y old, 4' 9¾" tall, dark complexion, scar on left hand above the upper joint of the forefinger abt 1" long, a scar on the front of the right leg, just below the knee, two scars on the forehead one immediately over each eye about 1" long & a small scar on the front of the chin
DATE	13 Aug 1845
RECORD #	1825
PAGE	21

Loudoun County, Virginia Register of Free Negroes 1844-1861

NAME	CROSS, John
PROOF	free man, or has the reputation as being so, as proved by the affirmation of Seth SMITH
DESCRIPTION	abt 25y old, 4' 9½" tall, bright mulatto, scar about 1" long between the right eye and ear, a small scar on the neck just under the chin, another caused by a burn on the middle of the throat, 2 scars on the cap of the right knee and one or two small ones on the cap of the left knee
DATE	13 Aug 1845
RECORD #	1826
PAGE	21

NAME	PAYNE, James Edward
PROOF	free boy, or has the reputation of being so, as proved by affirmation of Seth SMITH
DESCRIPTION	abt 19y old, 5' 9½" tall, dark complexion, prominent scar on the outer side of the left arm about 2" above the elbow, a small scar on the right side of the right leg opposite the knee, a scar in semi-circle form caused by a cut on the left side of the right foot, a small ___ on the forehead just over the right eye, a scar from a burn on the upper joint of the little finger of the right hand, no other scars or marks worth noticing
DATE	[14 Aug 1845]
RECORD #	1827
PAGE	22

NAME	SHARPER, Samuel
PROOF	free born as proved by oath of Samuel PURSEL Sr.
DESCRIPTION	23y old, light complexion, 5' 6" tall, scar on the front of the left leg just below the knee, a scar about 1" long about midway between the ankle and the knee on the left side of the left leg, a deep scar on the right side of the right leg near knee
DATE	14 Aug 1845
RECORD #	1828
PAGE	22

NAME	SHARPER, Daniel
PROOF	free born as proved by oath of Samuel PURSEL Sr.
DESCRIPTION	abt 21y old, 5' 2½" tall, light complexion, two round scars on the right side of the right leg below the knee, two small scars on the upper joints of the right fingers, a scar about the size of a half dollar on the left side of the left leg a little below the knee, no other marks worthy of notice
DATE	14 Aug 1845
RECORD #	1828
PAGE	22

NAME	DIMMY, Samuel
PROOF	free born as proved by oath of Samuel PURSEL Sr.
DESCRIPTION	22y old, 5' 7½" tall, somewhat light complexion, black mole in the middle of the breast, a small scar on the right side of the upper lip, two small scars on the right wrist just above the thumb, also several small scars on the right knee, no other marks worthy of notice
DATE	14 Aug 1845
RECORD #	1828
PAGE	22

NAME	DIMMY, Mary Ann
PROOF	free born as proved by oath of Samuel PURSEL Sr.
DESCRIPTION	abt 18y old, 5' 4" tall, quite a light complexion, scar 1½" long on left arm between the elbow & wrist, two scars from inoculation on the right arm above the elbow, a black mole on the upper part of the right breast and a small scar on the under lip, no other marks visible
DATE	14 Aug 1845
RECORD #	1828
PAGE	22

NAME	RICHARDSON, William (son of Hannah RICHARDSON)
PROOF	registered when a child, say 14 Sep 1829, and freedom proved by Dr. John H. McCABE now dec'd, and now by oath of William B. SULLIVAN
DESCRIPTION	24y old, 5' 8½" tall, brown colour, two scars leaving from the corner of the right eye nearly 1" long each, no other apparent mark or scar
DATE	14 Aug 1845
RECORD #	1829
PAGE	23

NAME	RICHARDSON, Jamima
PROOF	free born as proved by oath of Griffith W. PAXSON
DESCRIPTION	22y old, 5' 3" tall, dark complexion, scar caused by a burn in the middle of the back of the left hand, the little finger of the left hand crooked and stiff, also the little finger of the right hand somewhat crooked and stiff at the middle joint, a small scar at the outer end of the right eye brow, no other marks visible
DATE	14 Aug 1845
RECORD #	1830
PAGE	24

Loudoun County, Virginia Register of Free Negroes 1844-1861

NAME	RICHARDSON, Hannah Ann
PROOF	free born as proved by oath of Griffith W. PAXSON
DESCRIPTION	20y old, 5' 7½" tall, dark complexion, small scar on the upper joint of the little finger of the left hand, a small scar on the forehead nearly over the left eye, a small mole on the left side of the nose near the eye, no other distinguishing marks
DATE	14 Aug 1845
RECORD #	1830
PAGE	24

NAME	HULLS, Elizabeth
PROOF	free woman as proved by the affirmation of Joseph HOUGH
DESCRIPTION	abt 23y old, 5' 3 7/8" tall, bright mulatto very much freckled, long scar on the ball of the third finger from the thumb, lengthwise, and the thumb nail on the left hand injured and somewhat separated, a small scar in the centre of the forehead, and some moles on the neck, no other marks
DATE	8 Sep 1845
RECORD #	1331 [misnumbered]
PAGE	24

NAME	JACKSON, Annanias
PROOF	free man as proved by affirmation of Jonas JANNEY
DESCRIPTION	abt 21y old, 5' 10¼" tall, brown colour, small scar just above the left eye, several on his forefinger and thumb of the right hand & the thumb nail of the left hand split, and several small scars on same hand, and on the back of the wrist 3" or 4" above the hand a scar lengthwise ? the arm about ¾" long
DATE	8 Sep 1845
RECORD #	1332
PAGE	25

NAME	GANT, Nelson Talbert
PROOF	emancipated by will of John NIXSON dec'd admitted to record 8 Sep 1845 and by the direction of Ely JANNEY &Thomas NICHOLS two of the executors of said NIXON
DESCRIPTION	abt 23y old, 5' 9¾" tall, bright mulatto, with no particular scars or marks
DATE	9 Sep 1845
RECORD #	1333
PAGE	25

NAME	TALBERT, Ely
PROOF	emancipated by will of John NIXSON dec'd admitted to record 8 Sep 1845 and by the direction of Ely JANNEY & Thomas NICHOLS two of the executors of said NIXON
DESCRIPTION	abt 28y old, 5' 9¼" tall, dark brown colour, round scar just below the left ear, and a mole below the right corner of his mouth
DATE	9 Sep 1845
RECORD #	1334
PAGE	25

NAME	GANT, George
PROOF	emancipated by will of John NIXSON dec'd admitted to record 8 Sep 1845 and by the direction of Ely JANNEY & Thomas NICHOLS two of the executors of said NIXON
DESCRIPTION	abt 20y old, 5' 10 7/8" tall, brown colour, a remarkable scar on the left side of his neck and some dark streaks in the forehead & something like a scar in the left eye brow
DATE	9 Sep 1845
RECORD #	1335
PAGE	26

NAME	ANDERSON, Abraham
PROOF	emancipated by will of John NIXSON dec'd admitted to record 8 Sep 1845 and by the direction of Ely JANNEY & Thomas NICHOLS two of the executors of said NIXON
DESCRIPTION	abt 26y old, 5' 4" tall, black colour, scar on the left side of the forehead & one on the right cheek & a scar on the middle joint of the forefinger on the right hand
DATE	9 Sep 1845
RECORD #	1336
PAGE	26

NAME	JACKSON, Lewis
PROOF	emancipated by will of John NIXSON dec'd admitted to record 8 Sep 1845 and by the direction of Ely JANNEY & Thomas NICHOLS two of the executors of said NIXON
DESCRIPTION	abt 25y old, 5' 4½" tall, black complexion with a black mole on the lower extremity of the right ear and on the back of his right hand has a number of small scars
DATE	9 Sep 1845
RECORD #	1337
PAGE	26

NAME	GANT, Fenton
PROOF	emancipated by will of John NIXSON dec'd admitted to record 8 Sep 1845 and by the direction of Ely JANNEY & Thomas NICHOLS two of the executors of said NIXON
DESCRIPTION	abt 22y old, 5' 7½" tall, blackish complexion, long slim scar on the right wrist just above the thumb running lengthwise with the arm
DATE	9 Sep 1845
RECORD #	1338
PAGE	27

NAME	GANT, Daniel
PROOF	emancipated by will of John NIXSON dec'd admitted to record 8 Sep 1845 and by the direction of Ely JANNEY & Thomas NICHOLS two of the executors of said NIXON
DESCRIPTION	abt 18y old, 5' 11" tall, brown colour, two scars on the forefinger of the right hand, one on the first, and the other on the second joint
DATE	9 Sep 1845
RECORD #	1339
PAGE	27

NAME	ANDERSON, Wilson
PROOF	emancipated by will of John NIXSON dec'd admitted to record 8 Sep 1845 and by the direction of Ely JANNEY & Thomas NICHOLS two of the executors of said Nixon
DESCRIPTION	abt 29y old, 5' 6½" tall, dark brown colour, his right hand forefinger scarred and injured so that it forms a curve
DATE	9 Sep 1845
RECORD #	1340
PAGE	27

NAME	GANT, John Wm.
PROOF	emancipated by will of John NIXSON dec'd admitted to record 8 Sep 1845 and by the direction of Ely JANNEY & Thomas Nichols two of the executors of said NIXON
DESCRIPTION	abt 15y old, 5' 4" tall, bright brown colour, round scar in his breast
DATE	9 Sep 1845
RECORD #	1341
PAGE	28

NAME	GANT, Isaac
PROOF	emancipated by will of John NIXSON dec'd admitted to record 8 Sep 1845 and by the direction of Ely JANNEY & Thomas NICHOLS two of the executors of said NIXON
DESCRIPTION	abt 9y old, dark brown colour, scar on the right wrist
DATE	9 Sep 1845
RECORD #	1342
PAGE	28

NAME	GANT, Lloyd
PROOF	emancipated by will of John NIXSON dec'd admitted to record 8 Sep 1845 and by the direction of Ely JANNEY & Thomas NICHOLS two of the executors of said NIXON
DESCRIPTION	abt 8y old, light brown colour
DATE	9 Sep 1845
RECORD #	1343
PAGE	28

NAME	ANDERSON, Sarah
PROOF	emancipated by will of John NIXSON dec'd admitted to record 8 Sep 1845 and by the direction of Ely JANNEY & Thomas NICHOLS two of the executors of said NIXON
DESCRIPTION	abt 70y old, 4' 11½" tall, brown colour, no particular scars or marks
DATE	9 Sep 1845
RECORD #	1344
PAGE	29

NAME	ANDERSON, Eliza Ann
PROOF	emancipated by will of John NIXSON dec'd admitted to record 8 Sep 1845 and by the direction of Ely JANNEY & Thomas NICHOLS two of the executors of said Nixon
DESCRIPTION	abt 30y old, 5' ¾" tall, light brown colour
DATE	9 Sep 1845
RECORD #	1345
PAGE	29

NAME	ANDERSON, Mary Ann
PROOF	emancipated by will of John NIXSON dec'd admitted to record 8 Sep 1845 and by the direction of Ely JANNEY & Thomas NICHOLS two of the executors of said NIXON
DESCRIPTION	abt 11y old, bright mulatto, no particular scars
DATE	9 Sep 1845
RECORD #	1346
PAGE	29

Loudoun County, Virginia Register of Free Negroes 1844-1861

NAME	GANT, Eve
PROOF	emancipated by will of John NIXSON dec'd admitted to record 8 Sep 1845 and by the direction of Ely JANNEY & Thomas NICHOLS two of the executors of said NIXON
DESCRIPTION	abt 53y old, 5' 4½" tall, bright brown colour, her little finger on the right hand crooked
DATE	9 Sep 1845
RECORD #	1347
PAGE	29

NAME	ADAMS, Harriet Ann
PROOF	emancipated by will of John NIXSON dec'd admitted to record 8 Sep 1845, by the direction of Ely JANNEY & Thomas NICHOLS two executors of NIXON
DESCRIPTION	abt 27y old, 5' 4¾" tall, dark brown colour, no scars or marks
DATE	9 Sep 1845
RECORD #	1348
PAGE	30

NAME	ADAMS, Virginia Ann (daughter of Harriet Ann ADAMS)
PROOF	emancipated by will of John NIXSON dec'd admitted to record 8 Sep 1845, by the direction of Ely JANNEY & Thomas NICHOLS two executors of NIXON
DESCRIPTION	abt 4y old, bright mulatto
DATE	9 Sep 1845
RECORD #	1349
PAGE	30

NAME	ADAMS, Sally Ann
PROOF	emancipated by will of John NIXSON dec'd admitted to record 8 Sep 1845, by the direction of Ely JANNEY & Thomas NICHOLS two executors of NIXON
DESCRIPTION	abt 2y old, bright mulatto
DATE	9 Sep 1845
RECORD #	1350
PAGE	30

NAME	ADAMS, Amanda (daughter of Harriet Ann ADAMS)
PROOF	emancipated by will of John NIXSON dec'd admitted to record 8 Sep 1845 and by the direction of Ely JANNEY & Thomas NICHOLS two of the executors of said NIXON
DESCRIPTION	abt 5m old, bright mulatto
DATE	9 Sep 1845
RECORD #	1351
PAGE	31

NAME	GANT, Winefred Jane
PROOF	emancipated by will of John NIXSON dec'd admitted to record 8 Sep 1845 and by the direction of Ely JANNEY & Thomas NICHOLS two of the executors of said NIXON
DESCRIPTION	abt 17y old, 5' 3" tall, dark mulatto, dark spot on the left side of her neck a black mole on the right side of her breast
DATE	9 Sep 1845
RECORD #	1352
PAGE	31

NAME	GANT, Susan Ann
PROOF	emancipated by will of John NIXSON dec'd admitted to record 8 Sep 1845 and by the direction of Ely JANNEY & Thomas NICHOLS two of the executors of said Nixon
DESCRIPTION	abt 14y old, bright brown colour, no marks or scars
DATE	9 Sep 1845
RECORD #	1353
PAGE	31

NAME	GANT, Mary Francis
PROOF	emancipated by will of John NIXSON dec'd admitted to record 8 Sep 1845 and by the direction of Ely JANNEY & Thomas NICHOLS two of the executors of said Nixon
DESCRIPTION	2y old last March, bright mulatto, scar on the back of the left hand
DATE	9 Sep 1845
RECORD #	1354
PAGE	32

NAME	CRAVEN, Amanda
PROOF	free woman as proved by the oath of Charles SHREVE Esqr before James SINCLAIR Esqr
DESCRIPTION	abt 18y old, 5' 9¼" tall, bright mulatto, scar on back of right hand and a mole in the centre of her breast that rises above the skin and of a deep blue colour
DATE	10 Sep 1845
RECORD #	1355
PAGE	32

NAME	RANOLPH, Rosanna
PROOF	free born as proved by oath of William YOUNG
DESCRIPTION	abt 21y old, 5' 3" tall, dark mulatto or light brown colour, scar under the left jaw, somewhat freckled about the nose
DATE	13 Oct 1845
RECORD #	1356
PAGE	32

Loudoun County, Virginia Register of Free Negroes 1844-1861

NAME	GANT, George
PROOF	free man as proved by oath of James CRAIG
DESCRIPTION	abt 45y old, 5' 6" tall, dark mulatto or light brown colour, scar in the forehead and several remarkable marks on the breast that he says came naturally
DATE	13 Oct 1845
RECORD #	1357
PAGE	33

NAME	ADAMS, Charles
PROOF	this day set free by Thomas SANDERS by deed of emancipation this day admitted
DESCRIPTION	28y old the 12th of January next, 6' ½" tall, mulatto, large scar on the joint of the wrist of the right hand & a large dark scar on the right side of his face
DATE	14 Oct 1845
RECORD #	1358
PAGE	33

NAME	CRAVEN, John Henry (son of Amanda CRAVEN)
PROOF	free born as proved by oath of Charles SHREVE
DESCRIPTION	19m old
DATE	14 Oct 1845
RECORD #	1359
PAGE	33

NAME	JOHNSON, Malinda
PROOF	free woman as proved by oath of David LOVETT
DESCRIPTION	abt 19y old, 5' 2½" tall, with a scar on her left arm about 1" long a few inches above the hand on the back of the arm, the little fingers somewhat crooked & a mole between the forefinger & thumb of the right hand rather on the inside
DATE	30 Oct 1845
RECORD #	1360
PAGE	33

NAME	YOUNG, Margaret
PROOF	freedom proved by oath of George KEENE
DESCRIPTION	abt 16y old, 5' 4 ¾" tall, dark mulatto, plain scar in the centre of the forehead and somewhat freckled
DATE	12 Nov 1845
RECORD #	1361
PAGE	34

NAME	YOUNG, Doctor Franklin
PROOF	freedom proved by oath of George KEENE
DESCRIPTION	abt 14y old, dark mulatto, scar in the left eye brow
DATE	12 Nov 1845
RECORD #	1362
PAGE	34

NAME	YOUNG, Leven Burr
PROOF	freedom proved by oath of George KEENE
DESCRIPTION	going on 11y old, dark mulatto, scar across his left eye brow & a mark across his nose
DATE	12 Nov 1845
RECORD #	1362
PAGE	34

NAME	RIVERS, Susan
PROOF	emancipated by will of Peggy DOUGLAS as proved by oath of Charles B. TEBBS
DESCRIPTION	abt 26y old, 5' 3¼" tall, scar from a burn on her left arm near the elbow on the inside of the arm, with a small round scar about 4" above the wrist, also a scar on the left jaw and a small indentation near the left eye
DATE	12 Jan 1846
RECORD #	1363
PAGE	35

NAME	STEWART, John (son of Hester STEWART late WINTERS)
PROOF	free born as proved by oath of Jesse TIMMS now dec'd when John was abt 8y old, as appears by a register in May 1832
DESCRIPTION	21y old, 5' 8½" tall, nearly black, with a very small black mole about 1" above left eye brow, a small scar on back of hand where it joins wrist & another on wrist just above the hand on the inside nearly 2" long and several scars on his right hand
DATE	13 Jan 1846
RECORD #	1364
PAGE	35

NAME	HARPER, Samuel (son of Enoch & Elizabeth HARPER)
PROOF	proved by oath of Wm. THOMAS and by certificate of freedom on 14 Oct 1833 & No. 903
DESCRIPTION	abt 23y old, 5' 7" tall, bright mulatto, 2 scars over the left eye, a mole on right cheek opposite his mouth, scar on left hand near wrist joint & one on back of left hand, slightly freckled
DATE	13 Jan 1846
RECORD #	1365
PAGE	35

Loudoun County, Virginia Register of Free Negroes 1844-1861

NAME	THOMAS, Enoch
PROOF	free born as proved by oath of John C. MURRAY Esqr
DESCRIPTION	abt 27y old, 5' 9½" tall, brown colour, large scar on the lower part of the cap of his knee, with 2 or 3 small scars on the back part of his left hand
DATE	10 Mar 1846
RECORD #	1366
PAGE	36

NAME	THOMAS, Newman
PROOF	free born as proved by oath of John C. MURRAY Esqr
DESCRIPTION	abt 21y old, 5' 7¼" tall, brown colour, scar on the back of his head, a small scar near the outside corner of his left eye, another small scar just above the eye brow of his right eye and two small scars on the back of his left hand
DATE	10 Mar 1846
RECORD #	1367
PAGE	36

NAME	GILBERT, Margaret
PROOF	free born as proved by oath of Curtis R. SAUNDERS
DESCRIPTION	abt 20y old, 5' 2 3/8" tall, brown colour, no scars or marks
DATE	13 Apr 1846
RECORD #	1368
PAGE	37

NAME	PEYTON, William
PROOF	emancipated by will of Craven OSBURN dec'd as proved by oath of Joseph WORTHINGTON Esqr
DESCRIPTION	abt 25y old, 5' nearly 11" tall, black man, faint scar in his right eye brow & a scar across the bottom of his right foot & a round scar on the top of the same foot, and a very small scar on the top of the left foot, no other marks
DATE	12 May 1846
RECORD #	1369
PAGE	37

NAME	COOPER, Rachel
PROOF	emancipated by will of Craven OSBURN dec'd as proved by oath of Joseph WORTHINGTON Esqr
DESCRIPTION	abt 23y old, 5' 5" tall, black complexion, no material scars, has two moles on the left hand
DATE	12 May 1846
RECORD #	1370
PAGE	37

NAME	CROSS, Joseph
PROOF	free man as proved by oath of Mordecai C. KLINE
DESCRIPTION	abt 23y old, bright mulatto, small scar near the left corner of the right eye brow, no other mark or scar worth mentioning, straight hair, 5' ½" tall
DATE	[?? 12 May 1846 or 11 Aug 1846]
RECORD #	1371
PAGE	38

NAME	JONES, Beverly
PROOF	emancipated by deed executed by Mary VANDEVANTER bearing date 26 Aug 1845, affirmed by Noble S. BRADEN
DESCRIPTION	abt 38y old, scar above the middle of the under lip, scar on the upper joint of the left ?, abt 5' 5" tall, black complexion
DATE	11 Aug 1846
RECORD #	1372
PAGE	38

NAME	ALLEN, James (alias for Jim)
PROOF	liberated by will of Joseph LEWIS dec'd at Aug Court 1840, affirmation by John MEAD
DESCRIPTION	abt 20y old, 5' 7½" tall, dark complexion neither black or mulatto, small scar on the right side of the forehead, small scar over each eye brow, small scar on the back of the left hand
DATE	13 Aug 1846
RECORD #	1373
PAGE	39

NAME	CARTER, Samuel
PROOF	free born as appears from register record of 8 Dec 1832
DESCRIPTION	35y old the 5th of June last, 6' tall, dark mulatto complexion, scar between the two eye brows & no other apparent scars or marks
DATE	14 Sep 1846
RECORD #	1374
PAGE	39

NAME	SHARPER, Susan (alias DUNCAN)
PROOF	free born as proved by affirmation of John NICHOLS
DESCRIPTION	abt 23y old, 5' 2¼" tall, dark mulatto, has her ears bored, no other scars or marks
DATE	14 Sep 1846
RECORD #	1375
PAGE	39

Loudoun County, Virginia Register of Free Negroes 1844-1861

NAME　　　　　McDANIEL, Stephen
PROOF　　　　　free born as proved by Hunton (or Fenton) HOLMES
DESCRIPTION 32y old, 5' 8" tall, dark mulatto, scar on upper eye lash of left eye and another in eye brow of same or above same eye & on right arm a block of black appearance on inside near elbow & several small scars on back of fingers
DATE　　　　　14 Sep 1846
RECORD #　　　1376
PAGE　　　　　40

NAME　　　　　McDANIEL, Elizabeth (wife of the above Stephen)
PROOF　　　　　free born as proved by oath of Mary THYAR
DESCRIPTION 27y old, 5' 4" tall, bright mulatto, 6 or 7 small moles scattered over her face, no other scars or marks
DATE　　　　　14 Sep 1846
RECORD #　　　1377
PAGE　　　　　40

NAME　　　　　McDANIEL, Theodore (son of Stephen & Elizabeth)
PROOF　　　　　[as above ?]
DESCRIPTION 9y old
DATE　　　　　14 Sep 1846
RECORD #　　　1378
PAGE　　　　　40

NAME　　　　　McDANIEL, Casa Ann (daughter of Stephen & Elizabeth)
PROOF　　　　　[as above ?]
DESCRIPTION 7y old
DATE　　　　　14 Sep 1846
RECORD #　　　1378
PAGE　　　　　40

NAME　　　　　McDANIEL, Bernard (son of Stephen & Elizabeth)
PROOF　　　　　[as above ?]
DESCRIPTION 4y old
DATE　　　　　14 Sep 1846
RECORD #　　　1378
PAGE　　　　　40

NAME　　　　　McDANIEL, Mary Elizabeth (daughter of Stephen & Elizabeth)
PROOF　　　　　[as above ?]
DESCRIPTION 2y old next December
DATE　　　　　14 Sep 1846
RECORD #　　　1378
PAGE　　　　　40

NAME	CARTER, Mary Jane (formerly Mary Jane RIVERS)
PROOF	registered under the later name 15 Aug 1833, in that record proved to be free born by affirmation of Thomas PHILLIPS dec'd and proved now by affirmation of Amasa HOUGH
DESCRIPTION	28y old, 5' 4" tall, bright mulatto, scar on side of ancle on the right leg & scar on back of the forefinger near the upper joint & 2 moles on the right side of her neck
DATE	14 Sep 1846
RECORD #	1379
PAGE	41

NAME	JACKSON, Mary
PROOF	free born as proved by oath of Richard H. SUMMERS
DESCRIPTION	20y old next December, 5' 3½" tall, brown complexion, scar below the left eye near the nose, a long scar on the inside of the right arm just in the bend, and 3 raised moles on the back of the wrist on the same arm just above wrist joint
DATE	16 Sep 1846
RECORD #	1380
PAGE	41

NAME	TAYLOR, Margaret (daughter of Ann TAYLOR)
PROOF	free born as proved by affirmation of Jane JEWIT
DESCRIPTION	5y old on 29 Jul last, dark colour, 3 scars on right side of neck
DATE	[16 Sep 1846?]
RECORD #	1381
PAGE	41

NAME	DAVIS, Letitia (daughter of Maria DAVIS, emancipated by will of William HEPBURN at Alexandria Ct dated 24 May 1824)
PROOF	free born as proved by oath of John L. SULLIVAN
DESCRIPTION	18y old last August, 5' 4" tall, dark mulatto, on inside of wrist near the hand some dark scars and on the same arm near the elbow on the inside a remarkable appearance of light colour
DATE	26 Sep 1846
RECORD #	1382
PAGE	42

NAME	DAVIS, Marsalena (child of above Maria DAVIS, who has now married Joseph VENEY)
PROOF	free born as proved by oath of John L. SULLIVAN
DESCRIPTION	abt 4y old, bright mulatto, dark place quite small just above the right eye near the edge of the hair a small mole on the left arm inside a few inches above the hand & a faint scar just below the right jaw bone
DATE	26 Sep 1846
RECORD #	1383
PAGE	42

NAME	DAVIS, Dennis (child of above Maria DAVIS, who has now married Joseph VENEY)
PROOF	free born as proved by oath of John L. SULLIVAN
DESCRIPTION	abt 12y old, dark complexion, no scars or marks
DATE	26 Sep 1846
RECORD #	1383
PAGE	42

NAME	VENEY, Eliza Ann (child of above Maria DAVIS, who has now married Joseph VENEY)
PROOF	free born as proved by oath of John L. SULLIVAN
DESCRIPTION	5y old next March
DATE	26 Sep 1846
RECORD #	1383
PAGE	42

NAME	VENEY, Mary Bell (child of above Maria DAVIS, who has now married Joseph VENEY)
PROOF	free born as proved by oath of John L. SULLIVAN
DESCRIPTION	abt 3y old
DATE	26 Sep 1846
RECORD #	1383
PAGE	42

NAME	VENEY, James Moten (child of above Maria DAVIS, who has now married Joseph VENEY)
PROOF	free born as proved by oath of John L. SULLIVAN
DESCRIPTION	1y old in June last
DATE	26 Sep 1846
RECORD #	1383
PAGE	42

NAME	THORNTON, Cary Ann (daughter of Lavina THORNTON)
PROOF	free born as appears by affirmation of Joshua PUSEY
DESCRIPTION	abt 24y old, 5' 10" tall, dark complexion, scar in the forehead, two small scars on the right arm near the elbow, a disfigured nail on the little finger of the right hand and her left hand & wrist with the fingers on the left much scarred & disfigured by a burn
DATE	12 Oct 1846
RECORD #	1384
PAGE	42

NAME	JONES, Mary Ann
PROOF	free born as proved by affirmation of William TATE
DESCRIPTION	abt 17y old, 5' tall, bright mulatto, scar just below left eye and a long scar across the back of her left hand
DATE	12 Oct 1846
RECORD #	1384 [misnumbered]
PAGE	43

NAME	JONES, Sarah Virginia (infant child of Mary Ann JONES)
PROOF	free born as proved by affirmation of William TATE
DESCRIPTION	abt 4m old, about same colour as mother
DATE	12 Oct 1846
RECORD #	1384 [misnumbered]
PAGE	43

NAME	RANDOLPH, Hannah
PROOF	free born as proved by oath of Michael PLASTER
DESCRIPTION	25y old, 4' 11 3/8" tall, very dark mulatto, scar in the edge of the left eye brow & another on the back of the left hand
DATE	12 Oct 1846
RECORD #	1385
PAGE	43

NAME	HEATER, George Henry (son of Nancy HEATER)
PROOF	emancipated by will of Presley SAUNDERS dec'd as proved by oath of Presley SAUNDERS
DESCRIPTION	30y old, 5' nearly 7" tall, very dark complexion, several scars dispersed about his face, towit one in the edge of the hair in the right peak of the forehead, 2 or 3 just in the forehead, one on the nose & a small scar just below the right eye
DATE	12 Oct 1846
RECORD #	1386
PAGE	43

Loudoun County, Virginia Register of Free Negroes 1844-1861

NAME	CARTER, Elizabeth
PROOF	free born as proved by oath of James McILHANY Esqr
DESCRIPTION	nearly 15y old, 5' 2" tall, very dark mulatto, 2 very small moles on the right side of her neck & a newly made scar from a burn, near the end of the middle finger on the right hand & on top of it
DATE	9 Nov 1846
RECORD #	1387
PAGE	44

NAME	WRIGHT, Harriet
PROOF	free as proved by oath of Presley Saunders
DESCRIPTION	abt 36y old, 5' 4½" tall, dark complexion, two large scars on her right arm just below the elbow & some faint scars on the back of the same hand & two scars on the left just above the thumb and one in the edge of the hair in the forehead
DATE	10 Nov 1846
RECORD #	1388
PAGE	44

NAME	HOWARD, Armistead
PROOF	free born as proved by oath of Joseph S. HOUGH
DESCRIPTION	21y old the 26th of Jany next 1847, 5' 7" tall, bright mulatto, scar in the forehead near the hair upwards of an inch long, a faint scar on the right side of his face & 3 white looking spots on his neck
DATE	9 Nov 1846
RECORD #	1389
PAGE	44

NAME	MASON, John Henry
PROOF	manumitted by deed of emancipation executed by Catharine HULLS, dated 11 Aug 1830, recorded in Liber 3U folio 179
DESCRIPTION	abt 22y old, 5' 6¾" tall, mulatto, scar on the top of his nose and a long scar on the inside of the right hand above the thumb joint, no others of importance
DATE	10 Nov 1846
RECORD #	1390
PAGE	45

NAME	THOMAS, Sally Ann (alias Sally Ann HARPER)
PROOF	registered on 11 May 1840, a free woman as proved by oath of Richard H. SUMMERS
DESCRIPTION	17y old, 5' 3" tall, light mulatto, small indented mark in the corner of the left eye, small scar on the left side of the forehead, scar on the right cheek, small black mole on the left side of neck & a small scar on the last joint of the thumb on the left hand
DATE	10 Nov 1846
RECORD #	1391
PAGE	45

NAME	MASON, Jesse
PROOF	free born as proved by oath of William CARR
DESCRIPTION	upwards of 21y old, 5' 2" tall, black complexion, long scar running obliqly across the forehead, another on the right side of nose near the nostril, another on the right cheek, another on the left jaw bone & one on the left breast near the shoulder
DATE	11 Nov 1846
RECORD #	1392
PAGE	46

NAME	WRIGHT, Archibald (son of Nancy WRIGHT)
PROOF	free born as proved by oath of Duanna WATT, registered 14 Oct 1828 when he was 8y, and proved now by oath of Jas. McDONAUGH & John SMALE
DESCRIPTION	abt 26 old, 6' ½" tall, very dark mulatto, scar on the first joint of the forefinger on the left hand or very near the joint, and another scar on the shin of the right leg some 5 or 6 inches above the foot
DATE	15 Dec 1846
RECORD #	1393
PAGE	46

NAME	WRIGHT, George Benjamin
PROOF	free born as proved by oath of Duanna WATT, register made 14 Oct 1828 and proved now by oath of James McDONAUGH
DESCRIPTION	21y old the 16th of January next, 5' 11" tall, nearly black, large scar on the right shoulder in front caused by a burn & a scar on the inside of the left knee and a scar between the eye brows, also a scar rather obliqely across the end of his nose
DATE	9 Mar 1847
RECORD #	1394
PAGE	46

NAME	STEPTOE, Frederick
PROOF	emancipated by will of Presley SAUNDERS dec'd and proved by oath of Gunnell SAUNDERS
DESCRIPTION	31y old on 20 Dec 1846, 5' 11" tall, nearly black, scar on nose high up & running mostly on right side, another scar on upper lip long and slim, and another on left knee caused by a bile
DATE	15 Dec 1846
RECORD #	1395
PAGE	47

NAME	TIMBERS, Rutha
PROOF	freedom proved by oath of Margaret DORRELL
DESCRIPTION	54y old, 4' 11" tall, dark mulatto, scar in and across right eye brow and a scar on the right arm on the inside near the elbow
DATE	15 Dec 1846
RECORD #	1396
PAGE	47

NAME	TIMBERS, Matilda
PROOF	freedom proved by oath of Margaret DORRELL
DESCRIPTION	abt 31y old, 5' 1" tall, very dark mulatto, scar on top of nose & a long scar across her right arm a little below elbow
DATE	15 Dec 1846
RECORD #	1397
PAGE	48

NAME	TIMBERS, Betsy
PROOF	freedom proved by oath of Margaret DORRELL
DESCRIPTION	abt 29y old, very dark mulatto, scar on right arm & on chin
DATE	15 Dec 1846
RECORD #	1398
PAGE	48

NAME	GRAYSON, Amy (child of Jesse & Matilda GRAYSON)
PROOF	free born as proved by oath of Margaret DORRELL
DESCRIPTION	11y old, very dark mulatto
DATE	15 Dec 1846
RECORD #	1399
PAGE	48

NAME	GRAYSON, Jesse (child of Jesse & Matilda GRAYSON)
PROOF	free born as proved by oath of Margaret DORRELL
DESCRIPTION	7y old, very dark mulatto
DATE	15 Dec 1846
RECORD #	1399
PAGE	48

NAME   GRAYSON, Wesley (child of Jesse & Matilda GRAYSON)
PROOF   free born as proved by oath of Margaret DORRELL
DESCRIPTION 3y old, very dark mulatto
DATE   15 Dec 1846
RECORD #   1399
PAGE   48

NAME   GRAYSON, William (child of Jesse & Matilda GRAYSON)
PROOF   free born as proved by oath of Margaret DORRELL
DESCRIPTION nearly 2y old, very dark mulatto
DATE   15 Dec 1846
RECORD #   1399
PAGE   48

NAME   GRAYSON, Lee (child of Jesse & Matilda GRAYSON)
PROOF   free born as proved by oath of Margaret DORRELL
DESCRIPTION infant, very dark mulatto
DATE   15 Dec 1846
RECORD #   1399
PAGE   48

NAME   MORGAN, Andrew (son of Delila MORGAN)
PROOF   free born as proved by oath of Margaret DORRELL
DESCRIPTION going on 7y old, bright mulatto
DATE   15 Dec 1846
RECORD #   1400
PAGE   49

NAME   MORGAN, Rachel (daughter of Delila MORGAN)
PROOF   free born as proved by oath of Margaret DORRELL
DESCRIPTION going on 4y old, bright mulatto
DATE   15 Dec 1846
RECORD #   1400
PAGE   49

NAME   MORGAN, Charles Henry (son of Delila MORGAN)
PROOF   free born as proved by oath of Daniel MONDAY
DESCRIPTION abt 11y old, bright mulatto
DATE   15 Dec 1846
RECORD #   1401
PAGE   49

Loudoun County, Virginia Register of Free Negroes 1844-1861

NAME	MORGAN, Mary Catharine (daughter of Delila MORGAN)
PROOF	free born as proved by oath of Margaret DORRELL
DESCRIPTION	abt 15y old, 4' 11" tall, bright mulatto, scar bored left ear torn where it was bored, small scar on left jaw & between chin & mouth
DATE	15 Dec 1846
RECORD #	1402
PAGE	49

NAME	MORGAN, William Wright (son of Delila MORGAN)
PROOF	free born as proved by oath of Margaret DORRELL
DESCRIPTION	abt 2y old, nearly black
DATE	15 Dec 1846
RECORD #	1403
PAGE	49

NAME	MINOR, William Henry
PROOF	free born as proved by oath of Wm. RUSSELL
DESCRIPTION	abt 18y old, abt 5' 9 1/3" tall, dark mulatto, large scar on back part of his right arm half way between wrist and elbow, also small scar on right elbow, one small scar on first finger of his left hand near the lowest joint
DATE	11 Jan 1847
RECORD #	1404
PAGE	50

NAME	MUDD, Fletcher
PROOF	free man as proved by affirmation of Thos. NICHOLS in a former register made 9 Nov 1840, when he was abt 16y old, proved now by oath of Samuel PURSEL Jr.
DESCRIPTION	abt 22y old, 5' 6" tall, dark complexion, black mark on right side of neck just below ear abt 1" long and ¾" broad, scar in forehead in edge of hair, no other scars or marks to be seen
DATE	6 Jan 1847
RECORD #	1405
PAGE	50

NAME	GANT, Ann Maria (wife of Talbert GANT)
PROOF	emancipated by Charley Ann & Jane E. RUSSEL, freedom proved by affirmation of Thomas NICHOLS
DESCRIPTION	abt 19y old, 5' 1½" tall, mulatto, small mole in the forehead and another on right shoulder, and a faint mark on inside of the left arm below the wrist produced by a blister
DATE	8 Feb 1847
RECORD #	1406
PAGE	51

NAME	LANE, Cecelia (formerly RIVERS)
PROOF	freed by will of Peggy DOUGLAS dec'd, as proved by oath of Miss Eliz'th D. BINNS
DESCRIPTION	abt 25y old, 5' 6½" tall, dark colour, black? eyes, small scar in forehead & another on the upper lip, ditto on the back part of right wrist & a wart on the same wrist on the side of wrist & a large scar on the left breast burn, no other scars or marks
DATE	9 Feb 1847
RECORD #	1407
PAGE	51

NAME	LANE, Eliza (infant child of Cecelia LANE)
PROOF	free born, proved by the same
DESCRIPTION	nearly 6m old, mulatto, has something like a tit in the forehead
DATE	9 Feb 1847
RECORD #	1407
PAGE	51

NAME	CARTER, Andrew Jackson
PROOF	free born as proved by affirmation of David BIRDSALL
DESCRIPTION	abt 18y old, very dark mulatto, 5' 8" tall, some scars or marks on the right cheek, also a lightly colored mark on the left cheek, a mould on the back between the shoulders
DATE	9 Mar 1847
RECORD #	1408
PAGE	52

NAME	THOMAS, Ross
PROOF	free man as proved by oath of French SIMPSON, reference to Register 1232
DESCRIPTION	abt 21y old, 5' 7½" tall, bright mulatto, small dark mole on the left side of neck, also a small scar on the back of left hand near the wrist
DATE	12 Apr 1847
RECORD #	1409
PAGE	52

Loudoun County, Virginia Register of Free Negroes 1844-1861

NAME	BESICKS, Jesse
PROOF	emancipated from Elizabeth COSS? dated 22 Jan 1828 (see register 678), now proved by Joseph HILLIARD
DESCRIPTION	abt 55y old, 5' 6¾" tall, white spot right breast, a scar near the elbow of the right arm, one on right wrist, several scars on knuckles of right hand, scars on both arms where he was bled, several scars on back of neck, scar on the left arm where he vaccinated, 2 scars near the corner of the left eye, a scar in the middle of the forehead, a scar on the under lip on the right side of the mouth, a scar on the forefinger of the left hand, a very notable scar on the left leg, one on the right leg of a very dark complexion, no other apparent scar or mark
DATE	14 Apr 1847
RECORD #	1410
PAGE	53

NAME	SINKFIELD, Samuel Francis
PROOF	former register shows free born by oath of Ebenezer JACKSON & now proved by oath of Thomas L. HUMPHREY
DESCRIPTION	24y old on 11? Nov 1847, 5' 8 5/8" tall, dark brown colour, scar about 1" long running straight up from the 1st joint of the thumb & another on the finger next to little finger of the right hand, between the two last joints
DATE	11 May 1847
RECORD #	1411
PAGE	53

NAME	SINKFIELD, Thomas William
PROOF	former register shows free born by oath of Ebenezer JACKSON & now proved by oath of Thomas L. HUMPHREY
DESCRIPTION	21y old on 22 Apr 1847, 5' 10 5/8" tall, black complexion, plain scar on the right wrist & one inside his left hand
DATE	11 May 1847
RECORD #	1412
PAGE	54

NAME	JONES, Nelson
PROOF	free born as proved by oath of Wm. G. FURR
DESCRIPTION	22y old on 1 Feb 1847 5' 6" tall, black complexion, large broad scar caused by a burn above the temple in the hair in part on the left side
DATE	[10 May 1847]
RECORD #	1413
PAGE	54

NAME	TURLEY, Matilda
PROOF	court satisfied to be entitled to freedom
DESCRIPTION	27y old, 5' 7¾" tall, dark mulatto, very plain scar on the back of her right hand and a mole on the breast near the neck
DATE	10 May 1847
RECORD #	1414
PAGE	54

NAME	JONES, Riley
PROOF	free born as proved by oath of William G. FURR
DESCRIPTION	abt 27y old, 5' 7½" tall, very dark brown colour, small scar in the forehead and a scar on the inside of the left hand on the thick part just above the thumb
DATE	14 Jun 1847
RECORD #	1415
PAGE	55

NAME	HENRY, Maria
PROOF	free born as proved by Wm. G. FURR
DESCRIPTION	abt 25y old, very dark brown colour, 5' tall, scar on back between shoulders
DATE	14 Jun 1847
RECORD #	1416
PAGE	55

NAME	JINNINGS, Lewis
PROOF	registered formerly No. 690 made 9 Feb 1829 when he was abt 2y old, free born as proved by oath of James HARRIS
DESCRIPTION	not yet 21y old, scar 3" or 4" long obligely across the inside of the right hand running through the thick part of the hand above the thumb and onward into the wrist made from the cut of an axe, 5' 8¼" tall
DATE	15 Jun 1847
RECORD #	1417
PAGE	55

NAME	THOMAS, Frances
PROOF	free born as proved by oath of Robert ROOKWOOD
DESCRIPTION	abt 29y old, 5' 3½" tall, bright mulatto, small flesh mole about the size of a pin head on under lid of her left eye, scar across the inside of her right little finger and a faint scar about an inch long on the upper joint of the first finger on same hand
DATE	15 May 1847
RECORD #	1418
PAGE	56

NAME	THOMAS, Gustavus (son of Francis THOMAS)
PROOF	free born as proved by oath of Robert ROOKWOOD
DESCRIPTION	born 9 Jan 1834, bright mulatto, scar on the inside of his left wrist just above the hand & a dark scar under his left eye
DATE	15 Jun 1847
RECORD #	1419
PAGE	56

NAME	THOMAS, William (son of Francis THOMAS)
PROOF	free born as proved by oath of Robert ROOKWOOD
DESCRIPTION	born 30 Apr 1837, bright mulatto, scar above his left eye & in the forehead & another small scar on the middle joint of the first finger on the left hand
DATE	15 Jun 1847
RECORD #	1419
PAGE	56

NAME	THOMAS, John (son of Francis THOMAS)
PROOF	free born as proved by oath of Robert ROOKWOOD
DESCRIPTION	born 5 Mar 1839, considerably darker than brother, considerable scar under his left ear and a white streak running obliquely above his right eye
DATE	15 Jun 1847
RECORD #	1419
PAGE	56

NAME	THOMAS, Josiah (son of Francis THOMAS)
PROOF	free born as proved by oath of Robert ROOKWOOD
DESCRIPTION	born 30 Nov 1841, considerably darker than brother
DATE	15 Jun 1847
RECORD #	1419
PAGE	56

NAME	THOMAS, Henry (son of Francis THOMAS)
PROOF	free born as proved by oath of Robert ROOKWOOD
DESCRIPTION	born 30 Nov 1845, considerably darker than brother
DATE	15 Jun 1847
RECORD #	1419
PAGE	56

NAME	THROCKMORTON, Samuel
PROOF	liberated by Chas. B. HAMILTON Esqr by deed of emancipation on 10 May 1847 & proved by Samuel PRICE
DESCRIPTION	abt 55y old, 5' 9¾" tall, plain scar in the forehead 2 inches long
DATE	15 Jun 1847
RECORD #	1420
PAGE	57

NAME	CARTER, Helon
PROOF	emancipated by will of Ann SANDERS dec'd and proved by Wilson C. SANDERS [smeared]
DESCRIPTION	21y old on 28 Jun 1847, 4' 11¾" tall, black complexion
DATE	12 Jul 1847
RECORD #	1421
PAGE	57

NAME	CARTER, Jinny (child of Helon)
PROOF	emancipated by will of Ann SANDERS dec'd and proved by Wilson C. SANDERS [smeared]
DESCRIPTION	2y old in Aug next 1847, not quite so black
DATE	12 Jul 1847
RECORD #	1421
PAGE	57

NAME	HOLLIDAY, Kitty
PROOF	free born proved by oath of James BOWLES
DESCRIPTION	abt 22y old, 5' 4½" tall, light coloured, small mole between the eye brows nearest the left brow, the forefinger and on the two next on the inside of the left hand on each a scar caused by a cut of a knife
DATE	13 Jul 1847
RECORD #	1422
PAGE	57

NAME	MAHONY, Eliza Ann (daughter of Nelly CANADY)
PROOF	free born as proved by Catharine E. FOX
DESCRIPTION	21y or 22y old, bright mulatto, 5' 2¾" tall, scar under her right ear & a scar between the ear & left eye brow & a dark appearance just below the hair above the left eye brow & two small moles one on the back of the left hand & the other 6" or 7" above that on the arm
DATE	10 Aug 1847
RECORD #	1423
PAGE	58

NAME	WRIGHT, Rozannah (daughter of Nancy WRIGHT)
PROOF	emancipated by will of John A. BINNS dec'd as proved by oath of John SMALE, register on 14 Oct 1828
DESCRIPTION	24y old, 5' 4¾" tall, dark complexion, scar on the back of the left wrist above the joint, no other scar of importance
DATE	10 Aug 1847
RECORD #	1424
PAGE	58

NAME	WINTERS, Eliza (daughter of Grace alias Grace WINTERS)
PROOF	said to be emancipated by will of David LACEY dec'd as proved by oath of Leanner SINCLAIR
DESCRIPTION	22y old, 5' 2¾" tall, dark complexion, faint scar near the right eye brow, several scars made by cup[p]ing? on the left side of neck & two long faint scars on the back of her right hand
DATE	10 Aug 1847
RECORD #	1425
PAGE	59

NAME	CORAM, Benjamin
PROOF	certificate of freedom from Fauquier Co dated 23 Feb 1846
DESCRIPTION	abt 24y old, dark mulatto, small scar on the inside of the right little finger near the nail caused by a Mazh?, another scar on the inside of the left thumb extending upwards & caused by a cut with a knife
DATE	10 Aug 1847
RECORD #	1426
PAGE	59

NAME	THOMAS, Edward
PROOF	free man as proved by oath of John C. MURRAY Esqr
DESCRIPTION	21y? old the 24th June last past, 5' 7" tall, dark complexion, several scars in the face, to wit one on the upper lip one in the forehead and one near the corner of his left eye brow, one under the left side of his jaw, another under the right jaw, a long scar on the left hand above the thumb & one on the back of the thumb & a scar on the right hand caused by a burn between the two last fingers
DATE	10 Aug 1847
RECORD #	1427
PAGE	60

NAME	HARPER, Ignatius (son of Enoch HARPER)
PROOF	registered on 12 Mar 1834 with certificate of freedom and proved by Presley SAUNDERS
DESCRIPTION	33y old on 23 Jan 1847, 5' 9¼" tall, scar on the left cheek near the ear, the nail on the finger of the right hand next to the little finger crooked & is slightly marked in the face with the remains of the chicken pox
DATE	10 Aug 1847
RECORD #	1428
PAGE	60

NAME	HARPER, Frances Ann (late Frances Ann THOMAS, daughter of Elizabeth THOMAS)
PROOF	registered 11 May 1840 and proved to be free born by oath of Jane SWARTS
DESCRIPTION	abt 17y old, 5' 3½" tall, very light mulatto, slim scar more than half inch long on the upper lip running from the right nostril downward obliquely, a flesh mark near the corner of the left eye outward, several small moles about the face & neck & a long scar across the upper joint of the forefinger on the right hand & a small scar on the left hand above the joint of the first finger
DATE	10 Aug 1847
RECORD #	1429
PAGE	60

NAME	WATERS, Eliza [this entry was crossed out]
PROOF	[no information entered]
DESCRIPTION	[no information entered]
DATE	11 Aug 1847
RECORD #	1430
PAGE	61

NAME	THOMPSON, William H. (son of Franky THOMPSON)
PROOF	free born as proved by oath of David HIXSON
DESCRIPTION	abt 25y old, 5' 9½" tall, dark colour, scar on the under lip leaving a tit on it, caused by a cut, another scar in the corner of the left eye brow, one in the center of the forehead upward of an inch long, a round scar on left side of the upper lip, has holes bored in his ears, also a very plain scar on the breast 1½" long
DATE	12 Aug 1847
RECORD #	1431
PAGE	61

NAME	GUIDER, Joseph (son of Peter & Lydia GUIDER)
PROOF	free man as proved by oath of Margaret MAGRAK
DESCRIPTION	abt 22y or 23y old, 5' 7" tall, dark complexion, scars on both sides of his face not very plain about the depth of the skin appearing to be made by scratch with the nail of a human hand, scar on the forefinger of the right hand near or just above the middle joint a long scar on the left wrist on the outside running lengthwise, a very large scar on the skin of the left leg crosswise
DATE	13 Sep 1847
RECORD #	1432
PAGE	62

NAME	PERRY, Ralph
PROOF	emancipated by will of Joseph CLOWES dec'd and proved by affirmation of Thomas ROGERS
DESCRIPTION	abt 50y old, 5' 8" tall, black complexion, one scar just above the left eyebrow, the end of the second finger on the right hand is distorted having been cut off, a scar on the lowest joint of the left thumb, a bright narrow scar on the right ribs and one other scar on the left shoulder
DATE	13 Sep 1847
RECORD #	1433
PAGE	62

NAME	BUSH, Mary (alias BOYD)
PROOF	freedom proved by affidavit by Hester FOX
DESCRIPTION	dark mulatto, plain scar between the eye brow and a long scar commencing in the edge of the hair in the centre of the forehead & running obliquely downward about an inch long & a scar on the inside of the arm just above the wrist
DATE	14 Sep 1847
RECORD #	1434
PAGE	62

NAME	WRIGHT, Jane Eveline (daughter of Nancy WRIGHT)
PROOF	proved free by oath of John SMALE
DESCRIPTION	abt 31y or 32y old, 5' 5½" tall, very dark mulatto, mole or wart directly on the back of the neck in the edge of the hair, and a broad dark looking scar on the right hand between the thumb and forefinger
DATE	14 Sep 1847
RECORD #	1435
PAGE	63

NAME	FLORENCE, Betty
PROOF	emancipated by Fenton M. Love & Mary K.? LOVE by deed dated 13 Sep 1847
DESCRIPTION	abt 45y old, 5' tall, mark on top of the nose & a very small indentation between the eye brows
DATE	13 Sep 1847
RECORD #	1436
PAGE	63

NAME	FLORENCE, Smith (son of Betty FLORENCE)
PROOF	emancipated by Fenton M. LOVE & Mary K.? LOVE by deed dated 13 Sep 1847
DESCRIPTION	abt 14y old, light colour, scar at the corner of the left eye brow, small scar on the left side of nose and another in the forehead
DATE	13 Sep 1847
RECORD #	1436
PAGE	63

NAME	FLORENCE, Harrison (son of Betty FLORENCE)
PROOF	emancipated by Fenton M. LOVE & Mary K.? LOVE by deed dated 13 Sep 1847
DESCRIPTION	abt 12y old, light colour, very plain dark scar in the centre of the forehead, some dark spots on the left jaw & a scar 1½" long on the right hand between & above the forefinger & thumb
DATE	13 Sep 1847
RECORD #	1436
PAGE	63

NAME	FLORENCE, Sarah (daughter of Betty FLORENCE)
PROOF	emancipated by Fenton M. LOVE & Mary K.? LOVE by deed dated 13 Sep 1847
DESCRIPTION	abt 8y old, dark complexion, some marks around about her left ear
DATE	13 Sep 1847
RECORD #	1436
PAGE	63

NAME	FLORENCE, Louisa (daughter of Betty FLORENCE)
PROOF	emancipated by Fenton M. LOVE & Mary K.? LOVE by deed dated 13 Sep 1847
DESCRIPTION	abt 5y old, blue clouded appearances in the whites of her eyes
DATE	13 Sep 1847
RECORD #	1436
PAGE	63

NAME	STROTHER, William
PROOF	emancipated by David Fulton, proved by oath of Wm. FULTON
DESCRIPTION	abt 29y old, 5' 4¾" tall, dark complexion, one bright scar across the upper part of the right hand, one slight scar on the lower part of the forehead between the eyes on the right side of the nose & one large scar across the left side of the right knee
DATE	13 Sep 1847
RECORD #	1437
PAGE	64

NAME	ADAMS, Albert
PROOF	emancipated by will of David LACEY dec'd as proved by oath of Lucinda CONNER
DESCRIPTION	abt 28y old, 5' 9" tall, scar on the inside of the left hand & a scar on the skin of the left leg just below the knee
DATE	13 Sep 1847
RECORD #	1438
PAGE	64

NAME	WINTERS, John
PROOF	emancipated by will of David LACEY dec'd as proved by oath of Lucinda CONNER
DESCRIPTION	abt 28y old, 5' 6½" tall, scar on the thumb of the left hand just below the first joint, another across the little finger of the same hand between the 1st & 2nd joint & another on the end of the forefinger of the right hand, another on the forehead above the right eye brow & another below the left eye on the cheek
DATE	13 Sep 1847
RECORD #	1439
PAGE	65

NAME	ADAMS, William
PROOF	emancipated by will of David LACEY dec'd as proved by oath of Lucinda CONNER
DESCRIPTION	abt 30y old, 5' 10½" tall, dark brown colour, large black mark on the arm of the right hand upwards of 4" above the hand on the inside, a large scar on the back of his left hand, a small dark spot below the left eye near the outer corner with some minor scars
DATE	13 Sep 1847
RECORD #	1440
PAGE	65

NAME   STEWART, Elizabeth (daughter of Esther STEWART)
PROOF   free born as appears by oath of French SIMPSON
DESCRIPTION abt 30y old, 5' 3¾" tall, bright mulatto, two very small scars on the right hand caused by a burn, a small round white spot on the right side of the neck, and a small scar on the left arm caused by a burn
DATE   13 Sep 1847
RECORD #   1441
PAGE   65

NAME   MASON, Hannah (daughter of Fanny MASON)
PROOF   free woman as proved by affirmation of William SCHOOLEY
DESCRIPTION abt 30y old, 4' 10¾" tall, a considerable scar of dark appearance on the left side of neck and a small mole on the left hand above the thumb at the edge of the wrist
DATE   11 Oct 1847
RECORD #   1442
PAGE   66

NAME   POWELL, William
PROOF   emancipated by R. G. HICKS & proved by said HICKS
DESCRIPTION abt 31y old, 6' 3/8" tall, bright mulatto, scar on the first joint of the forefinger of the left hand about an inch long & one the last joint of the 3d finger a small scar causing it to be a little crooked, a ? [blotch of ink] in left eye brow caused by burn an the appearance of two scars on the right side of his nose
DATE   11 Oct 1847
RECORD #   1443
PAGE   66

NAME   SELF, Ann Virginia
PROOF   emancipated by her husband Duskin SELF & proved by R. G. HICKS
DESCRIPTION abt 18y old, 5' 3¼" tall, very bright or light mulatto, long mark in the forehead running upward from between the eye brows, several plain moles on the right side of her face & neck & another on the left side on the neck
DATE   11 Oct 1847
RECORD #   1444
PAGE   66

Loudoun County, Virginia Register of Free Negroes 1844-1861

NAME	THOMAS, Thadeus
PROOF	free born as appears by oath of William CARR Jr.
DESCRIPTION	abt 18y old, 5' 5" tall, a bright mulatto, scar in the right eye brow & another just above it & another in the corner of the forehead near the hair on the left side & a scar on the left hand above the thumb about an inch long and some other small scars on the forefinger
DATE	11 Oct 1847
RECORD #	1445
PAGE	67

NAME	THOMAS, Susan (daughter of Delila WRIGHT)
PROOF	free born as proved by oath of Margaret DORRELL
DESCRIPTION	upwards of 21y old, 5' ½" tall, bright mulatto, two moles on her breast, a scar on the first joint of the forefinger on the left hand some small moles on her neck & on each cheek a faint cross mark on the left cheek & her ears bored
DATE	11 Oct 1847
RECORD #	1446
PAGE	67

NAME	HUDLAND, Sarah
PROOF	free woman as proved by oath of Robert LOOKWOOD
DESCRIPTION	abt 22y old, 4' 10¼" tall, mulatto, very plainly pit[t]ed with a small pox
DATE	11 Oct 1847
RECORD #	1447
PAGE	67

NAME	THOMAS, Dotia Ann
PROOF	free woman as proved by oath of Robert LOOKWOOD
DESCRIPTION	abt 22y old, 5' 7/8" tall, mulatto, scar in centre of forehead & several scars one large on the left arm just above the hand caused by a burn
DATE	11 Oct 1847
RECORD #	1448
PAGE	68

NAME	NOKES, Malinda (daughter of Nancy NOKES)
PROOF	free born as proved by oath of Thomas WHITE
DESCRIPTION	abt 16y old, 5' 3½" tall, very dark mulatto, scar on her upper lip on the left side & another scar on the forefinger of her left hand
DATE	11 Oct 1847
RECORD #	1449
PAGE	68

NAME	MANLY, Enoch
PROOF	freedom as proved by Sampson HU[T]CHISON
DESCRIPTION	21y old on 23 Feb 1847, 5' 8" tall, bright mulatto, scar on upper wrist of right hand & on same side a scar on arm between the elbow & wrist
DATE	8 Nov 1847
RECORD #	1450
PAGE	68

NAME	McPHERSON, Charles William Cross (son of Ellen McPHERSON)
PROOF	free born as appears by oath of Jas. GARRISON
DESCRIPTION	abt 17y old, 5' 5¾" tall, dark mulatto, three dark small moles on left side of face and one on right side about centre of his cheek, a small scar across the knucles of 2d & 3d finger of left hand, no other apparent marks or scars
DATE	9 Nov 1847
RECORD #	1451
PAGE	69

NAME	McPHERSON, Eli Banks (son of Ellen McPHERSON)
PROOF	free born as appears by oath of Jas. GARRISON
DESCRIPTION	abt 15y old, 4' 11 1/8" tall, dark complexion, one small scar across his upper lip, one scar across left thumb and a large black mole on right breast, no other apparent scars or marks
DATE	9 Nov 1847
RECORD #	1451
PAGE	69

NAME	GOINGS, Lewis (son of Mary GOINGS)
PROOF	free born as per testimony of Susan A. LOVE
DESCRIPTION	15y old, 4' 11" tall, dark mulatto, several scars or dark spots and marks in his face, one directly in the outer corner of his left eye
DATE	8 Nov 1847
RECORD #	1452
PAGE	69

NAME	GOINGS, Mary Catharine (daughter of Mary Goings)
PROOF	free born as per testimony of Mrs. Catharine GLASGOW
DESCRIPTION	18y old, 5' 3 7/8" tall, freckled face & a large scar on the right arm just below the elbow
DATE	9 Nov 1847
RECORD #	1453
PAGE	70

NAME	CROSS, Priscilla (alias BISICKS)
PROOF	freedom proved by oath of Jane GIBBONS
DESCRIPTION	abt 30y old, 5' 4½" tall, light complexion, little freckles about the nose & has two very minute scars above the right eye
DATE	9 Nov 1847
RECORD #	1454
PAGE	70

NAME	CROSS, Rowena (alias BISICKS)
PROOF	freedom proved by oath of Jane GIBBONS
DESCRIPTION	abt 26y old, 5' 5" tall, dark complexion, plain scar above the hand on the left wrist, another above the right eye in the forehead, another in the left eye brow & one across the upper part of her nose
DATE	9 Nov 1847
RECORD #	1455
PAGE	70

NAME	WATSON, William (alias of Billy)
PROOF	emancipated by William B. JACKSON
DESCRIPTION	abt 50y old, 5' 7 7/8" tall, brown colour, strong scar above the left eye brow, and some dark blotches above the right eye & around it has a black mole on the inside of the left arm opposite the elbow
DATE	11 Sep 1849
RECORD #	1456
PAGE	71

NAME	PHILLIPS, Harriet
PROOF	freedom proved by oath of William HOUGH
DESCRIPTION	27y old, 5' 3" tall, brown color, scar on her cheek near her right ear & a mole on the neck left side of bluish colour & small
DATE	13 Mar 1848
RECORD #	1457
PAGE	71

NAME	MASON, Ama
PROOF	free born woman
DESCRIPTION	abt 25y old, 5' 3½" tall, yellow complexion, blue mole on right side of neck as large as a small pea
DATE	13 Mar 1848
RECORD #	1458
PAGE	71

NAME	LUCAS, Charles Wm.
PROOF	freedom proved by affirmation of Thomas NICHOLS
DESCRIPTION	upwards of 21y old, 5' 7 1/8" tall, very bright mulatto with light eyes, several small moles about the neck & three small indentations in the forehead
DATE	9 Aug 1848
RECORD #	1459
PAGE	71

NAME	LAWSON, Mahala
PROOF	free woman as proved by oath of Francis SIMPSON
DESCRIPTION	abt 46y old, 5' 5 1/8" tall, dark complexion, small scar on the upper lip & considerable scar on the left arm some 5" or 6" above the hand
DATE	14 Mar 1848
RECORD #	1460
PAGE	72

NAME	LAWSON, Elizabeth Ann
PROOF	free woman as proved by oath of Francis SIMPSON
DESCRIPTION	24y old, 5' 6¼" tall, dark complexion, two scars on her right cheek, a faint scar on the left cheek & a scar on the joint of the wrist on the left arm
DATE	14 Mar 1848
RECORD #	1561 [misnumbered]
PAGE	72

NAME	DADE, Henrietta
PROOF	registered in Fauquier Co.
DESCRIPTION	abt 35y old, 5' 3" tall, dark complexion, small scar on the first finger of the left hand between the first and second joint of the finger, with small ears
DATE	17 Mar 1848
RECORD #	1562
PAGE	72

NAME	ADDISON, Milly
PROOF	emancipated by James SINCLAIR
DESCRIPTION	abt 35y old, 4' 11½" tall, round indentation on the right cheek very small, a small black mole between the left eye & ear left side, and a scar on the left breast caused by a burn near the neck
DATE	29 Mar 1848
RECORD #	1563
PAGE	73

NAME	ADDISON, Richard (son of Milly ADDISON)
PROOF	emancipated by James SINCLAIR
DESCRIPTION	6y old last June
DATE	29 Mar 1848
RECORD #	1563
PAGE	73

NAME	ADDISON, Henrietta (daughter of Milly ADDISON)
PROOF	emancipated by James SINCLAIR
DESCRIPTION	5y old last July
DATE	29 Mar 1848
RECORD #	1563
PAGE	73

NAME	ADDISON, Sally Janney (daughter of Milly ADDISON)
PROOF	emancipated by James SINCLAIR
DESCRIPTION	2y old on 11 May next
DATE	29 Mar 1848
RECORD #	1563
PAGE	73

NAME	RAMSEY, Colvin
PROOF	freedom proved by James McILHANY Esqr
DESCRIPTION	abt 65y old, 6' 1" tall, scar in the forehead just above the left eye & another in the right eye brow & two other scars one on the ball of the right hand above the thumb & the other on the wrist of the same hand
DATE	10 Apr 1848
RECORD #	1564
PAGE	73

NAME	SWEENY, Edward (son of Leuisa SWEENY)
PROOF	proved to be free by oath of John CRIDLER
DESCRIPTION	3y old next October, mulatto colour
DATE	10 Apr 1848
RECORD #	1565
PAGE	74

NAME	GREEN, Lucy
PROOF	emancipated by will of John HAWLING dec'd as proved by the affirmation of Isaac W. HAWLING
DESCRIPTION	61y old, 5' 2" tall, very dark mulatto, some black moles about her face and arms
DATE	8 May 1848
RECORD #	1566
PAGE	74

NAME	GREEN, Westwood
PROOF	emancipated by will of John HAWLING dec'd as proved by the affirmation of Isaac W. HAWLING
DESCRIPTION	abt 42y old, 5' 4" tall, dark but not black complexion, faint scar on the forehead just above the left eye & a long scar on the forefinger of the left hand lengthwise across the middle joint
DATE	8 May 1848
RECORD #	1567
PAGE	74

NAME	JACKSON, Lewis Coaten
PROOF	born free, formerly registered, now proved by oath of Curtis R. SAUNDERS
DESCRIPTION	abt 25y old, 5' 6¾" tall, very dark complexion, scar on left great toe, and one in his forehead above left eye
DATE	15 Aug 1848
RECORD #	1568
PAGE	75

NAME	COLBERT, Leonard
PROOF	emancipated by will of John HAWLING dec'd, as proved by oath of Joseph Lewis HAWLING
DESCRIPTION	abt 50y old, 5' 8½" tall, dark mulatto, small scar above the left eye brow, another in the same eye brow running with it & a scar in the centre of the breast & a long scar on the inside of the wrist just above the hand
DATE	8 May 1848
RECORD #	1569
PAGE	75

NAME	THOMPSON, Archy
PROOF	free man proved by affirmation of Bernard TAYLOR
DESCRIPTION	abt 22y old, 5' 7" tall, dark colour, appearance of a scar in the left eye brow & a small scar in the corner of the same eye or near it & two round scars on his breast, and a black mole just below there, no other marks or scars worthy of notice
DATE	12 Jun 1848
RECORD #	1570
PAGE	75

NAME	GRAYSON, Jesse
PROOF	former register No. 735 and now proved by Margaret DORRELL
DESCRIPTION	abt 42y old, 5' 7 1/8" tall, black complexion, small scar on outside of the right wrist, an indistinct scar above the left eye & a small scar on the back of the middle finger of the right hand
DATE	16 Aug 1848
RECORD #	1571
PAGE	76

NAME	LANE, Charles William (son of Rachel LANE)
PROOF	Register No. 1163, now proved by oath of Margaret DORRELL
DESCRIPTION	abt 14y old, abt 4' 9¾" tall, very black complexion, small scar between the eyebrows, a large scar behind the left ear, is distinguished by a peculiar projection of the upper front teeth
DATE	16 Aug 1848
RECORD #	1572
PAGE	76

NAME	WRIGHT, Sarah Francis (daughter of Delilah WRIGHT)
PROOF	freedom proved by Margaret DORRELL
DESCRIPTION	14m old, dark complexion
DATE	15 Aug 1848
RECORD #	1573
PAGE	76

NAME	JONES, Levin Harrison
PROOF	freedom proved by oath of John MOORE
DESCRIPTION	upwards of 20y old, 5' 7" tall, bright mulatto, some moles on the neck and a sprangled scar on the upper lip & freckled in the face
DATE	15 Aug 1848
RECORD #	1574
PAGE	76

NAME	JONES, William Henry
PROOF	freedom proved by oath of John MOORE Esqr
DESCRIPTION	abt 13y old, scar above the left eye brow, and a large scar on the left cheek & on the back of his left hand caused by a burn, with some other inconsiderable scars
DATE	15 Aug 1848
RECORD #	1575
PAGE	77

NAME	CONTEE, George
PROOF	registered and proved by Jonathan WEAVER, now proved by oath of Daniel MILLER
DESCRIPTION	abt 17y old, 5' 7" tall, mulatto, large scar above his left eye brow, three small scars nearly in a centre of the forehead a small scar in his left thumb between the joints crosswise
DATE	15 Aug 1848
RECORD #	1576
PAGE	77

NAME	MAHONY, Elizabeth
PROOF	freedom proved by oath of Sarah MOLDON
DESCRIPTION	20y old, 5' 5" tall, dark mulatto, mark on the wrist of left hand from burn
DATE	14 Nov 1848
RECORD #	1577
PAGE	77

NAME	MAHONY, Catharine E. (daughter of Elizabeth MAHONY)
PROOF	freedom proved by oath of Sarah MOLDON
DESCRIPTION	going on 5y old, same colour as mother, scar under her chin & another on the left arm between the hand & elbow
DATE	14 Nov 1848
RECORD #	1577
PAGE	77

NAME	MAHONY, Eliza J. (daughter of Elizabeth MAHONY)
PROOF	freedom proved by oath of Sarah MOLDON
DESCRIPTION	going on 2y old, abt same colour as mother
DATE	14 Nov 1848
RECORD #	1577
PAGE	77

NAME	ADAMS, Amanda
PROOF	freedom proved by affirmation of William WILLIAMS
DESCRIPTION	21y old in Sept next, black complexion, 4' 10 3/8" tall, plain scar on the right arm between the wrist & elbow also a scar near the left eye brow & a black mole in the forehead rather on the left side
DATE	16 Nov 1848
RECORD #	1578
PAGE	78

NAME	HOPKINS, Elizabeth (daughter of Kitty BINNS)
PROOF	registered many years ago, proved now by oath of Wm. D. DRISH
DESCRIPTION	abt 56y old, 5' 4" tall, dark mulatto with some natural marks on the under lip
DATE	10 Oct 1848
RECORD #	1579
PAGE	78

NAME	THORNTON, Franklin
PROOF	proved by affirmation of Joshua PUSEY
DESCRIPTION	abt 22y old, 6' 1½" tall, dark colour, faint scar in the forehead, another on the back of the left hand & a large scar caused by a burn on the top of his left foot
DATE	11 Sep 1848
RECORD #	1580
PAGE	79

NAME	THORNTON, Eliza (alias Eliza PALMER)
PROOF	free born appears by affirmation of Abel JANNEY made 10 Jun 1833 and now proved by affirmation of David BROWN
DESCRIPTION	32y old last March, 5' 5¾" tall, dark complexion, small scar near the centre of the forehead
DATE	11 Sep 1848
RECORD #	1581
PAGE	79

NAME	PALMER, Wm. Henry (son of Eliza THORNTON alias PALMER)
PROOF	free born appears by affirmation of Abel JANNEY made 10 Jun 1833 and now proved by affirmation of David BROWN
DESCRIPTION	12y old last May, dark complexion, scar in the forehead
DATE	11 Sep 1848
RECORD #	1581
PAGE	79

NAME	PALMER, Frank (son of Eliza THORNTON alias PALMER)
PROOF	free born appears by affirmation of Abel JANNEY made 10 Jun 1833 and now proved by affirmation of David BROWN
DESCRIPTION	10y old
DATE	11 Sep 1848
RECORD #	1581
PAGE	79

NAME	PALMER, Abraham (son of Eliza THORNTON alias PALMER)
PROOF	free born appears by affirmation of Abel JANNEY made 10 Jun 1833 and now proved by affirmation of David BROWN
DESCRIPTION	8y old
DATE	11 Sep 1848
RECORD #	1581
PAGE	79

NAME	PALMER, Flavius (son of Eliza THORNTON alias PALMER)
PROOF	free born appears by affirmation of Abel JANNEY made 10 Jun 1833 and now proved by affirmation of David BROWN
DESCRIPTION	3y old
DATE	11 Sep 1848
RECORD #	1581
PAGE	79

NAME	PALMER, Bushrod (son of Eliza THORNTON alias PALMER)
PROOF	free born appears by affirmation of Abel JANNEY made 10 Jun 1833 and now proved by affirmation of David BROWN
DESCRIPTION	2y old
DATE	11 Sep 1848
RECORD #	1581
PAGE	79

NAME	WINTERS, Grace
PROOF	emancipated by will of David LACEY dec'd as proved by affirmation of Thomas ROGERS
DESCRIPTION	abt 45y old, 5' tall, dark colour, scar in the outer corner of each eye & another two on the elbow joint of the right arm
DATE	11 Sep 1848
RECORD #	1582
PAGE	79

NAME	WINTERS, Dennis (son of Grace WINTERS)
PROOF	proved by affirmation of Thomas ROGERS
DESCRIPTION	going on 19y old, 5' 4¾" tall, scar on the joint of the left arm elbow
DATE	11 Sep 1848
RECORD #	1583
PAGE	80

NAME	GORAM, George Washington (son of Elizabeth GORAM, a white woman)
PROOF	free born as proved by oath of James T. GORAM
DESCRIPTION	13y old the 24th of next Dec, bright mulatto, scar across his forefinger on the right hand between the two first joints & another small one on the next finger directly opposite
DATE	11 Sep 1848
RECORD #	1584
PAGE	80

NAME	SKINNER, Harriet
PROOF	free born proved by affirmation of Joshua PUSEY
DESCRIPTION	abt 48y old, 5' 6" tall, dark mulatto, a few small specks & moles scattered about her face
DATE	11 Sep 1848
RECORD #	1585
PAGE	80

NAME	WINTERS, George
PROOF	free man as proved by affirmation of Thos. ROGERS
DESCRIPTION	abt 25y old, 5' 5" tall, blackish colour, long scar on the ball of the left thumb, a small scar nearly in the centre of the forehead & another on the check bone just below the left eye
DATE	11 Sep 1848
RECORD #	1586
PAGE	81

NAME	WRIGHT, Amelia
PROOF	emancipated by deed executed by Oscar WRIGHT 13 Sep 1848
DESCRIPTION	abt 34y old, 5' 10¾" tall, dark complexion, scar on the right jaw bone about half way between the ear and chin
DATE	11 Sep 1848
RECORD #	1587
PAGE	81

NAME	McDANIEL, Travis Henry (son of Elizabeth McDANIEL)
PROOF	now registered, mother heretofore examined
DESCRIPTION	1y old 15 Jun 1848, yellow complexion
DATE	9 Oct 1848
RECORD #	1588
PAGE	82

NAME	HARPER, Charlotte (mother of Elizabeth McDANIEL & grandmother of Travis Henry McDANIEL)
PROOF	freedom proved by oath of William SUTTON
DESCRIPTION	54y old, 5' 6¾" tall, dark mulatto, a few moles about the face
DATE	9 Oct 1848
RECORD #	1588
PAGE	82

NAME	JINKINS, Mahala
PROOF	emancipated by Margaret PURSEL, by oath of Enos PURSEL
DESCRIPTION	40y old on 18 Aug last, 5' 2½" tall, dark colour, a dim scar across her nose high up & a small mole on the left side of her face about an inch from the eye toward the left ear
DATE	9 Oct 1848
RECORD #	1589
PAGE	82

NAME	LUCAS, Maria (formerly registered as Maria THORNTON)
PROOF	freedom proved by oath of Robert F. GOODIN
DESCRIPTION	abt 30y old, 5' 5¼" tall, small scar in upper lip, small mole left near nose, dark spot below right eye & faint scar on left cheek
DATE	14 Nov 1848
RECORD #	1590
PAGE	82

NAME	THORNTON, Ann R. (daughter of Maria LUCAS)
PROOF	freedom proved by oath of Robert F. GOODIN
DESCRIPTION	12y old last March, brown colour, flesh mark on the chin & a dark place about the left eye
DATE	14 Nov 1848
RECORD #	1590
PAGE	82

NAME	LUCAS, Jane S. (daughter of Maria LUCAS)
PROOF	freedom proved by oath of Robert F. GOODIN
DESCRIPTION	7y old last Dec, mulatto colour
DATE	14 Nov 1848
RECORD #	1590
PAGE	82

NAME	LUCAS, Jas. F. (son of Maria LUCAS)
PROOF	freedom proved by oath of Robert F. GOODIN
DESCRIPTION	5y old last Jan, very dark mulatto
DATE	14 Nov 1848
RECORD #	1590
PAGE	82

NAME	LUCAS, Eliza R. (daughter of Maria LUCAS)
PROOF	freedom proved by oath of Robert F. GOODIN
DESCRIPTION	3y old, same very dark mulatto
DATE	14 Nov 1848
RECORD #	1590
PAGE	82

NAME	LUCAS, Margaret E. (daughter of Maria LUCAS)
PROOF	freedom proved by oath of Robert F. GOODIN
DESCRIPTION	2y old in Oct 1848, scar on the left arm near the elbow caused by a burn
DATE	14 Nov 1848
RECORD #	1590
PAGE	82

NAME	LUCAS, Charles W. (son of Maria LUCAS)
PROOF	freedom proved by oath of Robert F. GOODIN
DESCRIPTION	infant born last Feb
DATE	14 Nov 1848
RECORD #	1590
PAGE	82

NAME	GORAM, John Henry (son of Elizabeth GORAM)
PROOF	[no information given]
DESCRIPTION	going on 17y old, bright mulatto, scar in centre of forehead just between eye brows & two other slight scars in face
DATE	[14 Nov 1848]
RECORD #	1591
PAGE	83

NAME	TIMBERS, Mariah
PROOF	free born as proved by oath of Margaret DORRELL
DESCRIPTION	abt 31y old, 4' 11½" tall, dark mulatto, two small scars on the right and left sides of the right eye, a small mole on the right cheek below the nose
DATE	10 Oct 1848
RECORD #	1592
PAGE	84

NAME	TIMBERS, Rutha (daughter of Maria TIMBERS)
PROOF	free born as proved by oath of Margaret DORRELL
DESCRIPTION	abt 7y old, dark complexion
DATE	10 Oct 1848
RECORD #	1592
PAGE	84

NAME	TIMBERS, Saml. Benjamin (son of Maria TIMBERS)
PROOF	free born as proved by oath of Margaret DORRELL
DESCRIPTION	abt 1y old, dark mulatto
DATE	10 Oct 1848
RECORD #	1592
PAGE	84

NAME	TIMBERS, Margaret
PROOF	free born as proved by oath of Margaret DORRELL
DESCRIPTION	abt 24y old, 5' ½" tall, light mulatto complexion, slight scar on the forehead near half way up the middle, small scar on the inside of the left arm near the elbow
DATE	10 Oct 1848
RECORD #	1593
PAGE	84

NAME	TIMBERS, Ann Maria (daughter of Margaret)
PROOF	free born as proved by oath of Margaret DORRELL
DESCRIPTION	6y old, bright mulatto
DATE	10 Oct 1848
RECORD #	1593
PAGE	84

NAME	TIMBERS, Betsy (daughter of Margaret)
PROOF	free born as proved by oath of Margaret DORRELL
DESCRIPTION	2y old, bright mulatto
DATE	10 Oct 1848
RECORD #	1593
PAGE	84

NAME	TIMBERS, Margaretta (daughter of Margaret)
PROOF	free born as proved by oath of Margaret DORRELL
DESCRIPTION	7m old, bright mulatto
DATE	10 Oct 1848
RECORD #	1593
PAGE	84

NAME	WINTERS, Mary Ellen (alias JACKSON)
PROOF	free born as proved by oath of Jno. A. BINNS (see Register No. 800) and now by oath of John ISETT
DESCRIPTION	abt 27y old, 5' 5" tall, very dark complexion, smallest finger on left hand slightly discoloured by old burn, no other scars
DATE	[10 Oct 1848]
RECORD #	1593 [misnumbered]
PAGE	84

Loudoun County, Virginia Register of Free Negroes 1844-1861

NAME	HULL, James William
PROOF	freedom proved by affirmation of Nathan WALKER
DESCRIPTION	abt 22y old, 5' 7 3/8" tall, bright mulatto, slight mark on the right cheek, a small mark or stripe about the middle of the right arm between wrist and elbow on the upper side, another scar across the middle of the left arm in same location
DATE	13 Mar 1849
RECORD #	1594
PAGE	85

NAME	MASON, Charles William
PROOF	freedom proved by oath of Presley SAUNDERS
DESCRIPTION	abt 23y old, 5' 7 3/8" tall, bright mulatto, without any scars or marks
DATE	14 Nov 1848
RECORD #	1595
PAGE	85

NAME	NEWMAN, Martha
PROOF	proved by affirmation of Benjamin BIRDSALL
DESCRIPTION	17y old, bright mulatto, 4' 11" tall, no scars or marks
DATE	13 Nov 1848
RECORD #	1596
PAGE	85

NAME	PEARSON, James (alias for James)
PROOF	emancipated by will of George ABEL dec'd and proved by oath of George ABEL
DESCRIPTION	abt 21y old, 5' 7½" tall, bright mulatto, scar above the right eye brow, the last finger of the right hand is crooked at the middle joint, no other apparent scars or marks
DATE	11 Dec 1848
RECORD #	1597
PAGE	86

NAME	DAVIS, Duana
PROOF	freedom proved by John JANNEY Esqr
DESCRIPTION	41y old, 5' 1¾" tall, dark complexion, two faint scars on the left hand & a dark spot on the right cheek
DATE	12 Dec 1848
RECORD #	1598
PAGE	86

NAME	THOMAS, Chandler
PROOF	freedom proved by the affirmation of Joshua NICHOLS
DESCRIPTION	abt 24y or 25y old, 5' 7½" tall, some scars above the left eye & his face freckled
DATE	12 Feb 1849
RECORD #	1599
PAGE	86

NAME	BRADY, Jane Ann
PROOF	free born as proved by affirmation of Joshua NICHOLS
DESCRIPTION	abt 20y old, 5' 2½" tall, dark mulatto, small black mole on the left cheek, some yellow marks in the outer corner of left eye and a small scar in the forehead rather above the right eye & a scar in the forefinger of the left hand on the middle joint
DATE	12 Feb 1849
RECORD #	1600
PAGE	87

NAME	MASON, Mary (alias HULLS)
PROOF	free woman as proved by oath of Edward HAMMATT
DESCRIPTION	abt 59y old, 5' 4½" tall, bright mulatto, large mole on the right side of the chin & three small ones on the nose
DATE	13 Mar 1849
RECORD #	1601
PAGE	87

NAME	MASON, Margaret Elizabeth (daughter of Mary MASON)
PROOF	freedom proved by oath of Edward HAMMATT
DESCRIPTION	abt 19y old, 5' 1¾" tall, bright mulatto, scar or small notch in the lower eyelid of the right eye & a very small black mole back of the same eye
DATE	13 Mar 1849
RECORD #	1602
PAGE	87

NAME	MASON, Mary Catharine (daughter of Mary MASON)
PROOF	freedom proved by oath of Edw'd HAMMATT)
DESCRIPTION	abt 17y old, 5' 2¼" tall, bright mulatto, black mole back of the corner of right eye & two other moles on her upper lip & one above it on the left of her nose & a black mole on the upper part of the wrist of the right hand
DATE	13 Mar 1849
RECORD #	1603
PAGE	87

NAME	MINOR, Sarah Ann (daughter of Nathan MINOR)
PROOF	freedom proved by Edward THOMPSON
DESCRIPTION	abt 18y old, 5' 3½" tall, brown complexion, long scar running lengthwise with the hand just above the thumb very faint
DATE	14 Mar 1849
RECORD #	1604
PAGE	88

NAME	JACKSON, Hezekiah
PROOF	proved to be free by affirmation of Seth SMITH
DESCRIPTION	going on 23y old, 6' 6½" tall, dark complexion each cheek somewhat of a mottle appearance
DATE	9 Apr 1849
RECORD #	1605
PAGE	88

NAME	GREENFIELD, James
PROOF	emancipated by Capt. John ROSE was registered 12 Jan 1841
DESCRIPTION	abt 58y old, 5' 9" tall, dark complexion, a large scar on his left wrist, a large dent in his forehead
DATE	10 Apr 1849
RECORD #	1606
PAGE	88

NAME	LUCAS, Job. Wm.
PROOF	proved to be free by oath of John HAMILTON
DESCRIPTION	abt 21y old, 5' 7¾" tall, bright mulatto, some small scars in the forehead near the hair & also on the back of his left hand
DATE	11 Jun 1849
RECORD #	1607
PAGE	89

NAME	JACKSON, Robert
PROOF	free born as proved by affidavit of John MOORE Esqr
DESCRIPTION	abt 28y old, 5' 6" tall, black complexion, long scar in the forehead running from the hair down toward the left eye brow another scar near the nose on the left side running from it & another scar on the thumb of the right hand near the ball of the hand
DATE	11 Jun 1849
RECORD #	1608
PAGE	89

NAME	JACKSON, Thomas
PROOF	free born as proved by affidavit of John MOORE Esqr
DESCRIPTION	abt 20y old, 5' 9" tall, dark mulatto, scar in the forehead about half way between the left eye brow & hair, a long scar on the right finger running from the upper joint downward and between that finger and the next
DATE	11 Jun 1849
RECORD #	1609
PAGE	89

NAME	CROSS, Betty (alias BROOKS)
PROOF	free born as proved by oath of Joseph HILLIARD
DESCRIPTION	27y old, 5' 2 5/8" tall, dark mulatto, scar in the hind of her left arm, a small black mole from the corner of her right eye a small indentation just above the eye brow of the same eye and another on her right cheek
DATE	12 Jun 1849
RECORD #	1610
PAGE	90

NAME	CROSS, Nancy (alias WINTERS)
PROOF	free born as proved by oath of Joseph HILLIARD
DESCRIPTION	abt 25y old, 5' 3½" tall, dark mulatto, scar near the corner of her right eye another on the left side of her nose and a mole on the left side of her nose, a small protruding mole on her nose near the corner of her right eye & some small scars on the back of each hand
DATE	12 Jun 1849
RECORD #	1611
PAGE	90

NAME	FENTON, Greenberry
PROOF	free born as proved by oath of John MOORE Esqr
DESCRIPTION	25y old the 10th of Jun 1849, 5' 6" tall, dark complexion, long scar just back of the left eye brow running into the edge of the hair and a very small one just in the edge of the same eye brow about the size of squirrel shot, a long scar under the right eye running crosswise, another caused by a burn below the last mentioned scar & nearer to the right ear
DATE	12 Jun 1849
RECORD #	1612
PAGE	90

Loudoun County, Virginia Register of Free Negroes 1844-1861

NAME	JACKSON, George Alexander
PROOF	free born as proved by oath of John MOORE Esqr
DESCRIPTION	abt 22y old, 5' 9 3/8" tall, dark mulatto, some black specks in the face & [? ink smear] mark in the centre of the forehead that may not continue & a scar across the right knee
DATE	12 Jun 1849
RECORD #	1613
PAGE	91

NAME	HOLLY, Martha Elizabeth (alias GRAYSON)
PROOF	registered in Augusta Co. VA
DESCRIPTION	abt 28y old, 5' 3½" tall, bright mulatto, a very small mole above the right thumb & a scar above the right forefinger
DATE	12 Jun 1849
RECORD #	1614
PAGE	91

NAME	GASKINS, Judy
PROOF	emancipated as proved by affirmation of William TATE
DESCRIPTION	abt 63y old, 5' 3" tall, scar just in the centre of the forehead, two small dark scars in the first and second knuckles of the right hand
DATE	9 Jul 1849
RECORD #	1615
PAGE	91

NAME	GASKINS, Areana
PROOF	emancipated as proved by affirmation of William TATE
DESCRIPTION	abt 16y old, 5' 2½" tall, brown colour, scar ½" long on left cheek & a spot scar on the right, quite fleshy
DATE	9 Jul 1849
RECORD #	1616
PAGE	92

NAME	GASKINS, Moses (son of Judy GASKINS)
PROOF	emancipated as proved by affirmation of William TATE
DESCRIPTION	abt 12y old, 4' 7½" tall, brown colour
DATE	9 Jul 1849
RECORD #	1617
PAGE	92

NAME	HAZLIP, Thomas
PROOF	free born as proved by certificate & affidavit of Eliz'th SULLIVAN and proved by Noble S. BRADEN
DESCRIPTION	abt 28y old, 6' 6½" tall, scar in the forehead on the left side running up into the hair & a small scar or two near the corner of the left eye, also a scar on the back of the hand & another large scar on the wrist of the right hand
DATE	13 Aug 1849
RECORD #	1618
PAGE	92

NAME	DAVIS, Washington
PROOF	free born as proved by affirmation of Henry T. GOVER
DESCRIPTION	24y old, 6' 1½" tall, very small scar just above the right eye brow flat at the end of his nose
DATE	14 Aug 1849
RECORD #	1619
PAGE	93

NAME	GILBERT, Phebe
PROOF	freedom proved by oath of Curtis R. SAUNDERS
DESCRIPTION	abt 21y old, 5' 2" tall, brown complexion, a small scar a little below her left nostril on the lip, a dark appearance on the back of her left hand & a long mark running up from between the thumb & forefinger up the wrist, both these last marks are caused by burn
DATE	14 Aug 1849
RECORD #	1620
PAGE	93

NAME	RIVERS, Stephen
PROOF	freedom proved by affirmation of Henry T. GOVER
DESCRIPTION	26y old, 5' 9" tall, dark complexion, small scar or two near the left eye brow, several scars on his hands, thick lips
DATE	14 Aug 1849
RECORD #	1621
PAGE	93

NAME	ADAMS, Hannah Elizabeth
PROOF	freedom proved by affirmation of Thomas ROGERS
DESCRIPTION	abt 25y old, 5' 4" tall, dark complexion, an indentation round mark, on her nose very near the corner of her right eye, and a scar on the back of her right wrist
DATE	14 Aug 1849
RECORD #	1622
PAGE	94

NAME	BRYANT, Lydia Ann (daughter of Eliza BRYANT)
PROOF	emancipated by will of Joseph LEWIS dec'd, free born as proved by oath of Aquilla MEAD
DESCRIPTION	abt 6y old
DATE	14 Aug 1849
RECORD #	1623
PAGE	94

NAME	RANDOLPH, Turner
PROOF	free man as proved by affirmation of Manly MEAD
DESCRIPTION	abt 27y old, 5' 3 1/3" tall, dark complexion, small scar in the forehead and a scar on the lower lip near the left corner of his mouth, the back of the right hand nearly crossed? with a scar from a burn & several scars on the back of the left hand
DATE	14 Aug 1849
RECORD #	1623 [misnumbered]
PAGE	94

NAME	BRYANT, Martha (alias Martha RANDOLPH)
PROOF	freedom proved by affirmation of Manly MEAD
DESCRIPTION	abt 21y old, 5' 2" tall, dark mulatto, small scar on the forehead, and a flesh mole on the left side of her neck
DATE	14 Aug 1849
RECORD #	1624
PAGE	95

NAME	BRYANT, Moses (son of Susan Bryant)
PROOF	freedom proved by oath of P. SAUNDERS
DESCRIPTION	abt 7y old, dark complexion, black looking scar on his left jaw bone
DATE	[14 Aug 1849]
RECORD #	1625
PAGE	95

NAME	BRYANT, James (son of Susan BRYANT)
PROOF	freedom proved by oath of P. SAUNDERS
DESCRIPTION	abt 4y old, scar on the joint bone of the wrist on the right hand
DATE	[14 Aug 1849]
RECORD #	1625
PAGE	95

NAME　　　　　　WINTERS, Mary Ellen
PROOF　　　　　 freedom proved by oath of James GARRISON
DESCRIPTION abt 23y old, 5' 5½" tall, has a white appearance caused by a burn on the two last fingers of her left hand
DATE　　　　　　15 Aug 1849
RECORD #　　　 1626
PAGE　　　　　　95

NAME　　　　　　THOMAS, William
PROOF　　　　　 freedom proved by oath of John E. STEWARD
DESCRIPTION abt 3y old, light colour
DATE　　　　　　15 Aug 1849
RECORD #　　　 1627
PAGE　　　　　　96

NAME　　　　　　ROBERTSON, Alfred Fitzallen (son of Margaret ROBERTSON)
PROOF　　　　　 free born as proved by oath of Albert H. JANNEY
DESCRIPTION abt 6y old, dark complexion
DATE　　　　　　15 Aug 1849
RECORD #　　　 1628
PAGE　　　　　　96

NAME　　　　　　ROBERTSON, John Jefferson (son of Margaret ROBERTSON)
PROOF　　　　　 free born as proved by oath of Albert H. JANNEY
DESCRIPTION abt 15m old, light mulatto
DATE　　　　　　15 Aug 1849
RECORD #　　　 1628
PAGE　　　　　　96

NAME　　　　　　WOOD, Townsend (son of Ann Maria WOOD)
PROOF　　　　　 free born as proved by oath of James BOWLES
DESCRIPTION abt 6y old, dark mulatto
DATE　　　　　　15 Aug 1849
RECORD #　　　 1629
PAGE　　　　　　96

NAME　　　　　　WOOD, Sarah Ellen (daughter of Ann Maria WOOD)
PROOF　　　　　 free born as proved by oath of James BOWLES
DESCRIPTION abt 3y old, dark mulatto
DATE　　　　　　15 Aug 1849
RECORD #　　　 1629
PAGE　　　　　　96

NAME	JONES, Leander (son of Mary Ann JONES)
PROOF	freedom proved by the affirmation of Albert H. JANNEY
DESCRIPTION	abt 1y old, bright mulatto
DATE	15 Aug 1849
RECORD #	1630
PAGE	96

NAME	ROBERTSON, Samuel (son of Maria ROBERTSON)
PROOF	freedom proved by affirmation of Albert H. JANNEY
DESCRIPTION	abt 13y old, light brown
DATE	15 Aug 1849
RECORD #	1631
PAGE	97

NAME	ROBERTSON, John (son of Maranda ROBERTSON)
PROOF	freedom proved by affirmation of Albert H. JANNEY
DESCRIPTION	abt 5y old, little bright brown
DATE	15 Aug 1849
RECORD #	1631
PAGE	97

NAME	CHAMBERS, Alven
PROOF	emancipated by deed from Joel CRAVEN
DESCRIPTION	abt 36y or 37y old, 5' 10" tall, two scars one directly in the outer corner of the right eye and the other a little larger a little below it
DATE	15 Aug 1849
RECORD #	1632
PAGE	97

NAME	CHAMBERS, Albina (child of Nancy CHAMBERS)
PROOF	free born as proved by oath of Joel CRAVEN
DESCRIPTION	5y old, dark mulatto
DATE	15 Aug 1849
RECORD #	1633
PAGE	97

NAME	CHAMBERS, John Henry (child of Nancy CHAMBERS)
PROOF	free born as proved by oath of Joel CRAVEN
DESCRIPTION	3y old, dark mulatto
DATE	15 Aug 1849
RECORD #	1633
PAGE	97

NAME   CHAMBERS, Burr Thomas (child of Nancy CHAMBERS)
PROOF   free born as proved by oath of Joel CRAVEN
DESCRIPTION   9m old, dark mulatto
DATE   15 Aug 1849
RECORD #   1633
PAGE   97

NAME   SKINNER, Isaac (son of Harriet SKINNER)
PROOF   free born as proved by oath of Margaret FULTON
DESCRIPTION   abt 11y old, dark complexion
DATE   11 Sep 1849
RECORD #   1634
PAGE   98

NAME   SKINNER, Armistead (son of Harriet SKINNER)
PROOF   free born as proved by oath of Margaret FULTON
DESCRIPTION   abt 8y old, dark complexion
DATE   11 Sep 1849
RECORD #   1634
PAGE   98

NAME   SKINNER, Eleanor (alias COX, daughter of Harriet
               SKINNER)
PROOF   free born as proved by oath of Marg[ar]et FULTON
DESCRIPTION   abt 22y old, 5' 2½" tall, dark complexion, no particular scars
               or marks
DATE   11 Sep 1849
RECORD #   1635
PAGE   98

NAME   SKINNER, Mary Elizabeth (daughter of Eleanor SKINNER)
PROOF   free born as proved by oath of Margaret FULTON
DESCRIPTION   infant mulatto
DATE   11 Sep 1849
RECORD #   1635
PAGE   98

NAME   SKINNER, Harriet Ann (daughter of Eleanor SKINNER)
PROOF   free born as proved by oath of Margaret FULTON
DESCRIPTION   infant mulatto
DATE   11 Sep 1849
RECORD #   1635
PAGE   98

Loudoun County, Virginia Register of Free Negroes 1844-1861

NAME	SKINNER, George (son of Harriet SKINNER)
PROOF	free born as proved by oath of Margaret FULTON
DESCRIPTION	abt 20y old, 5' 6½" tall, dark complexion, scar in each eye brow, scar on the back of his right hand recently made small & may ultimately disappear
DATE	11 Sep 1849
RECORD #	1636
PAGE	98

NAME	SKINNER, Harrison (son of Harriet SKINNER)
PROOF	free born as proved by oath of Margaret FULTON
DESCRIPTION	abt 17y old, 5' 7½" tall, dark mulatto, wart on the thumb of his left hand, two scars in & about the left eye brow, and some scars on his left ear made by the bite of a dog & a small black mole just above the left eye brow
DATE	11 Sep 1849
RECORD #	1637
PAGE	99

NAME	SKINNER, Sarah (daughter of Harriet SKINNER)
PROOF	free born as proved by oath of Margaret FULTON
DESCRIPTION	abt 14y old, 5' 1 " tall, scar just above the thumb of the left hand & a small mole on her left cheek
DATE	11 Sep 1849
RECORD #	1637 [misnumbered]
PAGE	99

NAME	BINNS, Sally
PROOF	free born as proved by oath of Thomas R. SAUNDERS
DESCRIPTION	abt 40y old, 5' 4" tall, dark complexion, small wart just above the ball of the thumb of the right hand, a little grey headed
DATE	11 Sep 1849
RECORD #	1638
PAGE	99

NAME	COX, George W.
PROOF	free born as proved by oath of Thomas R. SAUNDERS
DESCRIPTION	abt 27y old, 5' 10¾" tall, bright mulatto, circular scar on the thumb of the left hand, a scar on the upper lip another just above it & a scar in the inner edge of the right eye brow, a flesh mole on the left side of his neck
DATE	[11 Sep 1849]
RECORD #	1638 [misnumbered]
PAGE	100

NAME   RUTTER, Matilda (alias STINGER)
PROOF   free woman as proved by oath of Col. John SIMPSON
DESCRIPTION abt 40y old, 5' 6" tall, large scar on the right side of her neck, and another on the left side, caused by the Kings Girl?
DATE   11 Sep 1849
RECORD #   1639
PAGE   100

NAME   DAVIS, Charles
PROOF   free born as proved by oath of Jane TILLETT
DESCRIPTION abt 20y old, 5' 6¾" tall, black man, plain scar in the corner of his right eye outer corner
DATE   11 Sep 1849
RECORD #   1640
PAGE   100

NAME   DAVIS, Hannah Ann
PROOF   free born as proved by oath of Jane TILLETT
DESCRIPTION abt 18y old, 5' 3½" tall, black colour, scar just below left ear
DATE   11 Sep 1849
RECORD #   1641
PAGE   101

NAME   DAVIS, Jane
PROOF   free born as proved by oath of Jane TILLETT
DESCRIPTION abt 16y old, 5' 5¼" tall, brown colour, long scar on the left side of her face, another very small one just above it & a mole on the same side near the left ear
DATE   11 Sep 1849
RECORD #   1642
PAGE   101

NAME   STINGER, Thomas (child of Matilda RUTTER alias Stinger)
PROOF   free born as proved by oath of Jane TILLETT
DESCRIPTION abt 12y old
DATE   11 Sep 1849
RECORD #   1643
PAGE   101

NAME   STINGER, George (child of Matilda RUTTER alias STINGER)
PROOF   free born as proved by oath of Jane TILLETT
DESCRIPTION abt 10y old
DATE   11 Sep 1849
RECORD #   1643
PAGE   101

NAME	STINGER, Samuel (child of Matilda RUTTER alias STINGER)
PROOF	free born as proved by oath of Jane TILLETT
DESCRIPTION	abt 8y old
DATE	11 Sep 1849
RECORD #	1643
PAGE	101

NAME	STINGER, John (child of Matilda RUTTER alias STINGER)
PROOF	free born as proved by oath of Jane TILLETT
DESCRIPTION	abt 6y old
DATE	11 Sep 1849
RECORD #	1643
PAGE	101

NAME	STINGER, Enos (child of Matilda RUTTER alias STINGER)
PROOF	free born as proved by oath of Jane TILLETT
DESCRIPTION	abt 3y old
DATE	11 Sep 1849
RECORD #	1643
PAGE	101

NAME	REED, Alcinda (grandchild of Matilda RUTTER alias STINGER, mother is dead)
PROOF	free born as proved by oath of Jane TILLETT
DESCRIPTION	4y old
DATE	11 Sep 1849
RECORD #	1644
PAGE	102

NAME	REED, George Henry (grandchild of Matilda RUTTER alias STINGER, mother is dead)
PROOF	free born as proved by oath of Jane TILLETT
DESCRIPTION	2½y old
DATE	11 Sep 1849
RECORD #	1644
PAGE	102

NAME	THOMAS, Mary Ann (alias BIRKE, child of Mary Jane THOMAS alias BIRKE)
PROOF	free born as proved by oath of Ann LLOYD
DESCRIPTION	abt 6y old, nearly white
DATE	11 Sep 1849
RECORD #	1645
PAGE	102

NAME	THOMAS, Richard Henry (alias BIRKE, child of Mary Jane THOMAS alias BIRKE)
PROOF	free born as proved by oath of Ann LLOYD
DESCRIPTION	abt 4y old, bright mulatto
DATE	11 Sep 1849
RECORD #	1645
PAGE	102

NAME	THOMAS, James Wm. (alias BIRKE, child of Mary Jane THOMAS alias BIRKE)
PROOF	free born as proved by oath of Ann LLOYD
DESCRIPTION	abt 2y old, bright mulatto
DATE	11 Sep 1849
RECORD #	1645
PAGE	102

NAME	ALEXANDER, Jonathan H.
PROOF	freedom proved by oath of John CRIM
DESCRIPTION	22y old, 5' 8" tall, dark complexion, small indentation on the top of the nose & another near the outer corner of the left eye brow, some few unimportant scars on the back of the hands
DATE	[11 Sep 1849]
RECORD #	1646
PAGE	102

NAME	ALEXANDER, Wm. F.
PROOF	freedom proved by oath of John CRIM
DESCRIPTION	19y old, 5' 5" tall, lt brown colour, ½" scar across right brow
DATE	[11 Sep 1849]
RECORD #	1647
PAGE	103

NAME	ALEXANDER, Mary M.
PROOF	freedom proved by oath of John CRIM
DESCRIPTION	abt 18y old, 5' ½" tall, light brown colour
DATE	[11 Sep 1849]
RECORD #	1648
PAGE	103

NAME	ALEXANDER, Jane E. (sister of Samuel Thomas)
PROOF	freedom proved by oath of John CRIM
DESCRIPTION	16y old, 5' 2" tall, light brown colour
DATE	[11 Sep 1849]
RECORD #	1649
PAGE	103

NAME	ALEXANDER, Samuel Thomas (brother of Jane E.)
PROOF	freedom proved by oath of John CRIM
DESCRIPTION	10y old, light brown colour
DATE	[11 Sep 1849]
RECORD #	1649
PAGE	103

NAME	BIRKE, Lewis
PROOF	freedom proved by oath of Eli J. HAMILTON
DESCRIPTION	abt 25y old, 5' nearly 9" tall, dark colour, scar between the eye brow and several small scars n the back of his hands
DATE	11 Sep 1849
RECORD #	1650
PAGE	103

NAME	ROBERTSON, Susannah
PROOF	freedom proved by oath of [rest of entry blank]
DESCRIPTION	[no information given]
DATE	[11 Sep 1849]
RECORD #	1651
PAGE	104

NAME	MUDDARE?, Emily Jane (child of Fanny LUCAS alias MUDDARE?)
PROOF	free born as proved by affirmation of John W. GRIFFITH
DESCRIPTION	6y old, mulatto colour
DATE	11 Sep 1849
RECORD #	1651 [repeated]
PAGE	104

NAME	MUDDARE?, John Wm. (child of Fanny LUCAS alias MUDDARE?)
PROOF	free born as proved by affirmation of John W. GRIFFITH
DESCRIPTION	5y old, mulatto colour
DATE	11 Sep 1849
RECORD #	1651 [repeated]
PAGE	104

NAME	MUDDARE?, Delila Frances (child of Fanny LUCAS alias MUDDARE?)
PROOF	free born as proved by affirmation of John W. GRIFFITH
DESCRIPTION	4y old, mulatto colour
DATE	11 Sep 1849
RECORD #	1651 [repeated]
PAGE	104

NAME	MUDDARE?, Jas. Henry (child of Fanny LUCAS alias MUDDARE?)
PROOF	free born as proved by affirmation of John W. GRIFFITH
DESCRIPTION	2y old, mulatto colour
DATE	11 Sep 1849
RECORD #	1651 [repeated]
PAGE	104

NAME	RAMSEY, Wm. Wilson (child of Charlotte RAMSEY)
PROOF	free born as proved by oath of Mayo C. W. JANNEY
DESCRIPTION	6y old
DATE	11 Sep 1849
RECORD #	1652
PAGE	105

NAME	RAMSEY, Delilah Jane (child of Charlotte RAMSEY)
PROOF	free born as proved by oath of Mayo C. W. JANNEY
DESCRIPTION	4y old
DATE	11 Sep 1849
RECORD #	1652
PAGE	105

NAME	RAMSEY, Charlotte Ann
PROOF	free born as proved by oath of Mayo C. W. JANNEY
DESCRIPTION	abt 23y old, 5' 3" tall, black complexion, small appearance of scars on the face
DATE	11 Sep 1849
RECORD #	1653
PAGE	105

NAME	RAMSEY, Theodore Fry
PROOF	free born as proved by oath of Mayo C. W. JANNEY
DESCRIPTION	abt 19y old, 5' 6¾" tall, black complexion, mark in the forehead caused by falling against a hot stove
DATE	11 Sep 1849
RECORD #	1653 [repeated]
PAGE	105

NAME	RANDOLPH, Adolphus
PROOF	freedom proved by oath of Aquilla MEAD Jr
DESCRIPTION	abt 23y old, 5' 6½" tall, very dark mulatto, long scar about ½" long in the centre between his eye brows
DATE	11 Sep 1849
RECORD #	1654
PAGE	106

NAME	THOMAS, Mary Jane
PROOF	former register made when she was 16y old
DESCRIPTION	abt 25y old, 5' 3½" tall, mulatto, scar near outer corner of right eye, one on the left side of the forehead and a mole on the forefinger of the right hand near the upper joint or first joint
DATE	11 Sep 1849
RECORD #	1655
PAGE	106

NAME	JACKSON, America Mahala
PROOF	freedom proved by oath of Elizabeth HOUGH
DESCRIPTION	abt 20y old, 5' 4½" tall, black complexion, scar about 1" long near the outer corner of the right eye
DATE	11 Sep 1849
RECORD #	1655 [repeated]
PAGE	106

NAME	GOWAN, Martha Ann
PROOF	freedom proved by oath Eliz'th HOUGH
DESCRIPTION	24y old, 5' 3½" tall, black complexion, scar in the left eye brow & a scar on the back of the right hand
DATE	11 Sep 1849
RECORD #	1656
PAGE	107

NAME	GOWAN, Thos. H. Madison (son of Martha Ann GOWAN)
PROOF	freedom proved by oath Eliz'th HOUGH
DESCRIPTION	10y old, lighter in colour than mother
DATE	11 Sep 1849
RECORD #	1656
PAGE	107

NAME	GOWAN, Amanda E. (daughter of Martha Ann GOWAN)
PROOF	freedom proved by oath Eliz'th HOUGH
DESCRIPTION	6y old, lighter in colour than mother
DATE	11 Sep 1849
RECORD #	1656
PAGE	107

NAME	GOWAN, ___ (child of Martha Ann GOWAN)
PROOF	freedom proved by oath Eliz'th HOUGH
DESCRIPTION	3y old, lighter in colour than mother
DATE	11 Sep 1849
RECORD #	1656
PAGE	107

NAME	DOUGLASS, Ann (child of Harriet PHILLIPS)
PROOF	freedom proved by oath of Mary HOUGH
DESCRIPTION	abt 5y old, mulatto colour
DATE	11 Sep 1849
RECORD #	1657
PAGE	107

NAME	GANT, Milly (daughter of Lucy GANT)
PROOF	free born as proved by affirmation of John JANNEY Esqr and Joseph SINCLAIR Esqr
DESCRIPTION	23y old, 4' 11½" tall, dark complexion, scar over the right eye brow ½" long and one across the thick part of her left hand inside, mole on the inside of her left hand just above the little finger & another scar on the right hand between the thumb & finger
DATE	12 Sep 1849
RECORD #	1658
PAGE	107

NAME	GANT, Rachel Ann (daughter of Milly GANT)
PROOF	free born as proved by affirmation of John JANNEY Esqr and Joseph SINCLAIR Esqr
DESCRIPTION	6y old (? or 1y old)
DATE	12 Sep 1849
RECORD #	1658
PAGE	107

NAME	GANT, Robert Thorn (son of Milly GANT)
PROOF	free born as proved by affirmation of John JANNEY Esqr and Joseph SINCLAIR Esqr
DESCRIPTION	1y old (? or 6y old)
DATE	12 Sep 1849
RECORD #	1658
PAGE	107

NAME	WHEELER, Mary (daughter of Hester WHEELER)
PROOF	free born (No. 960) proved by oath of Landon WORTHINGTON
DESCRIPTION	39y old, 5' 2½" tall, dark complexion, very thick lips, prominent forehead, a very slight appearance of a scar under the left eye
DATE	8 Oct 1849
RECORD #	1659
PAGE	108

NAME	GANTT, Kezziah (daughter of Lucy GANTT, No. 797)
PROOF	formerly proved by affirmation of John SINCLAIR (No. 1258) and now by oath of John McCABE
DESCRIPTION	abt 27y old, 5' 1" tall, dark complexion, scar on the upper side of the left wrist above the thumb, a large scar on the right breast just on the top of collar bone, a long scar across the throat, a large scar behind the left ear
DATE	8 Oct 1849
RECORD #	1660
PAGE	108

NAME	GANTT, George Henry (son of Kezziah GANTT)
PROOF	formerly proved by affirmation of John SINCLAIR (No. 1258) and now by oath of John McCABE
DESCRIPTION	11y old
DATE	8 Oct 1849
RECORD #	1660
PAGE	108

NAME	GANTT, Alcinda (daughter of Kezziah GANTT)
PROOF	formerly proved by affirmation of John SINCLAIR (No. 1258) and now by oath of John McCABE
DESCRIPTION	5y old
DATE	8 Oct 1849
RECORD #	1660
PAGE	108

NAME	GANTT, Thomas (son of Kezziah GANTT)
PROOF	formerly proved by affirmation of John SINCLAIR (No. 1258) and now by oath of John McCABE
DESCRIPTION	4y old
DATE	8 Oct 1849
RECORD #	1660
PAGE	108

NAME	GANTT, Philip (son of Kezziah GANTT)
PROOF	[as with mother?]
DESCRIPTION	1y old
DATE	8 Oct 1849
RECORD #	1660
PAGE	108

NAME   GANTT, Annie (daughter of Kezziah GANTT)
PROOF   [as with mother?]
DESCRIPTION   2y old
DATE   8 Oct 1849
RECORD #   1660
PAGE   108

NAME   JONES, William Henry (son of Jane JONES)
PROOF   free born as proved by oath of Ann RYON
DESCRIPTION   abt 3y old, dark mulatto colour
DATE   8 Oct 1849
RECORD #   1661
PAGE   109

NAME   WRIGHT, James Fenton (son of Betty WRIGHT)
PROOF   free born as proved by oath of Noble S. BRADEN
DESCRIPTION   1y old, dark mulatto colour
DATE   8 Oct 1849
RECORD #   1662
PAGE   109

NAME   NORRIS, Wilson
PROOF   emancipated by deed from Keziah GANT
DESCRIPTION   abt 48y old, 5' 7½" tall, mulatto colour
DATE   8 Oct 1849
RECORD #   1663
PAGE   109

NAME   GANT, William
PROOF   free born proved by oath of John SINCLAIR in a former register made 11 Aug 1845
DESCRIPTION   abt 15y old, 4' 10" tall, dark complexion, round scar on the back of his right hand, there is an appearance on the lower part of his left ear of having been pierced
DATE   8 Oct 1849
RECORD #   1664
PAGE   110

NAME   WRIGHT, James William
PROOF   free born as proved by oath of Wm. HUNT
DESCRIPTION   abt 17y old, dark mulatto colour, nail of forefinger of right hand exhibits the mark of having been crushed, scar on the back of the same hand near the wrist, mole on the right cheek
DATE   8 Oct 1849
RECORD #   1665
PAGE   110

Loudoun County, Virginia Register of Free Negroes 1844-1861   81

NAME	MAGINIS, Charlotte Ann
PROOF	freedom proved by oath of Logan OSBURN
DESCRIPTION	abt 21y old, 5' 4½" tall, bright mulatto, small black mole on the right cheek and a scar on the middle joint of the forefinger on the right hand & some other very dim scars on both hands
DATE	[12 Nov 1849]
RECORD #	1666
PAGE	111

NAME	WINTERS, Thomas
PROOF	freedom proved by affirmation of Thomas ROGERS
DESCRIPTION	abt 22y old, 5' 2¾" tall, dark complexion, scar on the upper lip a little to right & below the right nostril of nose, another on the back of the left hand running from near the joint of the third finger upwards about 1" long and faint
DATE	12 Nov 1849
RECORD #	1667
PAGE	111

NAME	THOMPSON, Mary Jane
PROOF	free born as proved by oath of Sarah C. NOLAND
DESCRIPTION	abt 23y old, 5' tall, dark mulatto, scar of dark colour to the left of the left eye downward, two indebted scars near and below the right eye, two small moles to the left of her nose & a plainer one on the neck left side & 3 scars on the back of the left hand dispersed
DATE	12 Nov 1849
RECORD #	1668
PAGE	111

NAME	THOMPSON, Margaret (daughter of Mary Jane)
PROOF	free born as proved by oath of Sarah C. NOLAND
DESCRIPTION	abt 6y old with the mark of burn on the right cheek
DATE	12 Nov 1849
RECORD #	1668
PAGE	111

NAME	CROSS, Thomas William
PROOF	free man as proved by affirmation of Seth SMITH Esqr
DESCRIPTION	abt 24y old, 5' 8" tall, mulatto colour, defect in his left eye, somewhat freckled and a few small indentations in the face
DATE	10 Dec 1849
RECORD #	1669
PAGE	112

NAME	BALL, James Allison
PROOF	free born as proved by affirmation of Seth SMITH Esqr
DESCRIPTION	abt 15y old, dark mulatto, small scar in the right eye brow
DATE	10 Dec 1849
RECORD #	1670
PAGE	112

NAME	THOMAS, Richard Henry
PROOF	free born as proved by affirmation of Seth SMITH Esqr
DESCRIPTION	abt 6y old, light mulatto, scar in his right eye brow & a small scar on the upper lip
DATE	10 Dec 1849
RECORD #	1670
PAGE	112

NAME	DIGGS, Robert [this entry is crossed out]
PROOF	freedom proved by oath of P. SAUNDERS
DESCRIPTION	abt 21y old, 5' 7¾" tall, scar on upper eyelid of right eye, with some ½ doz small black moles scattered on face, little finger on both hands crooked
DATE	[10 Dec 1849]
RECORD #	1671
PAGE	112

NAME	THORNTON, Philip
PROOF	free man as proved by oath of Charles L. POWELL
DESCRIPTION	abt 65y old, 5' 5" tall, dark complexion, lost the end of his middle finger of the left hand & a finger next to it is crooked
DATE	[10 Dec 1849]
RECORD #	1672
PAGE	113

NAME	ALEXANDER, Thomas
PROOF	freedom proved by oath of George HEAD
DESCRIPTION	22y old next May, 5' 4¾" tall, dark complexion, very plain scar on the right cheek bone & a scar just above the knuckle of the two forefingers on the left hand his under jaw propels
DATE	10 Dec 1849
RECORD #	1673 [renewed 2338]
PAGE	113

Loudoun County, Virginia Register of Free Negroes 1844-1861

NAME	THOMPSON, George Albert
PROOF	free man as proved by affirmation of Benjamin BIRDSALL
DESCRIPTION	21y old in March next, 5' 7¾" tall, light complexion, three scars in the forehead one quite small, a dark spot on the right side of the nose, a small hole near the right ear, a little mark near the corner of the left eye & a long scar on the back of the left hand
DATE	10 Dec 1849
RECORD #	1674
PAGE	113

NAME	CHAMBERS, Letty
PROOF	emancipated this day by Amos WHITACRE
DESCRIPTION	abt 70y old, 5' ½" tall, dark colour, the back of her left hand a good deal scarified
DATE	11 Feb 1850
RECORD #	1675
PAGE	113

NAME	RIDOUT, Susan Jane (child of Mary Catharine RIDOUT)
PROOF	free born as proved by oath of James BOWLES
DESCRIPTION	abt 12y old, dark colour
DATE	11 Feb 1850
RECORD #	1676
PAGE	113

NAME	RIDOUT, John Wm. (child of Mary Catharine RIDOUT)
PROOF	free born as proved by oath of James BOWLES
DESCRIPTION	abt 3y old, dark colour
DATE	11 Feb 1850
RECORD #	1676
PAGE	113

NAME	RIDOUT, James Aaron (child of Mary Catharine RIDOUT)
PROOF	free born as proved by oath of James BOWLES
DESCRIPTION	abt 5m old, dark colour
DATE	11 Feb 1850
RECORD #	1676
PAGE	113

NAME	LEE, Hamilton
PROOF	free as proved by oath of James BOWLES
DESCRIPTION	38y old, 5' 10" tall, mulatto colour, mole on the left cheek and a scar on the right - a faint round mole in the forehead also a wart on the forefinger of the right hand and a wart on the inside of same hand
DATE	11 Feb 1850
RECORD #	1677
PAGE	113

NAME	DAVIS, Jefferson
PROOF	emancipated by John H. CRIM and proved by oath of Richard SPEAKS & Peter JACOBS
DESCRIPTION	40y old last March, 5' 10 1/3" tall, dark complexion, has a scar upwards of an inch long running from the corner of the left eye brow towards the ear, another below it on the cheek bone a small one
DATE	8 Apr 1850
RECORD #	1678
PAGE	114

NAME	GANT, Mary E. J. (daughter of Ann Maria GANT)
PROOF	proved to be the daughter by affirmation of Samuel JANNEY
DESCRIPTION	abt 20m old, now a large white looking scar in the forehead right side near the hair a small scar on the right jaw
DATE	8 Apr 1850
RECORD #	1679
PAGE	114

NAME	LUCAS, Anthony (son of Delila LUCAS)
PROOF	free born as proved by oath of Wm. HUGHES
DESCRIPTION	abt 20y old next June, 5' 8" tall, mulatto, scars on both of his shins of the legs & the ends of the two first fingers & thumb of the right hand cut off
DATE	8 Apr 1850
RECORD #	1680
PAGE	114

NAME	SAUNDERS, James
PROOF	emancipated by Tilghman GORE
DESCRIPTION	abt 57y old, 5' 8½" tall, dark colour, small scar just in the edge of the left eye brow, a scar on the left side of the nose, and a considerable scar on the back of the right hand
DATE	13 May 1850
RECORD #	1681
PAGE	115

NAME	THOMAS, Mary Elizabeth (daughter of Francis THOMAS)
PROOF	free born as proved by oath of Jonah HOOD
DESCRIPTION	15y old, 5' 2" tall, bright mulatto, a circular scar on her neck made by the scratch of a pin
DATE	13 May 1850
RECORD #	1682
PAGE	115

NAME	DAVIS, John Samuel Thomas (child of Elizabeth DAVIS)
PROOF	free born as proved by oath of John RITICOR
DESCRIPTION	abt 13y old, almost white
DATE	13 May 1850
RECORD #	1683
PAGE	115

NAME	DAVIS, Mary Elizabeth (child of Elizabeth DAVIS)
PROOF	free born as proved by oath of John RITICOR
DESCRIPTION	abt 10y old, dark mulatto
DATE	13 May 1850
RECORD #	1683
PAGE	115

NAME	DAVIS, William Cynthia (child of Elizabeth DAVIS)
PROOF	free born as proved by oath of John RITICOR
DESCRIPTION	abt 6y old, dark mulatto
DATE	13 May 1850
RECORD #	1683
PAGE	115

NAME	DAVIS, Ralph (child of Elizabeth DAVIS)
PROOF	free born as proved by oath of John RITICOR
DESCRIPTION	infant, dark mulatto
DATE	13 May 1850
RECORD #	1683
PAGE	115

NAME	BIRD, Caroline (child of James & Henrietta BIRD)
PROOF	emancipated by James BIRD
DESCRIPTION	abt 7y old, bright mulatto, two dark marks or scars under the right eye
DATE	11 Jun 1850
RECORD #	1684
PAGE	116

NAME	BIRD, Cecelia (child of James & Henrietta BIRD)
PROOF	emancipated by James BIRD
DESCRIPTION	abt 6y old, bright mulatto
DATE	11 Jun 1850
RECORD #	1684
PAGE	116

NAME	BUSH, Alsey Ann
PROOF	previously registered & proved by oath of Duanna WATT, now proved by P. SAUNDERS
DESCRIPTION	abt 26y old, 5' 7" tall, brown colour, small black mole inside left arm, two forefingers on each hand a little crooked at end
DATE	8 Jul 1850
RECORD #	1685
PAGE	116

NAME	BUSH, Amy Elenor
PROOF	previously registered & proved by oath of Duanna WATT, now proved by P. SAUNDERS
DESCRIPTION	abt 22y old, 5' 4" tall, two small round scars on the face under the left eye
DATE	8 Jul 1850
RECORD #	1686
PAGE	116

NAME	BUSH, Duanna
PROOF	previously registered & proved by oath of Duanna WATT, now proved by P. SAUNDERS
DESCRIPTION	abt 20y old, 5' 6¾" tall, small mole on the front of her neck
DATE	8 Jul 1850
RECORD #	1687
PAGE	116

NAME	COLBERT, Armistead (child of Amanda COLBERT)
PROOF	freedom proved by oath of Catharine RYAN
DESCRIPTION	abt 3y old
DATE	8 Jul 1850
RECORD #	1688
PAGE	117

NAME	RANDOLPH, Sarah E. (daughter of Rosana FORD)
PROOF	free born proved by oath of ___
DESCRIPTION	8y old, very light mulatto, white spot in the forehead
DATE	8 Jul 1850
RECORD #	1689
PAGE	117

Loudoun County, Virginia Register of Free Negroes 1844-1861

NAME	BUCKINGHAM, Thomas Henry
PROOF	registered in Sept 1850 and proved as free born by oath of Solomon SMITH
DESCRIPTION	abt 23y old, 5' 6 3/8" tall, dark mulatto, ears pierced, mole above the right eye brow, a small round indentation about 1" below the mole, a scar on the back of his right hand on the upper joint of the middle finger; resident of Loudoun; no permission has been granted to him to remain in state of Virginia
DATE	10 Sep 1850
RECORD #	1690
PAGE	118

NAME	BUCKINGHAM, Robert H.
PROOF	registered in Sept 1850 and proved as free born by oath of Solomon SMITH
DESCRIPTION	15y old, 5' 5" tall, dark mulatto, has always resided in Loudoun, scar in the inner corner of the left eye brow, a small one in the centre of his forehead and a dark or cloudy mark on the right jaw & a scar on each of his forefingers on either hand; no permission has been granted to him to remain in the state of Virginia
DATE	10 Sep 1850
RECORD #	1691
PAGE	118

NAME	LEE, Harriet
PROOF	emancipated by Verlinda PERRY
DESCRIPTION	abt 35y old, 5' 3¼" tall, bright mulatto, face freckled, on the right ear on the lower edge is a dark appearance, and on her left arm about 8", 9", or 10" above the wrist has a blue green lump; no permission has been granted them to remain in the state
DATE	17 Oct 1850
RECORD #	1692
PAGE	118

NAME	LEE, Wesley (child of Harriet)
PROOF	emancipated by Verlinda PERRY
DESCRIPTION	going on 11y old, mulatto darker than his mother, scar near the left temple & a round scar between the eye brows; no permission has been granted them to remain in the state of Virginia
DATE	17 Oct 1850
RECORD #	1692
PAGE	118

NAME	LEE, Arther (child of Harriet)
PROOF	emancipated by Verlinda PERRY
DESCRIPTION	going on 10y old, mulatto darker than his mother, small black mole on his left ear; no permission has been granted them to remain in the state of Virginia
DATE	17 Oct 1850
RECORD #	1692
PAGE	118

NAME	LEE, Mary (child of Harriet)
PROOF	emancipated by Verlinda PERRY
DESCRIPTION	going on 8y old, a shade lighter in colour, dark blotch on her breast near the neck on the right side; no permission has been granted them to remain in the state of Virginia
DATE	17 Oct 1850
RECORD #	1692
PAGE	118

NAME	LEE, Hannah (child of Harriet)
PROOF	emancipated by Verlinda PERRY
DESCRIPTION	going on 6y old, about the same colour as boys, dark spot on wrist a few inches above thumb on left side or arm; no permission has been granted them to remain in state of Va
DATE	17 Oct 1850
RECORD #	1692
PAGE	118

NAME	LEE, Amanda (child of Harriet)
PROOF	emancipated by Verlinda PERRY
DESCRIPTION	going on 5y old, perhaps 2 or 3 shades darker than the others, cavities below her eyes; no permission has been granted them to remain in the state of Virginia
DATE	17 Oct 1850
RECORD #	1692
PAGE	118

NAME	LEE, Martha (child of Harriet)
PROOF	born since mother's emancipation, and affirmed by oath of Elias HUGHES & Verlinda PERRY
DESCRIPTION	abt 2y old, considerably darker colour than the other children; no permission has been granted them to remain in the state of Virginia
DATE	17 Oct 1850
RECORD #	1692
PAGE	118

Loudoun County, Virginia Register of Free Negroes 1844-1861

NAME	LEE, Armistead (child of Harriet)
PROOF	born since mother's emancipation, and affirmed by oath of Elias HUGHES & Verlinda PERRY
DESCRIPTION	8m old, same colour of the first children; no permission has been granted them to remain in the state of Virginia
DATE	17 Oct 1850
RECORD #	1692
PAGE	118

NAME	HALL, Edward
PROOF	register Sept 1850 his freedom proved by oath of Squire BELL
DESCRIPTION	abt 20y old, 5' 10¾" tall, nearly black, a bumpy face, and a defective forefinger on the right hand and a small scar between that finger and the next finger next to the hand; no permission has been granted him for remaining in the state
DATE	14 Oct 1850
RECORD #	1693
PAGE	119

NAME	HALL, Nat.
PROOF	freedom proved by oath of Squire BELL at Sept Court 1850
DESCRIPTION	abt 17y old, 5' 9" tall, nearly black, no marks or scars; no permission to remain in the state of Va
DATE	14 Oct 1850
RECORD #	1694
PAGE	120

NAME	HALL, Eliza
PROOF	freedom proved by oath of Squire BELL
DESCRIPTION	abt 23y old, 5' 5 3/8" tall, dark mulatto, dark spot just below left eye & another just to the left & little finger on left hand crooked at the last joint; no permission to remain in state
DATE	15 Oct 1850
RECORD #	1695
PAGE	120

NAME	HALL, Mary Ann
PROOF	freedom proved by oath of John BEAVERS
DESCRIPTION	abt 26y old, 5' 3" tall, very dark mulatto, third finger on right hand is unusually large at end & has pout tooth in up jaw that projects & laps upon others; no permission to remain in state
DATE	15 Oct 1850
RECORD #	1696
PAGE	120

NAME	BURKE, Enos
PROOF	free born proved by affirmation of Dr. Daniel JANNEY
DESCRIPTION	abt 30y old, 5' 8½" tall, very dark mulatto, round indentation on the left side of the nose about the size of a squirrel shot & nose a little crooked, his right hand cut & tied up which may leave a scar
DATE	14 Oct 1850
RECORD #	1697
PAGE	120

NAME	BURK, Martha Jane (now GRAYSON)
PROOF	free born proved by affirmation of Dr. Daniel JANNEY
DESCRIPTION	abt 28y old, 5' 5¾" tall, very dark mulatto, ears have been pierced, no other visible scars or marks
DATE	14 Oct 1850
RECORD #	1698
PAGE	121

NAME	DIMY, Marcus
PROOF	free born proved by oath of James THOMPSON
DESCRIPTION	abt 20y old, 5' 7" tall, dark mulatto, a sort of fungus on the thumb of right hand produced by the use of the handle of tools with which he has been accustomed to work
DATE	14 Oct 1850
RECORD #	1699
PAGE	121

NAME	DIMY, Nimrod
PROOF	free born proved by oath of James THOMPSON
DESCRIPTION	abt 16y old, 5' 6" tall, mulatto, very small mole on the front of his neck
DATE	14 Oct 1850
RECORD #	1700
PAGE	121

NAME	DIMY, Turney (child of Marcus DIMY)
PROOF	free born as proved by oath of James THOMPSON
DESCRIPTION	abt 14y old, mulatto, scar across back of his right hand
DATE	14 Oct 1850
RECORD #	1701
PAGE	122

NAME	DIMY, Elizabeth (child of Marcus DIMY)
PROOF	free born as proved by oath of James THOMPSON
DESCRIPTION	abt 11y old, mulatto
DATE	14 Oct 1850
RECORD #	1701
PAGE	122

NAME	BALL, James Allison (child of Eliza BALL now dead)
PROOF	free born as proved by affirmation of Seth SMITH & John WEADON
DESCRIPTION	abt 15y old, very dark mulatto, scar in the right eye brow
DATE	14 Oct 1850
RECORD #	1702
PAGE	122

NAME	BALL, Richard Henry Thomas (child of Eliza BALL now dead)
PROOF	free born as proved by affirmation of Seth SMITH & John WEADON
DESCRIPTION	abt 8y old, bright mulatto, scar in the right eye brow
DATE	14 Oct 1850
RECORD #	1702
PAGE	122

NAME	JONES, Joseph Parkison (child of Philip & Sarah JONES)
PROOF	freedom proved by affirmation of Wm. TATE
DESCRIPTION	8y old, mulatto
DATE	14 Oct 1850
RECORD #	1702
PAGE	122

NAME	JONES, Asbury (child of Philip & Sarah JONES)
PROOF	freedom proved by affirmation of Wm. TATE
DESCRIPTION	6y old, mulatto
DATE	14 Oct 1850
RECORD #	1702
PAGE	122

NAME	JONES, George William (child of Philip & Sarah JONES)
PROOF	freedom proved by affirmation of Wm. TATE
DESCRIPTION	4y old, mulatto
DATE	14 Oct 1850
RECORD #	1702
PAGE	122

NAME	JONES, Margaret Ann (child of Philip & Sarah JONES)
PROOF	freedom proved by affirmation of Wm. TATE
DESCRIPTION	2y old, mulatto
DATE	14 Oct 1850
RECORD #	1702
PAGE	122

NAME	MADDISON, Frances
PROOF	free woman as proved by former register under the name of Frances MANLY (alias BIGBY) having married since, now proved by oath of Thomas L. HUMPHREY
DESCRIPTION	abt 43y old, 5' 4" tall, dark copper colour, scar on the inside of her right arm a few inches above the hand and a mole on the upper lip
DATE	15 Oct 1850
RECORD #	1703
PAGE	123

NAME	MADDISON, Levin
PROOF	emancipated by Frances MADDISON
DESCRIPTION	abt 40y? old [ink smeared], 5' 10" tall, dark copper colour, plain scar in the left eye brow & a scar on the back of left wrist
DATE	15 Oct 1850
RECORD #	1704
PAGE	123

NAME	McCARTY, Rachel
PROOF	freedom proved by oath of Squire BELL
DESCRIPTION	abt 30y old, 5' 2" tall, left eye is somewhat defective & differing in appearance from the other
DATE	9 Sep 1850
RECORD #	1705
PAGE	123

NAME	RUST, John Thomas (son of Betsy RUST formerly Betsy CROSS)
PROOF	free born as proved by oath of Isaac EATON
DESCRIPTION	21y old, 5' 11" tall, copper colour, scar in the inner corner of the right eye brow, some dark appearances about the face, a scar on the ball of the right thumb and a large scar on the left shoulder
DATE	15 Oct 1850
RECORD #	1706
PAGE	124

Loudoun County, Virginia Register of Free Negroes 1844-1861

NAME	RUST, Lydia E. (daughter of Betsy RUST formerly Betsy CROSS)
PROOF	free born as proved by oath of Isaac EATON
DESCRIPTION	19y old, 5' 3¾" tall, copper colour, scar in the forehead, one on the left cheek and then near the left eye brow outside & a scar on the inside of each wrist
DATE	15 Oct 1850
RECORD #	1707
PAGE	124

NAME	RIVERS, Jacob
PROOF	emancipated by Isaiah B. BEANS
DESCRIPTION	between 26y & 27y old, 5' 11½" tall, mulatto colour, black mole in the forehead, a small one on the right side of the nose, and a smaller one on the jaw near the right ear, some warts on his right hand, and a broad scar on the middle finger of the right hand between the two first joints on the back or upper part of the finger
DATE	13 Nov 1850
RECORD #	1708
PAGE	124

NAME	RIDOUT, Martha
PROOF	free born as proved by oath of James McILHANY Esqr
DESCRIPTION	abt 38y old, 5' 3½" tall, dark complexion, considerable mole on the left side of the neck, no other mark or scar
DATE	14 Nov 1850
RECORD #	1709
PAGE	125

NAME	RIDOUT, Sarah Winefred (daughter of Martha)
PROOF	free born as proved by oath of James McILHANY Esqr
DESCRIPTION	abt 11y old, 4' 11 7/8" tall, scar on the right cheek
DATE	14 Nov 1850
RECORD #	1709
PAGE	125

NAME	RIVERS, James Robert Rudolph (son of Dinah RIVERS)
PROOF	free as proved by oath of Susan BROOKS
DESCRIPTION	abt 20y old, 5' 11¼" tall, bright mulatto, scar in the centre of the forehead & two small ones to the right side of it and a small scar on the ridge of the nose
DATE	16 Nov 1850
RECORD #	1710
PAGE	125

NAME	JACKSON, Kitty
PROOF	emancipated by the will of Elizabeth G. BEATY
DESCRIPTION	abt 28y old, 5' 1¼" tall, bright mulatto, large scar in the forehead in the edge of the hair above the right eye caused by a burn, no other scars or marks
DATE	12 Nov 1850
RECORD #	1711
PAGE	126

NAME	JACKSON, Huldah (child of Kitty JACKSON)
PROOF	emancipated by the will of Elizabeth G. BEATY
DESCRIPTION	abt 8y old, considerably darker complexion than her mother
DATE	12 Nov 1850
RECORD #	1711
PAGE	126

NAME	JACKSON, Hannah Ann (child of Kitty JACKSON)
PROOF	emancipated by the will of Elizabeth G. BEATY
DESCRIPTION	abt 6y old, same complexion as sister
DATE	12 Nov 1850
RECORD #	1711
PAGE	126

NAME	JACKSON, Mary (child of Kitty JACKSON)
PROOF	emancipated by the will of Elizabeth G. BEATY
DESCRIPTION	abt 3y old, same complexion as sister
DATE	12 Nov 1850
RECORD #	1711
PAGE	126

NAME	WILLIAMS, Harriet
PROOF	emancipated by will of Elizabeth G. BEATY
DESCRIPTION	abt 45y or 46y old, 5' 2½" tall, ears have been pierced
DATE	12 Nov 1850
RECORD #	1712
PAGE	126

NAME	YOUNG, Henson
PROOF	emancipated by will of Jacob MOCK, proved by oath of George W. MOCK
DESCRIPTION	abt 38y old, 5' 4½" tall, mulatto complexion, some scars in the forehead & one on the left jaw and some scars on the left hand one on the back & the other on the thumb
DATE	9 Dec 1850
RECORD #	1713
PAGE	126

NAME	ALEXANDER, Henry
PROOF	freedom proved by oath of Thomas M. HUMPHREY
DESCRIPTION	23y old, 5' 8 7/8" tall, light mulatto, several scars in his forehead between the eyebrows, running up & down two in the left eye brow & some above it, a scar on the calf of his left leg caused by the bite of a dog, and a dark spot on the right hip
DATE	13 Jan 1851
RECORD #	1714
PAGE	127

NAME	COLEMAN, Robert
PROOF	mother free previously to the year 1806 as proved by oath of Catharine GLASGOW
DESCRIPTION	abt 22y old, 5' 8½" tall, dark mulatto, some black moles in face, a scar in the centre of his breast & a large scar on the outside of the left leg above the ancle
DATE	10 Feb 1851
RECORD #	1715
PAGE	127

NAME	PALMER, Daniel
PROOF	freedom proved by affirmation of Daniel JANNEY
DESCRIPTION	abt 20y old, 5' 4¾" tall, very dark mulatto, small scar running from the outer edge of his right eye brow & some small scars in the forehead and a long faint scar running across his forehead above the left eye brow barely visible
DATE	14 Oct 1850
RECORD #	1716
PAGE	127

NAME	MOXLEY, George
PROOF	freedom proved by oath of James THOMAS
DESCRIPTION	abt 23y old, 5' 3" tall, brown colour dark, scar in the forehead and a round scar on the left side of his nose a round scar in his right whisker
DATE	14 Apr 1851
RECORD #	1717
PAGE	128

NAME	LYONS, Leander
PROOF	free man emancipated by Mary M. FRAZIER and proved by oath of D. HIXSON
DESCRIPTION	abt 50y old, 5' 8" tall, nearly black, left leg shorter & smaller than the right walk lame, scar on the upper joint of little finger on the left hand, another scar on the forefinger of the right hand a little above the first joint & has a scar in the right corner of the right eye
DATE	14 Apr 1851
RECORD #	1718
PAGE	128

NAME	LEWIS, Ann
PROOF	freedom proved by oath of Wm. KEENE
DESCRIPTION	abt 37y old, 4' 11½" tall, nearly black, thickly pitted with the small pox, no other visible marks
DATE	12 May 1851
RECORD #	1719
PAGE	128

NAME	CARTER, Wm. H. (son of Joseph & Martha Ann CARTER)
PROOF	free born as proved by oath of Fenton M. LOVE
DESCRIPTION	abt 13y old, dark, though bright, mulatto, scar in the forehead over the left eye
DATE	9 Sep 1851
RECORD #	1720
PAGE	129

NAME	CARTER, John (son of Joseph & Martha Ann CARTER)
PROOF	free born as proved by oath of Fenton M. LOVE
DESCRIPTION	abt 9y old, same colour as his brother
DATE	9 Sep 1851
RECORD #	1720
PAGE	129

NAME	CARTER, Harriet Ann (daughter of Joseph & Martha Ann CARTER)
PROOF	free born as proved by oath of Fenton M. LOVE
DESCRIPTION	abt 5y old, same colour as her brothers
DATE	9 Sep 1851
RECORD #	1720
PAGE	129

Loudoun County, Virginia Register of Free Negroes 1844-1861

NAME	CARTER, Alcinda (daughter of Joseph & Martha Ann CARTER)
PROOF	free born as proved by oath of Fenton M. LOVE
DESCRIPTION	abt 3y old, same colour as her brothers
DATE	9 Sep 1851
RECORD #	1720
PAGE	129

NAME	CARTER, Joseph (son of Joseph & Martha Ann CARTER)
PROOF	free born as proved by oath of Fenton M. LOVE
DESCRIPTION	abt 1y old, same colour as siblings
DATE	9 Sep 1851
RECORD #	1720
PAGE	129

NAME	FIELDS, Susan
PROOF	freedom proved by oath of Wm. HOUGH
DESCRIPTION	abt 45y old, dark complexion, 5' 2" tall, no visible scars or marks
DATE	9 Sep 1851
RECORD #	1721
PAGE	129

NAME	FIELDS, Louisa (daughter of Susan FIELDS)
PROOF	freedom proved by oath of Wm. HOUGH
DESCRIPTION	abt 24y old, 5' 3½" tall, same colour as mother
DATE	9 Sep 1851
RECORD #	1721
PAGE	129

NAME	FIELDS, George Wm. (son of Susan FIELDS)
PROOF	freedom proved by oath of Wm. HOUGH
DESCRIPTION	abt 22y old, 6' 1½" tall, same colour as mother
DATE	9 Sep 1851
RECORD #	1721
PAGE	129

NAME	FIELDS, Ellen William (daughter of Susan FIELDS)
PROOF	freedom proved by oath of Wm. HOUGH
DESCRIPTION	abt 20y old, 5' 2" tall, same colour as mother
DATE	9 Sep 1851
RECORD #	1721
PAGE	129

Loudoun County, Virginia Register of Free Negroes 1844-1861

NAME   FIELDS, Martha (daughter of Susan FIELDS)
PROOF   freedom proved by oath of Wm. HOUGH
DESCRIPTION   abt 16y old, 5' 2" tall, same colour as mother
DATE   9 Sep 1851
RECORD #   1721
PAGE   129

NAME   FIELDS, James (son of Susan FIELDS)
PROOF   freedom proved by oath of Wm. HOUGH
DESCRIPTION   15y old, 5' 9½" tall, same colour as mother
DATE   9 Sep 1851
RECORD #   1721
PAGE   129

NAME   FIELDS, Aaron (son of Susan FIELDS)
PROOF   freedom proved by oath of Wm. HOUGH
DESCRIPTION   13y old, same colour as mother
DATE   9 Sep 1851
RECORD #   1721
PAGE   129

NAME   FIELDS, Sally (daughter of Susan FIELDS)
PROOF   freedom proved by oath of Wm. HOUGH
DESCRIPTION   abt 12y old, same colour as mother
DATE   9 Sep 1851
RECORD #   1721
PAGE   129

NAME   FIELDS, Winny (daughter of Susan FIELDS)
PROOF   freedom proved by oath of Wm. HOUGH
DESCRIPTION   abt 10y old, same colour as mother
DATE   9 Sep 1851
RECORD #   1721
PAGE   129

NAME   FIELDS, Susan (daughter of Susan FIELDS)
PROOF   freedom proved by oath of Wm. HOUGH
DESCRIPTION   abt 8y old, same colour as mother
DATE   9 Sep 1851
RECORD #   1721
PAGE   129

NAME   FIELDS, Hannah (daughter of Susan FIELDS)
PROOF   freedom proved by oath of Wm. HOUGH
DESCRIPTION abt 5y old, same colour as mother
DATE   9 Sep 1851
RECORD #   1721
PAGE   129

NAME   FIELDS, John (son of Susan FIELDS)
PROOF   freedom proved by oath of Wm. HOUGH
DESCRIPTION abt 2y old, same colour as mother
DATE   9 Sep 1851
RECORD #   1721
PAGE   129

NAME   FIELDS, Jane (daughter of Louisa FIELDS)
PROOF   freedom proved by Wm. HOUGH
DESCRIPTION 6y old, brown colour
DATE   9 Sep 1851
RECORD #   1922 [misnumbered]
PAGE   130

NAME   FIELDS, Catharine (daughter of Louisa FIELDS)
PROOF   freedom proved by Wm. HOUGH
DESCRIPTION 4y old, brown colour
DATE   9 Sep 1851
RECORD #   1922 [misnumbered]
PAGE   130

NAME   FIELDS, George (son of Louisa FIELDS)
PROOF   freedom proved by Wm. HOUGH
DESCRIPTION 1y old, brown colour
DATE   9 Sep 1851
RECORD #   1922 [misnumbered]
PAGE   130

NAME   WILLIAMS, John
PROOF   freedom proved by oath of Wm. HOUGH
DESCRIPTION 23y old, 5' 8½" tall, bright mulatto, visible scars except on the right side of the forehead
DATE   9 Sep 1851
RECORD #   1923
PAGE   130

NAME	McDANIEL, Ellen
PROOF	freedom proved by oath of Peggy MAGRAUGH
DESCRIPTION	abt 32y old, 5' 6" tall, dark mulatto, plain black mole on the left side of the neck and a scar above it on back of her ear
DATE	9 Sep 1851
RECORD #	1924
PAGE	130

NAME	PALMER, Samuel (child of John & Jane PALMER)
PROOF	freedom proved by affirmation of Joshua PUSEY
DESCRIPTION	13y old, dark complexion
DATE	13 Oct 1851
RECORD #	1925
PAGE	131

NAME	PALMER, Philip H. (child of John & Jane PALMER)
PROOF	freedom proved by affirmation of Joshua PUSEY
DESCRIPTION	6y old, dark complexion
DATE	13 Oct 1851
RECORD #	1925
PAGE	131

NAME	PALMER, Ann Elizabeth (child of John & Jane PALMER)
PROOF	freedom proved by affirmation of Joshua PUSEY
DESCRIPTION	3½y old, dark complexion
DATE	13 Oct 1851
RECORD #	1925
PAGE	131

NAME	PALMER, John William (child of John & Jane PALMER)
PROOF	freedom proved by affirmation of Joshua PUSEY
DESCRIPTION	1y old, dark complexion
DATE	13 Oct 1851
RECORD #	1925
PAGE	131

NAME	CARTER, Robert Isaac (son of Malinda CARTER)
PROOF	freedom proved by the affirmation of Joshua PUSEY
DESCRIPTION	1y old last May, dark colour
DATE	13 Oct 1851
RECORD #	1926
PAGE	131

Loudoun County, Virginia Register of Free Negroes 1844-1861

NAME	JENNINGS, Elias Edwd (son of John & Mary Ann JENNINGS)
PROOF	freedom proved by oath of David CARR
DESCRIPTION	12y old, dark mulatto
DATE	13 Oct 1851
RECORD #	1927
PAGE	131

NAME	JENNINGS, Ann Elizabeth (child of John & Mary Ann JENNINGS)
PROOF	freedom proved by oath of David CARR
DESCRIPTION	10y old, dark mulatto
DATE	13 Oct 1851
RECORD #	1927
PAGE	131

NAME	JENNINGS, Samuel Wm. (child of John & Mary Ann JENNINGS)
PROOF	freedom proved by oath of David CARR
DESCRIPTION	9y old, dark mulatto
DATE	13 Oct 1851
RECORD #	1927
PAGE	131

NAME	JENNINGS, Mary Ellen (child of John & Mary Ann JENNINGS)
PROOF	freedom proved by oath of David CARR
DESCRIPTION	6y old, dark mulatto
DATE	13 Oct 1851
RECORD #	1927
PAGE	131

NAME	JENNINGS, Lewis Fenton (child of John & Mary Ann JENNINGS)
PROOF	freedom proved by oath of David CARR
DESCRIPTION	4y old, dark mulatto
DATE	13 Oct 1851
RECORD #	1927
PAGE	131

NAME	JENNINGS, John Henry (son John & Mary Ann JENNINGS)
PROOF	freedom proved by oath of David CARR
DESCRIPTION	8m old, dark mulatto
DATE	13 Oct 1851
RECORD #	1927
PAGE	131

NAME	LUCAS, Noah (son of Sarah LUCAS)
PROOF	freedom proved by oath of Col. John LESLIE
DESCRIPTION	abt 16y old, bright mulatto, has a tit in the right ear & his eyes are rather light
DATE	14 Oct 1851
RECORD #	1928
PAGE	132

NAME	LUCAS, James (son of Bersheba LUCAS)
PROOF	freedom proved by oath of Col. John LESLIE
DESCRIPTION	abt 8y old, bright mulatto, small scar on the right side of nose
DATE	14 Oct 1851
RECORD #	1928
PAGE	132

NAME	RIDOUT, Wm.
PROOF	freedom proved by oath of Jas. McILHANY
DESCRIPTION	abt 32y old, 5' 6¼" tall, no visible scars or marks
DATE	14 Oct 1851
RECORD #	1929
PAGE	132

NAME	DAVIS, Charles
PROOF	freedom proved by oath of Saml. PURCEL
DESCRIPTION	18y old, 5' 7" tall, dark complexion, several scars in the centre of his forehead and a plain scar on right leg just below knee
DATE	14 Oct 1851
RECORD #	1932 [misnumbered]
PAGE	132

NAME	DAVIS, Courtney
PROOF	freedom proved by Samuel PURCEL
DESCRIPTION	abt 52y old, 5' 2½" tall, dark complexion, ears have been pierced, no other scar or mark worthy of note
DATE	14 Oct 1851
RECORD #	1930
PAGE	133

NAME	DAVIS. Mary A. (daughter of Courtney DAVIS)
PROOF	freedom proved by Samuel PURCEL
DESCRIPTION	abt 16y old, 5' 4" tall, no particular scar or mark
DATE	14 Oct 1851
RECORD #	1931
PAGE	133

NAME	DAVIS, John
PROOF	freedom proved by oath of Samuel PURCEL
DESCRIPTION	abt 14y old, a [? ink smear] appearance on his left cheek no other mark
DATE	14 Oct 1851
RECORD #	1932
PAGE	133

NAME	RIDOUT, Georgianna
PROOF	freedom proved by oath of Samuel PURSELL
DESCRIPTION	24y old, dark mulatto, 5' 5" tall, two scars in the forehead & a scar near the right corner of her mouth & another just below the right nostril
DATE	14 Oct 1851
RECORD #	1933
PAGE	133

NAME	RIDOUT, Mary Louisa (child of Georgianna)
PROOF	freedom proved by oath of Samuel PURSELL
DESCRIPTION	6y old, very dark mulatto
DATE	14 Oct 1851
RECORD #	1933
PAGE	133

NAME	RIDOUT, Sarah Wineford (child of Georgianna)
PROOF	freedom proved by oath of Samuel PURSELL
DESCRIPTION	4y old, very dark mulatto
DATE	14 Oct 1851
RECORD #	1933
PAGE	133

NAME	RIDOUT, Aaron Moses (child of Georgianna)
PROOF	freedom proved by oath of Samuel PURSELL
DESCRIPTION	3y old, very dark mulatto
DATE	14 Oct 1851
RECORD #	1933
PAGE	133

NAME	RIDOUT, Courtney Anna (child of Georgianna)
PROOF	freedom proved by oath of Samuel PURSELL
DESCRIPTION	6m old, very dark mulatto
DATE	14 Oct 1851
RECORD #	1933
PAGE	133

NAME	JACKSON, John
PROOF	freedom proved by oath of Wm. BALL
DESCRIPTION	28y old last March, 5' 9" tall, dark complexion, ears have been pierced, two scars in the forehead & a mole on the right cheek bone & a long scar across the back of his left hand
DATE	9 Sep 1851
RECORD #	1934
PAGE	134

NAME	DIGGS, Sarah
PROOF	freedom proved by oath of Joseph HILLIARD & deed of emancipation
DESCRIPTION	abt 50y old, 5' tall, brown complexion, some dark spots on her cheeks and a scar in her left eye brow & another between her eye brows nearest the left one
DATE	14 Oct 1851
RECORD #	1935
PAGE	134

NAME	DIGGS, William (son of Sarah)
PROOF	freedom proved by oath of Joseph HILLIARD & deed of emancipation
DESCRIPTION	abt 19y old, 5' 6" tall, same colour as mother, scar in the centre of the forehead & a mole on the right side of his cheek, a considerable fungus on the right side of his right foot sufficient to identify him
DATE	14 Oct 1851
RECORD #	1935
PAGE	134

NAME	DIGGS, Robert
PROOF	emancipated by Jno. DIGGS, proved by oath of Presley SAUNDERS
DESCRIPTION	abt 22y old, 5' 7¾" tall, dark mulatto, scar on the right upper eyelid with some ½ dozen small black moles scattered over his face, the little fingers of both hands crooked
DATE	12 Nov 1851
RECORD #	1936
PAGE	135

NAME	STEPTOE, Dorinda
PROOF	emancipated by will of Presly SAUNDERS to take effect at present age and proved by oath of James SINCLAIR Esqr
DESCRIPTION	abt 30y old, 5' ½" tall, ears are pierced with ear rings
DATE	11 Nov 1851
RECORD #	1937
PAGE	135

NAME	GALES, Lucinda
PROOF	freedom proved by oath of Christian STONEBURNER
DESCRIPTION	abt 30y old, 5' 2" tall, nearly black, walks lame caused by the white swelling when young
DATE	9 Feb 1852
RECORD #	1938
PAGE	135

NAME	WINTERS, Andrew
PROOF	freedom proved by Thomas ROGERS
DESCRIPTION	abt 19y old last August, 5' 7¼" tall, bumpy face and a scar on the left wrist
DATE	9 Feb 1852
RECORD #	1939
PAGE	136

NAME	JACKSON, Townsend (of Annanias & Martha JACKSON)
PROOF	freedom proved by affirmation of Thomas NICHOLS Esqr
DESCRIPTION	abt 5y old, dark complexion
DATE	10 Feb 1852
RECORD #	1940
PAGE	136

NAME	JACKSON, Sarah Pleasant (child of Annanias & Martha JACKSON)
PROOF	freedom proved by affirmation of Thomas NICHOLS Esqr
DESCRIPTION	abt 4y old, dark complexion
DATE	10 Feb 1852
RECORD #	1940
PAGE	136

NAME	JACKSON, Phebe Ann (child of Annanias & Martha JACKSON)
PROOF	freedom proved by affirmation of Thomas NICHOLS Esqr
DESCRIPTION	abt 3y old, dark complexion
DATE	10 Feb 1852
RECORD #	1940
PAGE	136

NAME	JACKSON, Martha Ellen (child of Annanias & Martha JACKSON)
PROOF	freedom proved by affirmation of Thomas NICHOLS Esqr
DESCRIPTION	abt 18m old, dark complexion
DATE	10 Feb 1852
RECORD #	1940
PAGE	136

NAME	FOX, William
PROOF	freedom proved by free papers obtained from Fairfax Co.
DESCRIPTION	abt 35y old, 5' 8½" tall, mulatto, scar running down into the right eyebrow, on the left nostril, one where the right hand joins the wrist & one on right forefinger running lengthwise
DATE	11 Feb 1851[2]
RECORD #	1941
PAGE	136

NAME	FLETCHER, Archilus
PROOF	freedom proved by oath of Ethelip RUSSEL
DESCRIPTION	abt 33y old, 5' 7½" tall, dark mulatto, scar on the nose and has lost his right eye
DATE	12 Apr 1852
RECORD #	1942
PAGE	137

NAME	FLETCHER, Mary
PROOF	freedom proved by oath of Ethelip RUSSELL
DESCRIPTION	abt 40y old, 5' 1" tall, mulatto, lump on her left ear
DATE	12 Apr 1852
RECORD #	1943
PAGE	137

NAME	WASHINGTON, Augustus
PROOF	freedom proved by oath of Wm. DAVIS
DESCRIPTION	abt 26y old, 5' 6½" tall, mulatto complexion, scar on the right side of his nose & a broad mark on the back of the right hands caused by a burn
DATE	12 Apr 1852
RECORD #	1944
PAGE	137

Loudoun County, Virginia Register of Free Negroes 1844-1861

NAME	CURTIS, Priscilla
PROOF	freedom proved by oath of Wm. DAVIS
DESCRIPTION	abt 48y old, 5' 3" tall, dark colour, scar on the left side of her face just below the nose, and a blemish in her right eye
DATE	12 Apr 1852
RECORD #	1945
PAGE	137

NAME	JOHNSON, Jacob
PROOF	emancipated by Jane MORGAN as by deed proved by A. S. TEBBS
DESCRIPTION	abt 32y old, [__] 9½" tall, high, dark mulatto, scar on the back of his right hand just above his little finger
DATE	12 Apr 1852
RECORD #	1946
PAGE	138

NAME	GAINES, Jane (daughter of Kitty GAINES)
PROOF	freedom proved by oath of William DAVIS
DESCRIPTION	abt 28y old, 5' 3¾" tall, nearly white or quite so in appearance, two of her upper front teeth gone, & earrings
DATE	12 Apr 1852
RECORD #	1947
PAGE	138

NAME	GAINES, Eliza (daughter of Kitty GAINES)
PROOF	freedom proved by oath of Wm. DAVIS
DESCRIPTION	abt 23y old, 5' 4" tall, very bright mulatto, black mole on the back of the left hand
DATE	12 Apr 1852
RECORD #	1948
PAGE	138

NAME	JACKSON, Joseph
PROOF	freedom proved by Richard H. SUMMERS
DESCRIPTION	abt 24y old, 6' tall, black, long plain scar on the right cheek with some scars on his hands
DATE	12 Apr 1852
RECORD #	1949
PAGE	139

NAME	PAYNE, Joseph A.
PROOF	freedom proved by affirmation of Garret WALKER
DESCRIPTION	abt 22y old, 5' 9½" tall, dark complexion, scar running from the edge of the right eye brow & a scar on his chin with some faint scars on his hands
DATE	13 Apr 1852
RECORD #	1950
PAGE	139

NAME	JOHNSON, Sarah Ann
PROOF	freedom proved by Thomas S. DORRELL
DESCRIPTION	24y old, scant 5' tall, brown complexion, no visible scars
DATE	10 May 1852
RECORD #	1951
PAGE	139

NAME	TRAMMELL, Joseph
PROOF	freedom proved by oath of Thomas S. DORRELL
DESCRIPTION	21y old, 5' 7" tall, dark complexion, small scar in the forehead & one on his left arm 6 or 8" above the wrist
DATE	10 May 1852
RECORD #	1952
PAGE	139

NAME	BURK, Louisa
PROOF	freedom proved by Joseph NICHOLS
DESCRIPTION	abt 24y old, 4' 11¼" tall, dark complexion, small scar in her forehead
DATE	10 May 1852
RECORD #	1953
PAGE	140

NAME	LEE, Helen
PROOF	freedom proved by oath of James THOMAS
DESCRIPTION	abt 40y old, 5' tall, dark complexion, scar on the right cheek & one over each eye & one on her left wrist
DATE	10 May 1852
RECORD #	1953 [misnumbered]
PAGE	140

NAME	LEE, John Wm. (child of Helen)
PROOF	freedom proved by oath of James THOMAS
DESCRIPTION	abt 11y old, very dark mulatto
DATE	10 May 1852
RECORD #	1953 [misnumbered]
PAGE	140

Loudoun County, Virginia Register of Free Negroes 1844-1861

NAME	LEE, Amanda Ellen (child of Helen)
PROOF	freedom proved by oath of James THOMAS
DESCRIPTION	abt 9y old
DATE	10 May 1852
RECORD #	1953 [misnumbered]
PAGE	140

NAME	LEE, Henry Clay (child of Helen)
PROOF	freedom proved by oath of James THOMAS
DESCRIPTION	abt 7y old, a bright mulatto
DATE	10 May 1852
RECORD #	1953 [misnumbered]
PAGE	140

NAME	LEE, Lydia Ann (child of Helen)
PROOF	freedom proved by oath of James THOMAS
DESCRIPTION	abt 5y old
DATE	10 May 1852
RECORD #	1953 [misnumbered]
PAGE	140

NAME	LEE, James Armistead (child of Helen)
PROOF	freedom proved by oath of James THOMAS
DESCRIPTION	between 2 & 3y old
DATE	10 May 1852
RECORD #	1953 [misnumbered]
PAGE	140

NAME	GRIMES, Jonathan (alias KENEDY)
PROOF	freedom proved by oath of Joshua PUSEY
DESCRIPTION	32y old the 16th of this month, 5' 6 7/8" tall, dark mulatto, faint scar under the right eye & some on the right hand
DATE	12 Jul 1852
RECORD #	1954
PAGE	141

NAME	JACKSON, Jeremiah
PROOF	freedom proved by oath of Seth SMITH
DESCRIPTION	24y old of next February, 5' 9" tall, dark complexion, two moles in his face & one on the left side of the nose & the other above the right eye brow
DATE	12 Jul 1852
RECORD #	1955
PAGE	141

NAME	CROSS, Charles William
PROOF	freedom proved by oath of James GARRISON
DESCRIPTION	abt 22y old, 5' 7" tall, mulatto, long scar on his right wrist inside running upward some scars on his fingers, has 3 prominent moles on his face & a good deal pitted by the small pox
DATE	10 Aug 1852
RECORD #	1956
PAGE	141

NAME	BANKS, Eli
PROOF	freedom proved by oath of James GARRISON
DESCRIPTION	abt 20y old, 5' 8" tall, dark complexion, scar on the first joint of his thumb of the left hand & some small scars on his left jaw & a mole in the breast
DATE	10 Aug 1852
RECORD #	1957
PAGE	142

NAME	MURRAY, Jas. Wesly
PROOF	freedom proved by the affirmation of Seth SMITH
DESCRIPTION	28y old, 5' 9¼" tall, brown color, scar across his forehead some 1½" long
DATE	13 Sep 1852
RECORD #	1958
PAGE	142

NAME	BURKE, Richard
PROOF	freedom proved by oath of Benj. T. FRANK
DESCRIPTION	27y old, 5' 5½" tall, brown colour, plain scar in the right eye brow a long scar above the left eye brow a long & broad scar on the back of his right & a long scar on the wrist of his left
DATE	13 Sep 1852
RECORD #	1959
PAGE	142

NAME	NOAKS, Malinda (now Malinda CARTER)
PROOF	registered (No. 948) when a child, now proved by Noble S. BRADEN
DESCRIPTION	21y old, 5' 3½" tall, dark mulatto, plain scar on her upper lip & a scar on her forefinger of the left hand
DATE	13 Sep 1852
RECORD #	1960
PAGE	143

Loudoun County, Virginia Register of Free Negroes 1844-1861   111

NAME	HOLLIDAY, Harvey
PROOF	freedom proved by oath of Thos. G. HUMPHREY
DESCRIPTION	son of a white woman, 21y old, 6' 1" tall, copper colour, scar on the left side of his nose a dim mole below the right eye a scar on his right wrist on the back part adjoining the hand, a round scar on the 1st joint of the thumb, and another between the two forefingers on the left hand
DATE	13 Sep 1852
RECORD #	1961
PAGE	143

NAME	STROTHER, John W. (child of Wm. & Charlotte STROTHER)
PROOF	freedom proved by Wm. FULTON
DESCRIPTION	abt 10y old, dark complexion, plain scar in the centre of the forehead
DATE	13 Sep 1852
RECORD #	1962
PAGE	143

NAME	STROTHER, Elisha T. (child of Wm. & Charlotte STROTHER)
PROOF	freedom proved by Wm. FULTON
DESCRIPTION	abt 7y old, dark complexion
DATE	13 Sep 1852
RECORD #	1962
PAGE	143

NAME	STROTHER, Catharine
PROOF	emancipated by Thomas ROGERS
DESCRIPTION	24y old, 4' 11½" tall, dark complexion, scar in her forehead and a scar on the inside of her forefinger on the right hand some 2" long
DATE	13 Sep 1852
RECORD #	1963
PAGE	144

NAME	STROTHER, Mary
PROOF	emancipated by will of Washington M. CARR dec'd and proved by oath of Isaac VANDEVANTER
DESCRIPTION	abt 12y old, 5' ½" tall, mulatto colour, small mole in the forehead & a small scar on the tip end of the thumb of the left hand
DATE	13 Sep 1852
RECORD #	1964
PAGE	144

NAME	THOMPSON, Elizabeth Ann
PROOF	freedom proved by affirmation of Nathan JANNEY
DESCRIPTION	25y old, 4' 11½" tall, dark complexion, cluster of small scars on her left cheek near the ear & a round scar on the right side & a cluster of scars in the same side these clusters of scars were produced by cupping
DATE	13 Sep 1852
RECORD #	1965
PAGE	144

NAME	THOMAS, Samuel
PROOF	freedom proved by James B. BEVERLY
DESCRIPTION	abt 22y old, 5' 9" tall, copper colour, scar running up from the nose between the eye brows nearly up to the hair, & a long scar nearly on the ball of the left hand above the thumb
DATE	13 Sep 1852
RECORD #	1966
PAGE	145

NAME	GUIDER, Mary
PROOF	freedom proved by oath of Joseph GIBSON
DESCRIPTION	25y old, 4' 11" tall, dark complexion very much freckled, scar in the forehead & some on her neck
DATE	13 Sep 1852
RECORD #	1967
PAGE	145

NAME	GUIDER, Eli (child of Mary)
PROOF	freedom proved by oath of Joseph GIBSON
DESCRIPTION	4y old, dark
DATE	13 Sep 1852
RECORD #	1967
PAGE	145

NAME	GUIDER, Lydia Alice (child of Mary)
PROOF	freedom proved by oath of Joseph GIBSON
DESCRIPTION	2y old, dark
DATE	13 Sep 1852
RECORD #	1967
PAGE	145

Loudoun County, Virginia Register of Free Negroes 1844-1861

NAME	GUIDER, Adolphus (child of Mary)
PROOF	freedom proved by oath of Joseph GIBSON
DESCRIPTION	11m old, dark
DATE	13 Sep 1852
RECORD #	1967
PAGE	145

NAME	PAYNE, Nancy
PROOF	freedom proved by oath of Washington BEAVERS & affirmation of Nathan JANNEY
DESCRIPTION	abt 18y old, 5' 3" tall, bright mulatto, defect apparently in the nail of the left forefinger
DATE	13 Sep 1852
RECORD #	1968
PAGE	145

NAME	PAYNE, James Henry (son of Nancy Payne)
PROOF	freedom proved by oath of Washington BEAVERS & affirmation of Nathan JANNEY
DESCRIPTION	6m old, bright mulatto
DATE	13 Sep 1852
RECORD #	1968
PAGE	145

NAME	GRAYSON, Jas. A. (child of Martha GRAYSON)
PROOF	registered this day
DESCRIPTION	7y old, dark colour, large scar from a burn in his forehead
DATE	13 Sep 1852
RECORD #	1969
PAGE	146

NAME	GRAYSON, Daniel (child of Martha GRAYSON)
PROOF	registered this day
DESCRIPTION	5y old, dark colour
DATE	13 Sep 1852
RECORD #	1969
PAGE	146

NAME	GRAYSON, Bushrod (child of Martha GRAYSON)
PROOF	registered this day
DESCRIPTION	3y old, dark colour
DATE	13 Sep 1852
RECORD #	1969
PAGE	146

NAME　　　　　GAINS, Issabella
PROOF　　　　 freedom proved by oath of Warner HALES
DESCRIPTION 49y old, 5' 4¼" tall, dark complexion, large scar on the throat, with two moles below the right eye
DATE　　　　　13 Sep 1852
RECORD #　　 1970
PAGE　　　　　146

NAME　　　　　JOHNSON, Francis
PROOF　　　　 free born as proved by oath of John ISETT
DESCRIPTION 19y old, 5' 3½ tall", small scar right eye brow & bumppy face
DATE　　　　　13 Sep 1852
RECORD #　　 1971
PAGE　　　　　146

NAME　　　　　CARR, Rebecca
PROOF　　　　 freedom proved by oath of David HIXSON
DESCRIPTION 30y old, 5' 2" tall, a crease between the eye brows & a small protruding mole on the chin
DATE　　　　　13 Sep 1852
RECORD #　　 1972
PAGE　　　　　146

NAME　　　　　MOXLEY, Sarah Ann
PROOF　　　　 emancipated by Daniel FRY
DESCRIPTION 34y old, 5' 2½" tall, brown colour, long scar on the inside of her left wrist or arm, ears are pierced with earrings
DATE　　　　　14 Sep 1852
RECORD #　　 1973
PAGE　　　　　147

NAME　　　　　JACKSON, Isabella (daughter of Sarah JACKSON)
PROOF　　　　 freedom proved by oath of Wm. HUNT
DESCRIPTION 15y old, 5' 1" tall, dark complexion, scar on upper joint of middle finger on right hand & some small scars on right cheek & one under her throat
DATE　　　　　14 Sep 1852
RECORD #　　 1974
PAGE　　　　　147

NAME　　　　　CROSS, Charles (son of Sarah CROSS)
PROOF　　　　 freedom proved by oath of James McDONAH
DESCRIPTION 5y old, dark complexion
DATE　　　　　14 Sep 1852
RECORD #　　 1975
PAGE　　　　　147

NAME	CROSS, James (son of Sarah CROSS)
PROOF	freedom proved by oath of James McDONAH
DESCRIPTION	3y old, dark complexion
DATE	14 Sep 1852
RECORD #	1975
PAGE	147

NAME	WINTERS, Emily (child of Mary Ellen WINTERS)
PROOF	freedom proved by oath of John W. HAMMERLY
DESCRIPTION	6y old, mulatto
DATE	14 Sep 1852
RECORD #	1976
PAGE	147

NAME	WINTERS, Charles Wm. (son of Mary Ellen WINTERS)
PROOF	freedom proved by oath of John SMALE
DESCRIPTION	11y old, bright mulatto
DATE	14 Sep 1852
RECORD #	1977
PAGE	148

NAME	WINTERS, Jane (daughter of Mary Ellen WINTERS)
PROOF	freedom proved by oath of Jno. M. ATHEY
DESCRIPTION	8y old, bright mulatto
DATE	14 Sep 1852
RECORD #	1977
PAGE	148

NAME	GANT, Charles
PROOF	freedom proved by oath of John BEAVERS
DESCRIPTION	24y old, 5' 10¾" tall, dark mulatto colour, mole on the left side of his nose, a small scar on the wrist of his right arm & one on the thumb of the same hand
DATE	11 Oct 1852
RECORD #	1978
PAGE	148

NAME	McPHERSON, Peter
PROOF	freedom proved by oath of John BEAVERS
DESCRIPTION	abt 23y old, 5' 7½" tall, dark complexion, bumppy face & some scars on the back of each hand
DATE	11 Oct 1852
RECORD #	1979
PAGE	148

NAME   McPHERSON, Henry
PROOF   freedom proved by oath of John BEAVERS
DESCRIPTION   abt 21y old, 5' 9" tall, nearly black colour, long scar above the right eye near the hair & a scar on the forefinger of the left hand
DATE   11 Oct 1852
RECORD #   1980
PAGE   149

NAME   THOMPSON, Frederick
PROOF   freedom proved by oath of Bernard TAYLOR
DESCRIPTION   abt 18y old, 5' 7" tall, dark complexion, scar at the left of his left eye a smaller one in the edge of the right eye brow & some promiscuous scars on the back of his right hand
DATE   11 Oct 1852
RECORD #   1981
PAGE   149

NAME   BEVER, Mary A. (or BENER)
PROOF   freedom proved by oath of Manly HAMMERLY
DESCRIPTION   abt 21y old, 5' 2½", brown colour, dark spot on the right side of her neck & a long scar on or near her right elbow
DATE   11 Oct 1852
RECORD #   1982
PAGE   149

NAME   BEVER, Geo. Wm. (or BENER, son of Mary A.)
PROOF   freedom proved by oath of Manly HAMMERLY
DESCRIPTION   infant, brown colour
DATE   11 Oct 1852
RECORD #   1982
PAGE   149

NAME   CARR, James H. (child of Rebecca & George CARR)
PROOF   freedom affirmed by Bernard TAYLOR
DESCRIPTION   abt 15y old, dark complexion, small scar at corner of right eye
DATE   11 Oct 1852
RECORD #   1983
PAGE   150

NAME   CARR, Geo. W. (child of Rebecca & George CARR)
PROOF   freedom affirmed by Bernard TAYLOR
DESCRIPTION   abt 14y old, dark complexion
DATE   11 Oct 1852
RECORD #   1983
PAGE   150

Loudoun County, Virginia Register of Free Negroes 1844-1861

NAME	CARR, Peggy Allen (child of Rebecca & George CARR)
PROOF	freedom affirmed by Bernard TAYLOR
DESCRIPTION	abt 12y old, dark complexion
DATE	11 Oct 1852
RECORD #	1983
PAGE	150

NAME	CARR, Phenias (child of Rebecca & George CARR)
PROOF	freedom affirmed by Bernard TAYLOR
DESCRIPTION	abt 4y old, dark complexion
DATE	11 Oct 1852
RECORD #	1983
PAGE	150

NAME	SHORES, Mary
PROOF	freedom proved by affirmation of Seth SMITH
DESCRIPTION	abt 19y old, 5' 4½" tall, dark mulatto complexion, small scar on the right nostril
DATE	11 Oct 1852
RECORD #	1984
PAGE	150

NAME	McDANIEL, James Wm.
PROOF	freedom proved by oath of David MILBOURN
DESCRIPTION	abt 31y old, 5' 9" tall, dark colour, long scar on the left cheek running downward, two scars on the right side of his face about a 1¼" a part near the eye, some scars on the left side of the neck, and a scar on the top of the first joint of the thumb of the right hand
DATE	12 Oct 1852
RECORD #	1985
PAGE	150

NAME	ROBERTSON, John M.
PROOF	freedom proved by affirmation of Seth SMITH
DESCRIPTION	abt 22y old, 5' 10" tall, fair mulatto, scar in the left eye brow & one in the edge of the hair on the left of his forehead, has some small scars on the first forefinger of the left hand
DATE	8 Nov 1852
RECORD #	1986
PAGE	150

NAME	LUCAS, Anthony
PROOF	registered on 13 Oct 1828, No. 693, proved by oath of Thomas L. HUMPHREY
DESCRIPTION	abt 40y old, 5' 5" tall, mulatto, a remarkable scar on right ear
DATE	13 Dec 1852
RECORD #	1987
PAGE	151

NAME	THOMPSON, Townsend
PROOF	freedom proved by affirmation of John S. PANCOAST
DESCRIPTION	abt 19y old, 5' 10" tall, black colour, rather thin virage?, no scar except one on the inside of little finger of the left hand
DATE	13 Dec 1852
RECORD #	1988
PAGE	151

NAME	RANDOLPH, Sarah E.
PROOF	freedom proved by affirmation of Thos. NICHOLS
DESCRIPTION	9y old, very light mulatto
DATE	13 Dec 1852
RECORD #	1989
PAGE	151

NAME	JONES, Nelson
PROOF	freedom proved by oath of Ashford WEADON
DESCRIPTION	abt 27y old, 5' 6" tall, large scar caused by a burn in the left side of his forehead running into the hair
DATE	13 Dec 1852
RECORD #	1990
PAGE	152

NAME	MANLY, Enoch
PROOF	freedom proved by affirmation of B. HUTCHISON
DESCRIPTION	abt 26y old, 5' 8¾" tall, dark mulatto, scar on the back of his right hand running up on the wrist
DATE	13 Dec 1852
RECORD #	1991
PAGE	152

NAME	WINTERS, James
PROOF	freedom proved by oath of James GARRISON
DESCRIPTION	abt 20y old, 5' 7¼" tall, scar in forehead above right eye & some on each cheek, pierced ears & a scar on left thumb
DATE	13 Dec 1852
RECORD #	1992
PAGE	152

NAME   FLETCHER, John Wm.
PROOF   freedom proved by affirmation of Oliver TAYLOR
DESCRIPTION   abt 24y old, 5' 5½" tall, bright mulatto, small mole near outer corner of left eye & two near left corner of mouth, & a dark spot on back of left hand near joint of middle finger
DATE   14 Dec 1852
RECORD #   1993
PAGE   153

NAME   MANLY, Gabriel
PROOF   freedom proved by oath of Robert P. SWART
DESCRIPTION   abt 22y, 5' 6" tall, dark mulatto, dark scar near the left temple with some other small scars scattering over the face
DATE   10 Jan 1853
RECORD #   1994
PAGE   153

NAME   BOYD, James
PROOF   freedom proved by affirmation of Joshua PUSEY
DESCRIPTION   abt 24y, 5' 11½" tall, mulatto, small [scar] near the centre of the forehead
DATE   10 Jan 1853
RECORD #   1995
PAGE   153

NAME   GUY, Joseph
PROOF   freedom proved by oath of W. C. SANDERS
DESCRIPTION   25y old, 5' 6", nearly black, has a tit near his right ear
DATE   14 Feb 1853
RECORD #   1996
PAGE   154

NAME   GUY, Harriet
PROOF   freedom proved by oath of W. C. SANDERS
DESCRIPTION   abt 22y old, 5' 1" tall, nearly black, no marks or scars that are perceivable
DATE   14 Feb 1853
RECORD #   1997
PAGE   154

Loudoun County, Virginia Register of Free Negroes 1844-1861

NAME	WINTERS, Henry C.
PROOF	freedom proved by oath of Alfred RYON
DESCRIPTION	14y old, very light mulatto, mole on the right cheek and a slight scar just above it & a slight scar on the left cheek
DATE	14 Feb 1853
RECORD #	1998
PAGE	154

NAME	JOHNSON, Samuel Benjamin
PROOF	freedom proved by oath of Dr. Thos. J. MARLOW
DESCRIPTION	abt 20y old, 5' 8" tall, black, large black mole on right cheek, a large protruding scar on right side of neck & near left ear
DATE	11 Apr 1853
RECORD #	1999
PAGE	155

NAME	NORRIS, Betty
PROOF	emancipated
DESCRIPTION	abt 57y old, 5' 6½" tall, brown colour, scar in the corner of the left eye & another above it
DATE	11 Apr 1853
RECORD #	2000
PAGE	155

NAME	BUSH, Nelson W.
PROOF	freedom proved by oath of David HIXSON
DESCRIPTION	abt 26y old, 5' 7½" tall, dark mulatto, black mole left side of nose
DATE	11 Apr 1853
RECORD #	2001
PAGE	155

NAME	PHILLIPS, Landon
PROOF	freedom proved by affirmation of Thomas ROGERS
DESCRIPTION	abt 34y old, 5' 6 5/8" tall, dark complexion, two slim scars across the forehead above the right eye
DATE	11 Apr 1853
RECORD #	2002
PAGE	156

NAME	PAYNE, Samuel Dade
PROOF	freedom proved by affirmation of Garrett WALKER
DESCRIPTION	abt 18y old, 5' 7", dark complexion, plain scar in right brow
DATE	11 Apr 1853
RECORD #	2003
PAGE	156

Loudoun County, Virginia Register of Free Negroes 1844-1861

NAME	MASON, Lee
PROOF	freedom proved by affirmation of Thos. J. NICHOLS
DESCRIPTION	abt 30y old, 5' 3½" tall, dark complexion, scar across nose, one on ball of left thumb & another on middle finger of same hand commencing at upper joint & running down finger
DATE	9 May 1853
RECORD #	2004
PAGE	156

NAME	FURR, Elzey
PROOF	free by deed of conveyance made by P. SAUNDERS to Joseph MEAD
DESCRIPTION	abt 30y old, 5' 6½" tall, scar on the 1st joint of thumb of right hand & some small ones above it
DATE	15 Jun 1853
RECORD #	2005
PAGE	157

NAME	FURR, Frances Ann
PROOF	freedom proved by Dr. DAVISON
DESCRIPTION	abt 21y old, 5' 1" tall, dark complexion, no visible scars
DATE	15 Jun 1853
RECORD #	2006
PAGE	157

NAME	FURR, Wm. Henry (child of Frances Ann)
PROOF	freedom proved by Dr. DAVISON
DESCRIPTION	abt 5y old, rather dark mulatto
DATE	15 Jun 1853
RECORD #	2006
PAGE	157

NAME	FURR, Robert (child of Frances Ann)
PROOF	freedom proved by Dr. DAVISON
DESCRIPTION	abt 3y old, very dark complexion
DATE	15 Jun 1853
RECORD #	2006
PAGE	157

NAME	FURR, Harriett Ann (child of Frances Ann)
PROOF	freedom proved by Dr. DAVISON
DESCRIPTION	going on 2y old, same complexion
DATE	15 Jun 1853
RECORD #	2006
PAGE	157

Loudoun County, Virginia Register of Free Negroes 1844-1861

NAME   TIMBERS, James Wm.
PROOF   freedom proved by oath of Jonah PURCELL
DESCRIPTION abt 22y old, 5' 5½" tall, dark mulatto, scar near the right eye brow & two or 3 small ones below the right eye
DATE   11 Jul 1853
RECORD #   2007
PAGE   157

NAME   McPHERSON, Sophia
PROOF   freedom proved by affirmation of Seth SMITH
DESCRIPTION abt 21y old, 5'½" tall, dark complexion, small scar on the chin & a dark spot under the chin & a scar on the top of the left forefinger
DATE   9 Aug 1853
RECORD #   2008
PAGE   158

NAME   JACKSON, Pleasant A. (child of Lewis C. JACKSON & Ann his wife late Ann GILBERT)
PROOF   freedom proved by Thomas W. EDWARDS
DESCRIPTION 6y old last May, very dark complexion, very small scar above the left eye
DATE   9 Aug 1853
RECORD #   2009
PAGE   158

NAME   JACKSON, Martha J. (child of Lewis C. JACKSON & Ann his wife late Ann GILBERT)
PROOF   freedom proved by Thomas W. EDWARDS
DESCRIPTION 5y old last April, same complexion, small scar on the forehead near the hair
DATE   9 Aug 1853
RECORD #   2009
PAGE   158

NAME   JACKSON, Andrew (child of Lewis C. JACKSON & Ann his wife late Ann GILBERT)
PROOF   freedom proved by Thomas W. EDWARDS
DESCRIPTION 2y old last May, same complexion, no scars
DATE   9 Aug 1853
RECORD #   2009
PAGE   158

Loudoun County, Virginia Register of Free Negroes 1844-1861

NAME	JACKSON, George W. (child of Lewis C. JACKSON & Ann his wife late Ann GILBERT)
PROOF	freedom proved by Thomas W. EDWARDS
DESCRIPTION	2m old, same complexion
DATE	9 Aug 1853
RECORD #	2009
PAGE	158

NAME	GANT, Cornelia E. (late Cornelia E. HOGAN)
PROOF	freed by deed of manumission from Patrick HOGAN
DESCRIPTION	abt 23y old, 5' 4½" tall, dark complexion, round face & prominent eyes, scar on the right wrist & a small one in the palm of the left hand
DATE	9 Aug 1853
RECORD #	2010
PAGE	158

NAME	HOGAN, Craven A.
PROOF	freed by deed of manumission from Patrick HOGAN
DESCRIPTION	30y old the 14 Feb last, 5' 8½" tall, dark complexion, high forehead & prominent eyes, small scar on the middle finger of the left hand
DATE	9 Aug 1853
RECORD #	2011
PAGE	159

NAME	HOGAN, Sarah V.
PROOF	freed by deed of manumission from Patrick HOGAN
DESCRIPTION	20y old the 11 Apr last, 5' 4" tall, dark complexion, large prominent eyes, small scar on the forehead just above the right eye brow, small scar on the right hand near the joint of the forefinger and a light spot on the same hand
DATE	9 Aug 1853
RECORD #	2012
PAGE	159

NAME	HOGAN, Ann Maria
PROOF	freed by deed of manumission from Patrick HOGAN
DESCRIPTION	will be 18y old on 9 Sep 1853, 5' 2½" tall, dark complexion, prominent eyes, small black mole on the left side of nose, small scar on the left hand near the thumb joint
DATE	9 Aug 1853
RECORD #	2013
PAGE	160

NAME   HOGAN, James Henry
PROOF   freed by deed of manumission from Patrick HOGAN
DESCRIPTION will be 15y old on 19 Sep 1853, dark complexion, high round forehead, prominent eyes, small scar in centre of forehead
DATE   9 Aug 1853
RECORD #   2014
PAGE   161

NAME   GUIDER, Richard
PROOF   freedom proved by oath of Henry GLASGOW
DESCRIPTION upwards of 21y old, 5' 8½" tall, bright mulatto, scar in the right eye brow
DATE   12 Sep 1853
RECORD #   2015
PAGE   161

NAME   ALLEN, Leroy
PROOF   freedom proved by oath of Chas. F. FADELY
DESCRIPTION abt 21y old, 5' 4½" tall, dark mulatto, dark scar on the left cheek and a scar on the right hand just above the forefinger
DATE   12 Sep 1853
RECORD #   2016
PAGE   162

NAME   GUIDER, Thomas
PROOF   freedom proved by Henry GLASGOW
DESCRIPTION abt 17y old, 5' tall, bright mulatto, scar in centre of forehead at hair edge & 5 or 6 moles in face, 3 in cluster near right nostril
DATE   12 Sep 1853
RECORD #   2017
PAGE   162

NAME   JONES, Jane (now Jane STEWART)
PROOF   freedom proved by affirmation of W. E. CUMMINGS
DESCRIPTION abt 37y old, 5' tall, mulatto, scar under her right jaw & one in the left eyebrow
DATE   10 Oct 1853
RECORD #   2018
PAGE   162

NAME   STEWART, Alfred (son of Jane, formerly Jane JONES)
PROOF   freedom proved by affirmation of Wm. E. CUMMINGS
DESCRIPTION 9y old next Feby, darker mulatto than his mother
DATE   10 Oct 1853
RECORD #   2018
PAGE   162

Loudoun County, Virginia Register of Free Negroes 1844-1861

NAME	JONES, Sarah
PROOF	freedom proved by affirmation of Joseph NICHOLS
DESCRIPTION	abt 55y old [with a 2y old child??], 5' 3½" tall, bright mulatto, plain mole low down in the centre of the neck
DATE	10 Oct 1853
RECORD #	2019
PAGE	163

NAME	JONES, Martha Ellen (daughter of Sarah Jones)
PROOF	freedom proved by affirmation of Joseph NICHOLS
DESCRIPTION	2y old, about same colour as mother
DATE	10 Oct 1853
RECORD #	2019
PAGE	163

NAME	JONES, James Wesley
PROOF	freedom proved by affirmation of Wm. E. CUMMINGS
DESCRIPTION	abt 23y old, 5' 8½" tall, very dark mulatto, something like a mark or scar to the left of his left eye
DATE	10 Oct 1853
RECORD #	2220 [misnumbered]
PAGE	163

NAME	JONES, Charles Henry
PROOF	freedom proved by affirmation of Wm. E. CUMMINGS
DESCRIPTION	21y old, 6' ½" tall, very dark mulatto, scar in the centre of the forehead and one on the first joint of his forefinger of the left hand
DATE	10 Oct 1853
RECORD #	2221
PAGE	163

NAME	JONES, Saml. Washington
PROOF	freedom proved by affirmation of Wm. E. CUMMINGS
DESCRIPTION	17y old, 5' 8" tall, dark complexion, small scar in the forehead & two moles one close to the right eye brow & the other on the right side of his nose
DATE	10 Oct 1853
RECORD #	2222
PAGE	163

Loudoun County, Virginia Register of Free Negroes 1844-1861

NAME   JONES, Benj. Franklin
PROOF   freedom proved by affirmation of Wm. E. CUMMINGS
DESCRIPTION   abt 14y or 15y old, dark complexion, mole on the left corner of his mouth & a very small mole just below the left nostril
DATE   10 Oct 1853
RECORD #   2222
PAGE   163

NAME   WINTERS, Dennis
PROOF   emancipated by David LACY, re-registered by affirmation of Thomas ROGERS
DESCRIPTION   abt 22y old, 5' 5" tall, nearly black, has a small scar in the corner of the right eye
DATE   10 Oct 1853
RECORD #   2223
PAGE   164

NAME   DIXSON, Elizabeth
PROOF   freedom proved by oath of James McDONOUGH
DESCRIPTION   abt 17y old, 4' 11" tall, bright mulatto, small mole & small scar on the right cheek
DATE   10 Oct 1853
RECORD #   2224
PAGE   164

NAME   WINTERS, Charles W. (child of Mary, 29y old, 5' 3 ½" tall)
PROOF   freedom proved by oath of Thos. S. DORRELL
DESCRIPTION   14y old, dark complexion, natural mark in the breast
DATE   10 Oct 1853
RECORD #   2225
PAGE   164

NAME   WINTERS, George H. (child of Mary, 29y old, 5' 3 ½" tall)
PROOF   freedom proved by oath of Thos. S. DORRELL
DESCRIPTION   13y old, same complexion
DATE   10 Oct 1853
RECORD #   2225
PAGE   164

NAME   WINTERS, James E. (child of Mary, 29y old, 5' 3 ½" tall)
PROOF   freedom proved by oath of Thos. S. DORRELL
DESCRIPTION   8y old, same colour
DATE   10 Oct 1853
RECORD #   2225
PAGE   164

NAME	WINTERS, Sarah (child of Mary, 29y old, 5' 3 ½" tall)
PROOF	freedom proved by oath of Thos. S. DORRELL
DESCRIPTION	9y old, same colour
DATE	10 Oct 1853
RECORD #	2225
PAGE	164

NAME	WINTERS, Saml. F. (child of Mary, 29y old, 5' 3 ½" tall)
PROOF	freedom proved by oath of Thos. S. DORRELL
DESCRIPTION	18m old, same colour
DATE	10 Oct 1853
RECORD #	2225
PAGE	164

NAME	BURKE, Jane (child of Enos BURKE)
PROOF	freedom proved by affirmation of Joseph NICHOLS
DESCRIPTION	abt 9y old, dark complexion with a scar on the left hand, just above the forefinger, also a scar on the left arm just below the elbow
DATE	14 Nov 1853
RECORD #	2226
PAGE	165

NAME	BURKE, Mary Cornelia (child of Enos BURKE)
PROOF	freedom proved by affirmation of Joseph NICHOLS
DESCRIPTION	abt 7y old, same colour as sister, scar on the right cheek and one on the right arm between the wrist & elbow
DATE	14 Nov 1853
RECORD #	2226
PAGE	165

NAME	BURKE, Elias William (child of Enos BURKE)
PROOF	freedom proved by affirmation of Joseph NICHOLS
DESCRIPTION	abt 5y old, same colour as sister, no marks
DATE	14 Nov 1853
RECORD #	2226
PAGE	165

NAME	BURKE, Susan Mahala (child of Enos BURKE)
PROOF	freedom proved by affirmation of Joseph NICHOLS
DESCRIPTION	abt 3y old, same colour as sister, scar on the inside of the right elbow
DATE	14 Nov 1853
RECORD #	2226
PAGE	165

NAME	BURKE, James Wesley (child of Enos BURKE)
PROOF	freedom proved by affirmation of Joseph NICHOLS
DESCRIPTION	abt 9m old, same colour as sister, no marks
DATE	14 Nov 1853
RECORD #	2226
PAGE	165

NAME	SENATE, Elmina (child of Wm. & Eliza SENATE)
PROOF	mother was manumitted by David LACEY and never has obtained permission to reside in the state, proved by oath of H. S. TAYLOR
DESCRIPTION	abt 5y old, dark mulatto, horizontal scar across the nose between the eyes
DATE	15 Nov 1853
RECORD #	2227
PAGE	165

NAME	SENATE, Oscar (child of Wm. & Eliza SENATE)
PROOF	mother was manumitted by David LACEY and never has obtained permission to reside in the state, proved by oath of H. S. TAYLOR
DESCRIPTION	abt 4y old, dark mulatto, scar about the middle of forehead
DATE	15 Nov 1853
RECORD #	2227
PAGE	165

NAME	MANLEY, William Henry
PROOF	free born as proved by oath of A. D. LEE
DESCRIPTION	abt 28y old, 5' 7½" tall, brown colour, small scar about ½" above the left eye brow and another just behind that running into the wool, about 1½" long running upwards, and a round scar on the breast & one on the middle finger of the right hand near the end, also a scar above the right eye near the hair
DATE	12 Dec 1853
RECORD #	2228
PAGE	166

NAME	STEWARD, John
PROOF	deed of emancipation from Elizabeth O. CARTER
DESCRIPTION	abt 66y old, 5' 8½" tall, light brown colour, horizontal scar on the left wrist
DATE	14 Mar 1854
RECORD #	2229
PAGE	166

NAME	THOMAS, Enoch
PROOF	free born as certified on 10 Mar 1846 (see No. 1366), identified by Seth SMITH Esqr
DESCRIPTION	abt 32y old, 5' 9½" tall, brown colour, large scar on the lower part of the cap of right knee, with 2 or 3 small scars on the back of his left hand and a scar near the left corner of mouth
DATE	15 Mar 1854
RECORD #	2230
PAGE	166

NAME	CROSS, Priscilla (alias BESICKS)
PROOF	freedom proved by Jane GIBBINS
DESCRIPTION	abt 33y old, 5' 4¾" tall, dark mulatto colour, no scars worth naming
DATE	15 Mar 1854
RECORD #	2231
PAGE	167

NAME	JACKSON, Obediah Dixon
PROOF	freedom proved by affirmation of Seth SMITH
DESCRIPTION	between 20y and 21y old, 5' 7", dark brown, scar on the left arm between the elbow and wrist
DATE	10 Apr 1854
RECORD #	2232
PAGE	167

NAME	DAVIS, Thomas
PROOF	freedom proved by oath of James M. KILGOUR; [notation as register hereto from No. 1390]
DESCRIPTION	abt 31y old, 5' 10½" tall, brown colour, mole on right cheek, scar supposed to be caused by the Kine Pox on the left, and a large scar on the inside of his right wrist a few inches above the hand
DATE	10 Apr 1854
RECORD #	2233
PAGE	167

NAME	JACKSON, Milly E. (child of Edmond & Sarah JACKSON)
PROOF	freedom proved by oath of Lewis HUNT Esqr
DESCRIPTION	between 9y & 10y old, brown colour, scar on the left cheek
DATE	11 Apr 1854
RECORD #	2234
PAGE	168

NAME	JACKSON, Edmond (child of Edmond & Sarah JACKSON)
PROOF	freedom proved by oath of Lewis HUNT Esqr
DESCRIPTION	abt 6y old, brown colour, scar over each eye, two small scars on the right side of his neck and two on his breast
DATE	11 Apr 1854
RECORD #	2234
PAGE	168

NAME	WINTERS, Sarah (alias Sarah JACKSON)
PROOF	freedom proved by oath of Lewus HUNT Esqr; [notation as registered No. 1021]
DESCRIPTION	abt 39y old, 5' 6½" tall, dark mulatto, scar on the breast, one on the right arm just below the elbow supposed to be caused by a burn, and one on back of the two forefingers of the right hand
DATE	11 Apr 1854
RECORD #	2235
PAGE	168

NAME	FIELDS, Clary
PROOF	free born as certified on 10 Aug 1841 (No. 1283), now identified by oath of George HEAD Esqr
DESCRIPTION	abt 39y old, 5' 5" tall, dark brown colour, scar on the back of the right hand, one on the side of the right arm above the elbow, a small one below, one other on the left arm near the elbow, one on the forefinger of the left hand and one on the thumb of the same
DATE	11 Apr 1854
RECORD #	2236
PAGE	169

NAME	MASON, Cosmelia (child of Hannah MASON)
PROOF	freedom proved by oath of Thomas NICHOLS
DESCRIPTION	abt 11y old, dark mulatto
DATE	8 May 1854
RECORD #	2237
PAGE	169

NAME	MASON, Samuel (child of Hannah MASON)
PROOF	freedom proved by oath of Thomas NICHOLS
DESCRIPTION	abt 7y old, dark brown colour, scar on his forehead
DATE	8 May 1854
RECORD #	2237
PAGE	169

NAME	MASON, James William (child of Hannah MASON)
PROOF	freedom proved by oath of Thomas NICHOLS
DESCRIPTION	abt 6y old, same colour as brother, horizontal scar over left eye
DATE	8 May 1854
RECORD #	2237
PAGE	169

NAME	MASON, John W. (child of Hannah MASON)
PROOF	freedom proved by oath of Thomas NICHOLS
DESCRIPTION	between 2y & 3y old, mulatto colour
DATE	8 May 1854
RECORD #	2237
PAGE	169

NAME	RIVERS, Daniel
PROOF	freedom proved by oath of Archibald N. DOUGLAS
DESCRIPTION	abt 28y old, 5' 7½" tall, black with an indentation on the left side of the thumb nail on the right hand and a small scar near the end of the 3rd finger on the left hand
DATE	13 Jun 1854
RECORD #	2238
PAGE	170

NAME	THORNTON, Bushrod Washington Muse (son of Ann THORNTON alias Nancy)
PROOF	named in Register No. 1338 and proved by oath of Seth SMITH
DESCRIPTION	32y old, 5' 8" tall, black colour, number of small scars on back of right hand, scar on each of the two last joints of his forefinger on same hand and scar on the forefinger of the left hand, with a scar from a burn on the left arm below the elbow and a scar on the right eye brow & a scar on the lower lip
DATE	10 Jul 1854
RECORD #	2239
PAGE	170

NAME	THORNTON, Alfred Dangerfield
PROOF	freedom proved by oath of Seth SMITH
DESCRIPTION	29y old, 5' 6" tall, dark colour, scar on the left side of his chin with a burn on his right hand & one on the forefinger of the left hand & one on the last joint of the thumb on the same hand and scar on the back of the same hand
DATE	10 Jul 1854
RECORD #	2240
PAGE	170

NAME	THORNTON, Welby Debuts
PROOF	freedom proved by oath of Seth SMITH
DESCRIPTION	17y old, 5' tall, light black colour, scar near the neck and a scar on the left hand near the thumb, scar on the forehead
DATE	10 Jul 1854
RECORD #	2241
PAGE	171

NAME	THORNTON, James Douglas
PROOF	freedom proved by oath of Seth SMITH
DESCRIPTION	20y old, 5' 5" tall, black colour, small scar on left cheek or side of face and very small scar on his neck in front
DATE	10 Jul 1854
RECORD #	2242
PAGE	171

NAME	RIVERS, Sarah
PROOF	emancipated by M. H. D. TEBBS on 5 Jan 1830
DESCRIPTION	abt 26y old, 5' 5½" tall, dark complexion, scar on the back of the right hand, one on the right side of the chin
DATE	15 Aug 1854
RECORD #	2243
PAGE	171

NAME	LUCUS, Sarah Elizabeth
PROOF	freedom proved by affirmation of Seth SMITH
DESCRIPTION	22y old, 5' 4¼" tall, bright mulatto
DATE	11 Sep 1854
RECORD #	2244
PAGE	172

NAME	GOWEN, Thomas H. (son of Martha Ann GOWEN)
PROOF	freedom proved by Mary A. RIPPEN (see No. 1656)
DESCRIPTION	abt 15y old, mulatto, scar corner of left eye & on forehead
DATE	11 Sep 1854
RECORD #	2245
PAGE	172

NAME	JACKSON, Wm. Price (child of America Mahalah T. JACKSON)
PROOF	freedom proved by oath of Mary A. RIPPEN
DESCRIPTION	abt 6y old, black complexion
DATE	11 Sep 1854
RECORD #	2246
PAGE	172

Loudoun County, Virginia Register of Free Negroes 1844-1861

NAME	JACKSON, George A. (child of America Mahalah T. JACKSON)
PROOF	freedom proved by oath of Mary A. RIPPEN
DESCRIPTION	abt 3y old, black complexion
DATE	11 Sep 1854
RECORD #	2246
PAGE	172

NAME	JACKSON, John T. (child of America Mahalah T. JACKSON)
PROOF	freedom proved by oath of Mary A. RIPPEN
DESCRIPTION	abt 1y old, black complexion
DATE	11 Sep 1854
RECORD #	2246
PAGE	172

NAME	MASON, Amy
PROOF	freedom proved by oath of Amos DENHAM
DESCRIPTION	abt 31y old, 5' 3½" tall, bright mulatto colour, black mole on the right side of the neck about the size of a pea
DATE	11 Sep 1854
RECORD #	2247
PAGE	173

NAME	MASON, Mary (child of Amy MASON)
PROOF	freedom proved by oath of Amos DENHAM
DESCRIPTION	abt 14y old, bright mulatto, no scars worth named
DATE	11 Sep 1854
RECORD #	2248
PAGE	173

NAME	MASON, Ellen Douglas (child of Amy MASON)
PROOF	freedom proved by oath of Amos DENHAM
DESCRIPTION	abt 11y old, bright mulatto, no scars worth naming
DATE	11 Sep 1854
RECORD #	2248
PAGE	173

NAME	MASON, Eliza French (child of Amy MASON)
PROOF	freedom proved by oath of Amos DENHAM
DESCRIPTION	abt 9y old, scar in the left hand caused by a burn
DATE	11 Sep 1854
RECORD #	2248
PAGE	173

NAME   BRICE, John
PROOF   freedom proved by affirmation of Amasa HOUGH Esqr
DESCRIPTION abt 23y old, 5' 10" tall, scar on the left wrist and a small on over the left eye
DATE   11 Sep 1854
RECORD #   2249
PAGE   173

NAME   ALLEN, Betsy
PROOF   registered in Pr. Wm. Co., freedom proved by oath of Hampton R. BREWEN
DESCRIPTION abt 50y old, 5' 3" tall, black color
DATE   11 Sep 1854
RECORD #   2250
PAGE   174

NAME   ALLEN, Wm.
PROOF   freedom proved by oath of Hampton R. BREWEN
DESCRIPTION abt 24y old, 5' 7¾" tall, dark complexion, scar near the corner of the left eye and one near the corner of the mouth
DATE   11 Sep 1854
RECORD #   2251
PAGE   174

NAME   ALLEN, Narcissa
PROOF   no freedom information given
DESCRIPTION abt 20y old, 5' tall, black, no scars worth naming
DATE   11 Sep 1854
RECORD #   2252
PAGE   174

NAME   ALLEN, Uginta (child of Narcissa)
PROOF   no freedom information given
DESCRIPTION 18m old, black, no scars worth naming
DATE   11 Sep 1854
RECORD #   2252
PAGE   174

NAME   ALLEN, Mary
PROOF   freedom proved by oath of Hampton R. BREWEN
DESCRIPTION abt 16y old, 5' 2½" tall, black colour
DATE   11 Sep 1854
RECORD #   2253
PAGE   175

NAME	ALLEN, Catharine (daughter of Mary Allen)
PROOF	freedom proved by oath of Hampton R. BREWEN
DESCRIPTION	18m old, lighter complexion than mother
DATE	11 Sep 1854
RECORD #	2253
PAGE	175

NAME	ALLEN, Alex (son of Amanda ALLEN)
PROOF	freedom proved by oath of Hampton R. BREWEN
DESCRIPTION	abt 19y old, 5' 8½" tall, dark mulatto colour, small scar on his left arm and one on his right foot
DATE	11 Sep 1854
RECORD #	2254
PAGE	175

NAME	MINOR, Lewis
PROOF	freedom proved by oath of Wm. DENSMORE
DESCRIPTION	abt 17y old, 5' 8½" tall, bright black boy, scar on his right cheek near the eye
DATE	11 Sep 1854
RECORD #	2255
PAGE	175

NAME	JACKSON, George (son of Kern JACKSON)
PROOF	freedom proved by oath of Mary RIPPEN
DESCRIPTION	abt 27y old, 5' 8" tall, black colour, small scar on his right arm just above the hand and one on the middle finger of the same hand and a stiffness in his right knee supposed to be caused by a white swelling
DATE	11 Sep 1854
RECORD #	2256
PAGE	176

NAME	JOHNSON, Fenton (child of Amanda JOHNSON)
PROOF	freedom proved by affirmation of Joshua PURSEY
DESCRIPTION	6y old, mulatto
DATE	9 Oct 1854
RECORD #	2257
PAGE	176

NAME	JOHNSON, George Aaron (child of Amanda JOHNSON)
PROOF	freedom proved by affirmation of Joshua PURSEY
DESCRIPTION	4y old, mulatto
DATE	9 Oct 1854
RECORD #	2257
PAGE	176

NAME	JOHNSON, Harriet Ann (child of Amanda JOHNSON)
PROOF	freedom proved by affirmation of Joshua PUSEY
DESCRIPTION	17m old, mulatto
DATE	9 Oct 1854
RECORD #	2257
PAGE	176

NAME	WITTINGHAM, Dilcey Ann
PROOF	freedom proved by affirmation of Jonah SANDS
DESCRIPTION	abt 27y old, 5' 4½" tall, black colour, scar of her right hand
DATE	9 Oct 1854
RECORD #	2258
PAGE	176

NAME	WITTINGHAM, Mary Alice (child of Dilcey Ann)
PROOF	freedom proved by affirmation of Jonah SANDS
DESCRIPTION	6y old, mulatto
DATE	9 Oct 1854
RECORD #	2258
PAGE	176

NAME	WITTINGHAM, Rodney (child of Dilcey Ann)
PROOF	freedom proved by affirmation of Jonah SANDS
DESCRIPTION	3y old, mulatto
DATE	9 Oct 1854
RECORD #	2258
PAGE	176

NAME	WITTINGHAM, Preccella Jane (child of Dilcey Ann)
PROOF	freedom proved by affirmation of Jonah SANDS
DESCRIPTION	1y old, mulatto
DATE	9 Oct 1854
RECORD #	2258
PAGE	176

NAME	CANNADY, Elizabeth
PROOF	freedom proved by affirmation of Joshua PUSEY
DESCRIPTION	abt 20y old, 5' 1" tall, mulatto colour, scar under the left jaw, two moles on the left cheek and a mole on the right ear
DATE	9 Oct 1854
RECORD #	2259
PAGE	177

Loudoun County, Virginia Register of Free Negroes 1844-1861

NAME   CANNADY, James
PROOF   freedom proved by affirmation of Joshua PUSEY
DESCRIPTION   abt 14y old, 5' 3" tall, mulatto colour
DATE   9 Oct 1854
RECORD #   2260
PAGE   177

NAME   PARMER, Israel
PROOF   freedom proved by affirmation of David CARR
DESCRIPTION   abt 23y old, 5' 3" tall, dark mulatto colour, scar on his breast &
                two scars on the left leg
DATE   13 Nov 1854
RECORD #   2261
PAGE   177

NAME   CRAVEN, Allison
PROOF   emancipated by will of Washington M. CARR dec'd as proved
                by oath of Isaac VANDEVANTER
DESCRIPTION   abt 21y old, 6' 2" tall, yellow colour, small scar on his
                forehead over the left eye, a scar on his left leg
DATE   13 Nov 1854
RECORD #   2262
PAGE   178

NAME   THOMPSON, James
PROOF   freedom proved by affirmation of Bernard TAYLOR
DESCRIPTION   abt 24y old, 5' 9" tall, black colour, scar on right arm, scar on
                right shoulder, scar on right leg, small scar on left side of face
DATE   13 Nov 1854
RECORD #   2263
PAGE   178

NAME   STEWART, Fenton (son of Adeline JONES)
PROOF   freedom proved by affirmation of Seth SMITH
DESCRIPTION   abt 22y old, 5' 8" tall, mulatto colour, scar over his right eye
                and left eye has but one eye
DATE   11 Dec 1854
RECORD #   2264
PAGE   178

NAME   JACKSON, Clarissa
PROOF   freedom proved by oath of Jno. MOORE
DESCRIPTION   abt 21y old, 5' 7" tall, bright mulatto colour
DATE   8 Jan 1855
RECORD #   2265
PAGE   179

NAME	JOHNSON, John
PROOF	freedom proved by oath of Wm. HUNT
DESCRIPTION	abt 21y old, 5' 5" tall, dark colour, no fingers on his right hand and on the left but three fingers, scar on right elbow & one on the right shoulder
DATE	8 Jan 1855
RECORD #	2266
PAGE	179

NAME	NICKENS, James H.
PROOF	freedom proved by oath of Fielding LITTLETON
DESCRIPTION	abt 25y old, 5' 11" tall, mulatto colour, scar over his right eye, scar on his left thumb below the nail
DATE	8 Jan 1855
RECORD #	2267
PAGE	179

NAME	BROOKS, James
PROOF	produced the certificate from Hampshire Co. dated 28 Jun 1842, freedom proved by oath of Geo. K. FOX
DESCRIPTION	abt 35y old, 5' 7" tall, mulatto colour, scar on the right arm, scar on the left cheek, scar on the right thumb
DATE	9 Jan 1855
RECORD #	2268
PAGE	180

NAME	DADE, McGill
PROOF	freedom proved by oath of F. LITTLETON
DESCRIPTION	abt 21y old, 5' 7" tall, mulatto colour, scar in left eye brow, scar on the neck below the ear
DATE	9 Jan 1855
RECORD #	2269
PAGE	180

NAME	CRAVEN, Giles
PROOF	emancipated by will of John CARR dec'd as proved by oath of Isaac VANDEVANTER
DESCRIPTION	abt 32y old, 5' 11" tall, bright colour, scar at the corner of his right eye brow
DATE	12 Feb 1855
RECORD #	2270
PAGE	181

Loudoun County, Virginia Register of Free Negroes 1844-1861

NAME	SIMMS, Charita
PROOF	emancipated by will of Joseph CLOWES dec'd as proved by oath of Benjamin F. TAYLOR
DESCRIPTION	abt ___ y old, 5' 1" tall, black colour
DATE	12 Mar 1855
RECORD #	2271
PAGE	181

NAME	DEVAWL, Charles
PROOF	emancipated by will of Joseph CLOWES dec'd as proved by oath of Benjamin F. TAYLOR
DESCRIPTION	abt 28y old, 5' 6" tall, black colour, scar on the right shoulder
DATE	12 Mar 1855
RECORD #	2272
PAGE	181

NAME	SIMMS, Betsy
PROOF	emancipated by will of John VANDEVANTER dec'd as proved by oath of Eli JANNEY
DESCRIPTION	abt ___ y old, 5' tall, black colour
DATE	12 Mar 1855
RECORD #	2273
PAGE	182

NAME	PALMER, Townsend
PROOF	freed by deed from Eli JANNEY
DESCRIPTION	abt 28y old, 5' 3" tall, black colour, scar over the right eye brow
DATE	12 Mar 1855
RECORD #	2274
PAGE	182

NAME	PALMER, Lee
PROOF	freedom proved by oath of Eli JANNEY
DESCRIPTION	abt 26y old, 5' 2" tall, black colour, bump behind the right ear
DATE	12 Mar 1855
RECORD #	2275
PAGE	182

NAME	ROBINSON, Counsel C.
PROOF	freedom proved by oath of Joseph GIBSON
DESCRIPTION	abt 23y old, 5' 6" tall, brown colour
DATE	14 May 1855
RECORD #	2276
PAGE	183

NAME   ROBINSON, Susannah
PROOF   freedom proved by oath of Joseph GIBSON
DESCRIPTION abt 30y old, 5' 2" tall, mulatto colour
DATE   14 May 1855
RECORD #   2277
PAGE   183

NAME   ROBINSON, Alice T.
PROOF   freedom proved by oath of Joseph GIBSON
DESCRIPTION abt 24y old, 5' 2½" tall, mulatto colour
DATE   14 May 1855
RECORD #   2278
PAGE   183

NAME   JONES, Mary (daughter of Jane JONES)
PROOF   freedom proved by oath of Geo. K. FOX
DESCRIPTION abt 19y old, 5y 2½" tall, mulatto colour, scar on back of neck
DATE   15 May 1855
RECORD #   2279
PAGE   184

NAME   WATSON, Sally
PROOF   freedom proved by oath of Jas. SINCLAIR
DESCRIPTION abt 22y old, 5' 3" tall, mulatto colour, scar on the lip, a lump
             on the right wrist
DATE   12 Jun 1855
RECORD #   2280
PAGE   184

NAME   CLAGGETT, Daniel (child of Fanny CLAGGETT)
PROOF   mother emancipated since 1806, freedom proved by oath of J.
             S. HARRIS
DESCRIPTION 9y old, brown colour, blind
DATE   10 Jul 1855
RECORD #   2281
PAGE   184

NAME   CLAGGETT, Mary E. (child of Fanny CLAGGETT)
PROOF   mother emancipated since 1806, freedom proved by oath of J.
             S. HARRIS
DESCRIPTION 7y old, brown colour
DATE   10 Jul 1855
RECORD #   2281
PAGE   184

Loudoun County, Virginia Register of Free Negroes 1844-1861

NAME THOMPSON, Mary Jane (wife of J. E. THOMPSON)
PROOF freedom proved by oath of Bernard TAYLOR
DESCRIPTION 5' 4" tall, mulatto colour
DATE 14 Aug 1855
RECORD # 2282
PAGE 185

NAME THOMPSON, Sarah (child of Mary Jane THOMPSON)
PROOF freedom proved by oath of Bernard TAYLOR
DESCRIPTION 14y old, 5' tall, bright mulatto colour
DATE 14 Aug 1855
RECORD # 2282
PAGE 185

NAME THOMPSON, Susannah (child of Mary Jane THOMPSON)
PROOF freedom proved by oath of Bernard TAYLOR
DESCRIPTION 11y old, dark mulatto colour, scar on her temple
DATE 14 Aug 1855
RECORD # 2282
PAGE 185

NAME THOMPSON, Nathan (child of Mary Jane THOMPSON)
PROOF freedom proved by oath of Bernard TAYLOR
DESCRIPTION 9y old, dark mulatto colour, small scar near the left eye
DATE 14 Aug 1855
RECORD # 2282
PAGE 185

NAME THOMPSON, Alice (child of Mary Jane THOMPSON)
PROOF freedom proved by oath of Bernard TAYLOR
DESCRIPTION 7y old, dark mulatto colour, scar on the left side of her nose
DATE 14 Aug 1855
RECORD # 2282
PAGE 185

NAME THOMPSON, Semore (child of Mary Jane THOMPSON)
PROOF freedom proved by oath of Bernard TAYLOR
DESCRIPTION 6y old, dark mulatto colour
DATE 14 Aug 1855
RECORD # 2282
PAGE 185

NAME	THOMPSON, Mary Catharine (child of Mary Jane THOMPSON)
PROOF	freedom proved by oath of Bernard TAYLOR
DESCRIPTION	3y old, dark mulatto colour, scar near the left eye
DATE	14 Aug 1855
RECORD #	2282
PAGE	185

NAME	THOMPSON, Mary Jane (wife of Wm. THOMPSON)
PROOF	freedom proved by oath of Bernard TAYLOR
DESCRIPTION	5' 4" tall, bright mulatto colour
DATE	14 Aug 1855
RECORD #	2283
PAGE	185

NAME	THOMPSON, Archibald Washington (child of Mary Jane THOMPSON)
PROOF	freedom proved by oath of Bernard TAYLOR
DESCRIPTION	6y old, dark mulatto, 2 scars on his forehead
DATE	14 Aug 1855
RECORD #	2283
PAGE	185

NAME	THOMPSON, Asa Moore (child of Mary Jane THOMPSON)
PROOF	freedom proved by oath of Bernard TAYLOR
DESCRIPTION	4y old, dark mulatto, scar over his right eye
DATE	14 Aug 1855
RECORD #	2283
PAGE	185

NAME	THOMPSON, John Harrison (child of Mary Jane THOMPSON)
PROOF	freedom proved by oath of Bernard TAYLOR
DESCRIPTION	2y old, mulatto colour
DATE	14 Aug 1855
RECORD #	2283
PAGE	185

NAME	LUCUS, Lewis (alias GOINGS, son of Mary Ann LUCUS)
PROOF	freedom proved by oath of Susan A. BROOKS
DESCRIPTION	abt 22y old, 5' 4" tall, dark mulatto colour, scar on the corner of his left eye
DATE	14 Aug 1855
RECORD #	2284
PAGE	186

NAME	KENNEDY, Nancy (daughter of Nelly MAHONEY alias KENNEDY)
PROOF	freedom proved by affirmation of Joshua PUSEY
DESCRIPTION	abt 18y old, 5' 2½" tall, bright mulatto colour, scar from a burn on the left cheek near the ear, scar on the thumb
DATE	10 Sep 1855
RECORD #	2285
PAGE	186

NAME	GASKIN, Elisa (wife of Harrison GASKIN)
PROOF	emancipated by will of Jno. ONEALE dec'd since 1806, as proved by oath of Thomas FRED
DESCRIPTION	abt 39y old, 5' 4" tall, mulatto colour,
DATE	10 Sep 1855
RECORD #	2286
PAGE	187

NAME	GASKIN, Margaret (child of Elisa GASKIN)
PROOF	freedom proved by affirmation of Thomas FRED
DESCRIPTION	14y old, 5' 2" tall, bright mulatto colour
DATE	10 Sep 1855
RECORD #	2286
PAGE	187

NAME	GASKIN, Joseph (child of Elisa GASKIN)
PROOF	freedom proved by affirmation of Thomas Fred
DESCRIPTION	13y old, mulatto colour, scar on the back of the left hand
DATE	10 Sep 1855
RECORD #	2286
PAGE	187

NAME	GASKIN, Nelson (child of Elisa GASKIN)
PROOF	freedom proved by affirmation of Thomas FRED
DESCRIPTION	11y old, mulatto colour, scar on the forehead
DATE	10 Sep 1855
RECORD #	2286
PAGE	187

NAME	GASKIN, William F. (child of Elisa GASKIN)
PROOF	freedom proved by affirmation of Thomas FRED
DESCRIPTION	9y old, bright mulatto colour
DATE	10 Sep 1855
RECORD #	2286
PAGE	187

NAME	THOMPSON, John H.
PROOF	freedom proved by oath of Thomas NICHOLS
DESCRIPTION	abt 29y old, 5' 10" tall, dark brown colour, scar on back of the right hand
DATE	10 Sep 1855
RECORD #	2287
PAGE	187

NAME	THOMPSON, Elisa (wife of Samuel THOMAS)
PROOF	freedom proved by affirmation of Thomas NICHOLS
DESCRIPTION	abt 25y old, 5' 3½" tall, mulatto colour, scar on right jaw
DATE	10 Sep 1855
RECORD #	2288
PAGE	188

NAME	THOMAS, William H. (child of Elisa THOMAS)
PROOF	freedom proved by affirmation of Thomas NICHOLS
DESCRIPTION	5y old, brown colour
DATE	10 Sep 1855
RECORD #	2288
PAGE	188

NAME	THOMAS, John N. (child of Elisa THOMAS)
PROOF	freedom proved by affirmation of Thomas NICHOLS
DESCRIPTION	1y old, bright mulatto colour
DATE	10 Sep 1855
RECORD #	2288
PAGE	188

NAME	PIERCE, Martha
PROOF	freedom proved by oath of Thomas NICHOLS
DESCRIPTION	abt 19y old, 4' 11" tall, brown colour, scar on the forehead, scar on the forefinger of the left hand, scar on the right arm
DATE	10 Sep 1855
RECORD #	2289
PAGE	188

NAME	RICHARDSON, Hannah Ann
PROOF	freedom proved by oath of Wm. RUSSELL
DESCRIPTION	abt 30y old, 5' 6' tall, dark colour, small scar above the left brow in the forehead, very black small mole between her eyes & one under her left eye & with a large nose
DATE	10 Sep 1855
RECORD #	2290
PAGE	189

NAME	RICHARDSON, Helen E. (child of Hannah Ann RICHARDSON)
PROOF	freedom proved by oath of Wm. RUSSELL
DESCRIPTION	9y old, dark colour
DATE	10 Sep 1855
RECORD #	2290
PAGE	189

NAME	RICHARDSON, Corida? (child of Hannah Ann RICHARDSON)
PROOF	freedom proved by oath of Wm. RUSSELL
DESCRIPTION	2y 6m old, dark colour
DATE	10 Sep 1855
RECORD #	2290
PAGE	189

NAME	CROSS, Sarah (daughter of Polly CROSS)
PROOF	freedom proved by oath of James McDONOUGH
DESCRIPTION	abt 40y old, 5' 5" tall, brown colour
DATE	11 Sep 1855
RECORD #	2291
PAGE	189

NAME	CROSS, Charles (son of Sarah CROSS)
PROOF	freedom proved by oath of James McDONOUGH
DESCRIPTION	4y old, brown colour
DATE	11 Sep 1855
RECORD #	2291
PAGE	189

NAME	PAYNE, Robert (son of Ann Payne)
PROOF	freedom proved by oath of William BROWN
DESCRIPTION	abt 22y old, 5' 5½" tall, dark brown, scar on left wrist & one on the right arm ½ way between the wrist & elbow
DATE	11 Sep 1855
RECORD #	2292
PAGE	189

NAME	FLETCHER, William (son of Mary FLETCHER)
PROOF	freedom proved by affirmation of Yardley TAYLOR
DESCRIPTION	abt 17y old, 5' 5" tall, brown colour
DATE	8 Oct 1855
RECORD #	2293
PAGE	190

NAME	COOK, Josiah (child of Mary COOK alias Mary DORSEY)
PROOF	freedom proved by oath of James E. McCABE
DESCRIPTION	abt 18y old, 5' 1" tall, brown colour, scar in the left eyebrow & is lame
DATE	8 Oct 1855
RECORD #	2294
PAGE	190

NAME	COOK, Robert (child of Mary COOK alias Mary DORSEY)
PROOF	freedom proved by oath of James E. McCABE
DESCRIPTION	15y old, 5' 2" tall, brown colour
DATE	8 Oct 1855
RECORD #	2294
PAGE	190

NAME	COOK, Mary Jane (child of Mary COOK alias Mary DORSEY)
PROOF	freedom proved by oath of James E. McCABE
DESCRIPTION	13y old, 4' 9" tall, brown colour
DATE	8 Oct 1855
RECORD #	2294
PAGE	190

NAME	ADAMS, Charles
PROOF	freedom proved by affirmation of James M. WALKER
DESCRIPTION	abt 21y old, 5' 8½" tall, dark colour, burnt scar on right thigh, also a scar back of the right ear
DATE	12 Nov 1855
RECORD #	2295
PAGE	191

NAME	DAVIS, Maria
PROOF	freedom proved by affirmation of James M. WALKER
DESCRIPTION	abt 52y old, 5' 6" tall, dark colour, scar under the right eye, also a scar on the back of each wrist
DATE	12 Nov 1855
RECORD #	2296
PAGE	191

NAME	DAVIS, Dennis (child of Maria DAVIS)
PROOF	freedom proved by affirmation of James M. WALKER
DESCRIPTION	abt 19y old, 5' 11¾" tall, dark colour, large mole on the side of the left foot
DATE	12 Nov 1855
RECORD #	2296
PAGE	191

Loudoun County, Virginia Register of Free Negroes 1844-1861

NAME	DAVIS, Eliza Ann
PROOF	freedom proved by affirmation of James M. WALKER
DESCRIPTION	abt 14y old, 5' ½" tall, dark colour, no scars about her person
DATE	12 Nov 1855
RECORD #	2296
PAGE	191

NAME	DAVIS, Reamless
PROOF	freedom proved by affirmation of James M. WALKER
DESCRIPTION	abt 4y old, abt 3' tall, dark colour, scar of a dark colour above the left wrist
DATE	12 Nov 1855
RECORD #	2296
PAGE	191

NAME	MORGAN, Mary
PROOF	freedom proved by affirmation of Thomas NICHOLS
DESCRIPTION	abt 21y old, abt 5' tall, bright mulatto colour
DATE	12 Nov 1855
RECORD #	2297
PAGE	192

NAME	MORGAN, Drusilla (child of Mary MORGAN)
PROOF	freedom proved by affirmation of Thomas NICHOLS
DESCRIPTION	abt 5y old, 3' 2" tall, no scars about her person, bright mulatto colour
DATE	12 Nov 1855
RECORD #	2297
PAGE	192

NAME	MORGAN, James William (child of Mary MORGAN)
PROOF	freedom proved by affirmation of Thomas NICHOLS
DESCRIPTION	abt 3y old, 2' 10" tall, bright mulatto colour
DATE	12 Nov 1855
RECORD #	2297
PAGE	192

NAME	MORGAN, Archelus [? ink smear] (child of Mary MORGAN)
PROOF	freedom proved by affirmation of Thomas NICHOLS
DESCRIPTION	abt 10m old, 2' 3" tall, bright mulatto colour, no scars to be seen
DATE	12 Nov 1855
RECORD #	2297
PAGE	192

NAME	GANT, Elizabeth
PROOF	freedom proved by affirmation of Elisha JANNEY
DESCRIPTION	abt 48y old, 5' 1½" tall, dark colour, small scar between the elbow and wrist of the right arm
DATE	12 Nov 1855
RECORD #	2298
PAGE	192

NAME	GANT, John Thomas (child of Elizabeth GANT)
PROOF	freedom proved by affirmation of Elisha JANNEY
DESCRIPTION	abt 19y old, 5' 8" tall, black colour, burnt scar on the left side of his face above the temple
DATE	12 Nov 1855
RECORD #	2298
PAGE	192

NAME	GANT, Julia Ann (child of Elizabeth GANT)
PROOF	freedom proved by affirmation of Elisha JANNEY
DESCRIPTION	abt 15y old, 5' 3" tall, dark colour
DATE	12 Nov 1855
RECORD #	2298
PAGE	192

NAME	GANT, Mary Elizabeth (child of Elizabeth GANT)
PROOF	freedom proved by affirmation of Elisha JANNEY
DESCRIPTION	abt 17y old, 5' 4¼" tall, dark colour, small scar above the right wrist
DATE	12 Nov 1855
RECORD #	2298
PAGE	192

NAME	GANT, Nancy Catharine (child of Elizabeth GANT)
PROOF	freedom proved by affirmation of Elisha JANNEY
DESCRIPTION	abt 13y old, 5' 1" tall, dark colour, no scars about her person
DATE	12 Nov 1855
RECORD #	2298
PAGE	192

NAME	GANT, Frances Amelia (child of Elizabeth GANT)
PROOF	freedom proved by affirmation of Elisha JANNEY
DESCRIPTION	abt 11y old, 4' 5" tall, no scars to be seen
DATE	12 Nov 1855
RECORD #	2298
PAGE	192

Loudoun County, Virginia Register of Free Negroes 1844-1861   149

NAME	GANT, Charles Elwood (child of Elizabeth GANT)
PROOF	freedom proved by affirmation of Elisha JANNEY
DESCRIPTION	9y old, 4' 1½" tall, light complexion
DATE	12 Nov 1855
RECORD #	2298
PAGE	192

NAME	GANT, Martha Ellen (child of Elizabeth GANT)
PROOF	freedom proved by affirmation of Elisha JANNEY
DESCRIPTION	abt 7y old, 4' tall, dark colour, small dark scar below left ear
DATE	12 Nov 1855
RECORD #	2298
PAGE	192

NAME	GANT, Sarah Love (child of Elizabeth GANT)
PROOF	freedom proved by affirmation of Elisha JANNEY
DESCRIPTION	abt 5y old, 3' 7" tall, dark colour, no scars about her person
DATE	12 Nov 1855
RECORD #	2298
PAGE	192

NAME	BIGSBY, Peter
PROOF	freedom proved by oath of Thomas J. NICHOLS
DESCRIPTION	abt 55y old, 5' 6" tall, dark colour
DATE	12 Nov 1855
RECORD #	2299
PAGE	193

NAME	GANT, Amanda Jane
PROOF	freedom proved by oath of ____
DESCRIPTION	abt 25y old, 4' 11½" tall, dark colour
DATE	12 Nov 1855
RECORD #	2300
PAGE	193

NAME	THOMPSON, Delia
PROOF	freedom proved by affirmation of Bernard TAYLOR
DESCRIPTION	abt 45y old, 5' 4" tall, very dark colour, no scars to be seen
DATE	12 Nov 1855
RECORD #	2301
PAGE	194

Loudoun County, Virginia Register of Free Negroes 1844-1861

NAME	THOMPSON, John Eskridge (child of Delia THOMPSON)
PROOF	freedom proved by affirmation of Bernard TAYLOR
DESCRIPTION	abt 20y old, 5' 9¾" tall, dark colour, small scar above right eye
DATE	12 Nov 1855
RECORD #	2301
PAGE	194

NAME	THOMPSON, James William (child of Delia THOMPSON)
PROOF	freedom proved by affirmation of Bernard TAYLOR
DESCRIPTION	abt 17y old, 5' 4½" tall, dark colour, scar on right forefinger
DATE	12 Nov 1855
RECORD #	2301
PAGE	194

NAME	THOMPSON, Samuel Francis (child of Delia THOMPSON)
PROOF	freedom proved by affirmation of Bernard TAYLOR
DESCRIPTION	abt 15y old, 5' 4" tall, dark colour, small scar caused by a burn on the back of his right hand
DATE	12 Nov 1855
RECORD #	2301
PAGE	194

NAME	THOMPSON, Frances Ann (child of Delia THOMPSON)
PROOF	freedom proved by affirmation of Bernard TAYLOR
DESCRIPTION	abt 15y old, 5' 2" tall, dark colour, scar on the left forefinger and blind in the left eye
DATE	12 Nov 1855
RECORD #	2301
PAGE	194

NAME	THOMPSON, George Henry (child of Delia THOMPSON)
PROOF	freedom proved by affirmation of Bernard TAYLOR
DESCRIPTION	abt 12y old, 4' 11" tall, dark colour, dark scar on the back of the right hand
DATE	12 Nov 1855
RECORD #	2301
PAGE	194

NAME	THOMPSON, Carlisle (son of Delia THOMPSON)
PROOF	freedom proved by affirmation of Bernard TAYLOR
DESCRIPTION	abt 10y old, 4' 8" tall, dark colour, a burnt scar on the inside of his right wrist and also a scar about the middle of his forehead
DATE	12 Nov 1855
RECORD #	2301
PAGE	194

NAME THOMPSON, Sarah Elizabeth (child of Delia THOMPSON)
PROOF freedom proved by affirmation of Bernard TAYLOR
DESCRIPTION abt 9y old, 4' 4¾" tall, dark colour, no scars to be seen
DATE 12 Nov 1855
RECORD # 2301
PAGE 194

NAME THOMPSON, Ardella Ringold (child of Delia THOMPSON)
PROOF freedom proved by affirmation of Bernard TAYLOR
DESCRIPTION abt 5y old, 3' 9½" tall, small scar over the left eye
DATE 12 Nov 1855
RECORD # 2301
PAGE 194

NAME THOMPSON, Louisa
PROOF freedom proved by affirmation of Bernard TAYLOR
DESCRIPTION abt 48y old, 5' 4½" tall, dark colour, scar on back of right hand
DATE 12 Nov 1855
RECORD # 2302
PAGE 195

NAME THOMPSON, Geo. William Annamore
PROOF freedom proved by affirmation of Bernard TAYLOR
DESCRIPTION abt 18y old, 5' 11" tall, dark mulatto, large scar on right thumb
DATE 12 Nov 1855
RECORD # 2302
PAGE 195

NAME THOMPSON, Alfred
PROOF freedom proved by affirmation of Bernard TAYLOR
DESCRIPTION abt 17y old, 5' 5¾" tall, dark colour, several scars on both
sides of the neck caused by the scroffula
DATE 12 Nov 1855
RECORD # 2302
PAGE 195

NAME THOMPSON, Georgeanna
PROOF freedom proved by affirmation of Bernard TAYLOR
DESCRIPTION abt 12y old, 5' ½" tall, dark colour, small scar on the forehead
DATE 12 Nov 1855
RECORD # 2302
PAGE 195

NAME	THOMPSON, Rebecca Dallas
PROOF	freedom proved by affirmation of Bernard TAYLOR
DESCRIPTION	abt 10y old, 4' 7½" tall, mulatto colour, 2 moles on the right side of the neck
DATE	12 Nov 1855
RECORD #	2302
PAGE	195

NAME	THOMPSON, Cordelia
PROOF	freedom proved by affirmation of Bernard TAYLOR
DESCRIPTION	abt 15y old, 5' 4½" tall, dark colour, scar near the left temple caused by a burn
DATE	12 Nov 1855
RECORD #	2302
PAGE	195

NAME	SMITH, Rozilla
PROOF	freedom proved by affirmation of Leven RICHARDS
DESCRIPTION	abt 20y old, 5' ½" tall, dark mulatto, no scars whatever
DATE	12 Nov 1855
RECORD #	2303
PAGE	196

NAME	GAINES, Mary Elizabeth
PROOF	freedom proved by oath of Geo. K. FOX
DESCRIPTION	abt 20y old, 5' ½" tall, dark colour, scar on the left arm near the elbow, also a large lump on the left side of the neck
DATE	13 Nov 1855
RECORD #	2304
PAGE	196

NAME	GAINES, Nelly Ann
PROOF	freedom proved by oath of Geo. K. FOX
DESCRIPTION	abt 25y old, 5' tall, mulatto, straight hair, right eye contracted and disfigured, also a scar on the right wrist
DATE	13 Nov 1855
RECORD #	2305
PAGE	196

NAME	GAINES, Ann Elizabeth
PROOF	freedom proved by oath of Geo. K. FOX
DESCRIPTION	abt 9y old, 4' 3" tall, very bright mulatto, straight hair, no scars about her person
DATE	13 Nov 1855
RECORD #	2305
PAGE	196

NAME	GAINES, Josephine
PROOF	freedom proved by oath of Geo. K. FOX
DESCRIPTION	abt 6y old, mulatto colour, no scars about her person
DATE	13 Nov 1855
RECORD #	2305
PAGE	196

NAME	GAINES, Edwin
PROOF	freedom proved by oath of Geo. K. FOX
DESCRIPTION	abt 5y old, mulatto colour, scar on the upper part of his forehead
DATE	13 Nov 1855
RECORD #	2305
PAGE	196

NAME	GAINES, Armstead
PROOF	freedom proved by oath of Geo. K. FOX
DESCRIPTION	abt 2y old, dark mulatto colour, scar on right side of the forehead caused by a burn
DATE	13 Nov 1855
RECORD #	2305
PAGE	196

NAME	CROSS, Priscilla Elizabeth (otherwise called JONES, daughter of Priscilla CROSS)
PROOF	freedom proved by oath of George WOODARD
DESCRIPTION	abt 16y old, 5' 7½" tall, bright mulatto colour, small scar on the right eye brow, also a very dark spot on the side of the right ear
DATE	13 Nov 1855
RECORD #	2306
PAGE	197

NAME	CROSS, James Maddison (otherwise called JONES)
PROOF	freedom proved by oath of George WOODARD
DESCRIPTION	abt 20y old, 5' 5½" tall, dark colour, small scar on his left eyebrow and also a small scar on the left arm above the wrist
DATE	13 Nov 1855
RECORD #	2306
PAGE	197

NAME	CROSS, Jesse (otherwise called JONES)
PROOF	freedom proved by oath of George WOODARD
DESCRIPTION	abt 12?y old, dark complexion, scar on right thumbs also a scar on the left arm both caused by a burn
DATE	13 Nov 1855
RECORD #	2306
PAGE	197

NAME	CROSS, Victoria (otherwise called JONES)
PROOF	freedom proved by oath of George WOODARD
DESCRIPTION	abt 9y old, dark colour, no scars about her person
DATE	13 Nov 1855
RECORD #	2306
PAGE	197

NAME	RUST, Betsey
PROOF	freedom proved by oath of Dr. J. EATON
DESCRIPTION	abt 43y old, 5' 5" tall, dark mulatto colour
DATE	10 Dec 1855
RECORD #	2307
PAGE	197

NAME	RUST, Lucinda Catharine
PROOF	freedom proved by oath of Dr. J. EATON
DESCRIPTION	in her 16y of age, 5' 7½" tall, dark color, a perceptible scar over the right temple
DATE	10 Dec 1855
RECORD #	2307
PAGE	197

NAME	RUST, Martha
PROOF	freedom proved by oath of Dr. J. EATON
DESCRIPTION	abt 14y old, 5' 1" tall, dark mulatto color
DATE	10 Dec 1855
RECORD #	2307
PAGE	197

NAME	RUST, George Wm.
PROOF	freedom proved by oath of Dr. J. EATON
DESCRIPTION	22y old, 5' 6½" tall, dark copper color, without any particular marks or scars
DATE	10 Dec 1855
RECORD #	2307
PAGE	197

NAME	RUST, Samuel Manley
PROOF	freedom proved by oath of Joseph McFARLAND
DESCRIPTION	23y old, 5' 6½" tall, dark copper color, scar on the left leg below the knee from a dog bite
DATE	10 Dec 1855
RECORD #	2307
PAGE	197

NAME	CURTIS, Mary Catharine
PROOF	freedom proved by oath of Israel MYERS
DESCRIPTION	38y old, 5' 4" tall, dark copper color, small scar on left cheek near the mouth
DATE	10 Dec 1855
RECORD #	2308
PAGE	198

NAME	CURTIS, Mary Martha (child of Mary Catharine CURTIS)
PROOF	freedom proved by oath of Israel MYERS
DESCRIPTION	13y old, dark copper color, small scar on her right hand from a burn
DATE	10 Dec 1855
RECORD #	2308
PAGE	198

NAME	CURTIS, Ann Elizabeth (child of Mary Catharine CURTIS)
PROOF	freedom proved by oath of Israel MYERS
DESCRIPTION	10y old, dark copper color, without scars or marks
DATE	10 Dec 1855
RECORD #	2308
PAGE	198

NAME	CURTIS, Hannah Maranda (child of Mary Catharine CURTIS)
PROOF	freedom proved by oath of Israel MYERS
DESCRIPTION	nearly 8y old, dark copper color, without marks or scars
DATE	10 Dec 1855
RECORD #	2308
PAGE	198

NAME	MAHONEY, Eliza C.
PROOF	freedom proved by oath of Charles F. ANDERSON
DESCRIPTION	5' 6" tall, bright copper color, long straight hair, slight scar in the centre of her forehead
DATE	11 Feb 1856
RECORD #	2309
PAGE	199

NAME	MAHONEY, Bushrod (child of Eliza C.)
PROOF	freedom proved by oath of Charles F. ANDERSON
DESCRIPTION	in his 11th year, nearly white
DATE	11 Feb 1856
RECORD #	2309
PAGE	199

NAME	MAHONEY, Charles Henry (child of Eliza C.)
PROOF	freedom proved by oath of Charles F. ANDERSON
DESCRIPTION	in his 10th year, nearly white
DATE	11 Feb 1856
RECORD #	2309
PAGE	199

NAME	MAHONEY, Richard Jno.? (child of Eliza C.)
PROOF	freedom proved by oath of Charles F. ANDERSON
DESCRIPTION	in his 6th year, nearly white
DATE	11 Feb 1856
RECORD #	2309
PAGE	199

NAME	MAHONEY, Catharine (child of Eliza C.)
PROOF	freedom proved by oath of Charles F. ANDERSON
DESCRIPTION	in her 5th year, nearly white
DATE	11 Feb 1856
RECORD #	2309
PAGE	199

NAME	MAHONEY, Wesley (child of Eliza C.)
PROOF	freedom proved by oath of Charles F. ANDERSON
DESCRIPTION	in his 4th year, nearly white
DATE	11 Feb 1856
RECORD #	2309
PAGE	199

NAME	MAHONEY, William (child of Eliza C.)
PROOF	freedom proved by oath of Charles F. ANDERSON
DESCRIPTION	in his 1st year, nearly white
DATE	11 Feb 1856
RECORD #	2309
PAGE	199

Loudoun County, Virginia Register of Free Negroes 1844-1861

NAME	MAHONEY, John
PROOF	freedom proved by oath of Lewin F. JONES
DESCRIPTION	abt 34y old, 5' 4" tall, copper color with straight brown hair, no scars
DATE	11 Mar 1856
RECORD #	2310
PAGE	199

NAME	PERRY, Jefferson
PROOF	freedom proved by oaths of Dr. T. LEITH & Ludwell LUCKETT
DESCRIPTION	in his 26th year, 5' 8" tall, copper color with black hair nearly straight, slight scar on the little finger of the left hand
DATE	11 Mar 1856
RECORD #	2311
PAGE	199

NAME	GILES, Samuel
PROOF	deed of emancipation received this day
DESCRIPTION	abt 46y old, 5¾' tall, very dark color, scar in the right wrist also one at the end of the middle finger of the right hand
DATE	14 Apr 1856
RECORD #	2312
PAGE	200

NAME	COATES, Daniel
PROOF	freedom proved by oath of Daniel T. CRAWFORD
DESCRIPTION	between 18y & 19y old, 5' 7" tall, dark copper color, no particular marks except on the last joint of the little finger on the left hand
DATE	14 Apr 1856
RECORD #	2313
PAGE	200

NAME	LUCUS, Melissa Ann
PROOF	freedom proved by oath of W. B. NOLAND
DESCRIPTION	28y old, 5' 6" tall, bright mulatto color, many freckles on her face, no scars
DATE	14 Apr 1856
RECORD #	2314
PAGE	200

NAME	FLETCHER, Mary
PROOF	freedom proved by oath of Elizabeth RUSSELL
DESCRIPTION	abt 22y old, 5' 2" tall, bright mulatto color with long black hair, slight scar on the thumb of the left hand
DATE	12 May 1856
RECORD #	2315
PAGE	200

NAME	GRAYSON, Charles F. (of Martha HOLLY alias GRAYSON)
PROOF	freedom proved by oath of David CARR
DESCRIPTION	13y old
DATE	12 May 1856
RECORD #	2316
PAGE	201

NAME	GRA[Y]SON, Benson (child of Martha HOLLY alias GRAYSON)
PROOF	freedom proved by oath of David CARR
DESCRIPTION	in his 11th year
DATE	12 May 1856
RECORD #	2316
PAGE	201

NAME	GRAYSON, Parfarla (child of Martha HOLLY alias GRAYSON)
PROOF	freedom proved by oath of David CARR
DESCRIPTION	7y old
DATE	12 May 1856
RECORD #	2316
PAGE	201

NAME	GRAYSON, Georgiana (child of Martha HOLLY alias GRAYSON)
PROOF	freedom proved by oath of David CARR
DESCRIPTION	4y old
DATE	12 May 1856
RECORD #	2316
PAGE	201

NAME	GRAYSON, Marshall W. (child of Martha HOLLY alias GRAYSON)
PROOF	freedom proved by oath of David CARR
DESCRIPTION	in his 3rd year
DATE	12 May 1856
RECORD #	2316
PAGE	201

NAME   PARMER, George Sr.
PROOF   freedom proved by oath of Nathan H. JANNEY
DESCRIPTION   55y old, 5' 4" tall, nearly black
DATE   12 May 1856
RECORD #   2317
PAGE   201

NAME   PARMER, Jesse (son of George PARMER Sr. by first wife)
PROOF   freedom proved by oath of Nathan H. JANNEY
DESCRIPTION   in his 19th year, very dark copper color
DATE   12 May 1856
RECORD #   2317
PAGE   201

NAME   PALMER, George Jr. [not PARMER]
PROOF   freedom proved by oath of Nathan H. JANNEY
DESCRIPTION   21y old, 5' 5½" tall, dark copper color, two scars on right arm between the elbow and the wrist
DATE   12 May 1856
RECORD #   2318
PAGE   201

NAME   SMITH, Mary Frances (child of late Percilla SMITH now Percilla PARMER)
PROOF   freedom proved by Nathan H. JANNEY
DESCRIPTION   20y old
DATE   12 May 1856
RECORD #   2319
PAGE   201

NAME   SMITH, Corian (child of late Percilla SMITH now Percilla PARMER)
PROOF   freedom proved by Nathan H. JANNEY
DESCRIPTION   18y old
DATE   12 May 1856
RECORD #   2319
PAGE   201

NAME   SMITH, John (child of late Percilla SMITH now Percilla PARMER)
PROOF   freedom proved by Nathan H. JANNEY
DESCRIPTION   16y old
DATE   12 May 1856
RECORD #   2319
PAGE   201

NAME	PARMER, Percilla
PROOF	freedom proved by oath of Nathan H. JANNEY
DESCRIPTION	47y old, 5' 4½" tall, very dark copper color, scar on left wrist
DATE	12 May 1856
RECORD #	2320
PAGE	202

NAME	PARMER, Levi (child of Percilla PARMER)
PROOF	freedom proved by oath of Nathan H. JANNEY
DESCRIPTION	in his 12th year, dark copper color
DATE	12 May 1856
RECORD #	2320
PAGE	202

NAME	PARMER, Jonah (child of Percilla PARMER)
PROOF	freedom proved by oath of Nathan H. JANNEY
DESCRIPTION	in his 10th year, dark copper color
DATE	12 May 1856
RECORD #	2320
PAGE	202

NAME	PARMER, Joseph (child of Percilla PARMER)
PROOF	freedom proved by oath of Nathan H. JANNEY
DESCRIPTION	in his 6th year, dark copper color, slight scar over his left eye
DATE	12 May 1856
RECORD #	2320
PAGE	202

NAME	PARMER, Allen (child of Percilla PARMER)
PROOF	freedom proved by oath of Nathan H. JANNEY
DESCRIPTION	nearly 4y old, dark copper color
DATE	12 May 1856
RECORD #	2320
PAGE	202

NAME	PARMER, Ruth Hannah (child of Percilla PARMER)
PROOF	freedom proved by oath of Nathan H. JANNEY
DESCRIPTION	in her 2nd year, dark copper color
DATE	12 May 1856
RECORD #	2320
PAGE	202

Loudoun County, Virginia Register of Free Negroes 1844-1861

NAME	ROBINSON, Kitty Ann
PROOF	freedom proved by oath of Nathan H. JANNEY
DESCRIPTION	25y old, 5' 5½" tall, very dark copper color
DATE	12 May 1856
RECORD #	2321
PAGE	202

NAME	ROBINSON, Hamilton (child of Kitty Ann ROBINSON)
PROOF	freedom proved by oath of Nathan H. JANNEY
DESCRIPTION	10y old, dark copper color, 2 or 3 scars in the back of the head
DATE	12 May 1856
RECORD #	2321
PAGE	202

NAME	ROBINSON, Leanna (child of Kitty Ann ROBINSON)
PROOF	freedom proved by oath of Nathan H. JANNEY
DESCRIPTION	8y old, dark copper color, no scars
DATE	12 May 1856
RECORD #	2321
PAGE	202

NAME	ROBINSON, Isaiah (child of Kitty Ann ROBINSON)
PROOF	freedom proved by oath of Nathan H. JANNEY
DESCRIPTION	3y old, dark copper color, no scars
DATE	12 May 1856
RECORD #	2321
PAGE	202

NAME	ROBINSON, Isaac (child of Kitty Ann ROBINSON)
PROOF	freedom proved by oath of Nathan H. JANNEY
DESCRIPTION	nearly 1y old, dark copper color
DATE	12 May 1856
RECORD #	2321
PAGE	202

NAME	GANT, Alexander
PROOF	freedom proved by affirmation of Robert A. ISH
DESCRIPTION	20y old, 5' 5½" tall, dark copper color, scar on each eye brow
DATE	12 May 1856
RECORD #	2322
PAGE	202

NAME	JACKSON, Jerry
PROOF	freedom proved by oath of William B. MARSHALL
DESCRIPTION	abt 21y old, 5' 9" tall, bright mulatto color, dark brown hair nearly straight
DATE	12 May 1856
RECORD #	2323
PAGE	203

NAME	BRADEY, Frances
PROOF	freedom proved by oath of James GARRISON
DESCRIPTION	29y old, 5' 3" tall, mulatto color, no marks or scars
DATE	13 May 1856
RECORD #	2324
PAGE	203

NAME	McCARTY, Mary Jane (child of Rachel McCARTY)
PROOF	mother registered 9 Sep 1850 No. 1705, child proved by oath of Alfred CLINE
DESCRIPTION	15y? old [ink botch covers part], dark copper color like mother
DATE	15 Jul 1856
RECORD #	2325
PAGE	203

NAME	McCARTY, Charles William (child of Rachel McCARTY)
PROOF	mother registered 9 Sep 1850 No. 1705, child proved by oath of Alfred CLINE
DESCRIPTION	13y old, dark copper color like mother, scar under the left jaw
DATE	15 Jul 1856
RECORD #	2325
PAGE	203

NAME	McCARTY, Elizabeth (child of Rachel McCARTY)
PROOF	mother registered 9 Sep 1850 No. 1705, child proved by oath of Alfred CLINE
DESCRIPTION	11y old, dark copper color like mother
DATE	15 Jul 1856
RECORD #	2325
PAGE	203

NAME	McCARTY, Susannabel (child of Rachel McCARTY)
PROOF	mother registered 9 Sep 1850 No. 1705, child proved by oath of Alfred CLINE
DESCRIPTION	6y old, dark copper color like mother
DATE	15 Jul 1856
RECORD #	2325
PAGE	203

Loudoun County, Virginia Register of Free Negroes 1844-1861

NAME	McCARTY, Louisa Ellen (child of Rachel McCARTY)
PROOF	mother registered 9 Sep 1850 No. 1705, child proved by oath of Alfred CLINE
DESCRIPTION	2y old, dark copper color like mother
DATE	15 Jul 1856
RECORD #	2325
PAGE	203

NAME	POLAND, Julia Ann
PROOF	freedom proved by oath of Stacy M. NICHOLS
DESCRIPTION	abt 19y old, 5' 1" tall, nearly white, scar on forefinger on the right hand & scar on the thumb of the same hand
DATE	11 Aug 1856
RECORD #	2326
PAGE	204

NAME	FIELDS, Charles
PROOF	freedom proved by oath of A. F. OSBURN
DESCRIPTION	abt 21y old, 5' 7" tall, mulatto color, scar on lower lip, scar on second finger of right hand & scar on forefinger of left hand
DATE	11 Aug 1856
RECORD #	2327
PAGE	204

NAME	MANLY, Nancy (alias Nancy ARNETT)
PROOF	registered 13 Aug 1841 as proved by oath of Joel L. NIXON
DESCRIPTION	[no information given]
DATE	12 Aug 1856
RECORD #	2328
PAGE	204

NAME	BROOKS, David
PROOF	emancipated by will of Nancy WRIGHT dec'd
DESCRIPTION	abt 50y old, 5' 11½" tall, very dark color, scar at the root of each thumb on the outside
DATE	12 Aug 1856
RECORD #	2329
PAGE	205

NAME	FIELDS, Amanda (wife of George Wm. FIELDS)
PROOF	freedom proved by oath of James GRUBB
DESCRIPTION	in her 28th year, 5' 1½" tall, mulatto color
DATE	12 Aug 1856
RECORD #	2330
PAGE	205

NAME	FIELDS, John William (child of Amanda FIELDS)
PROOF	freedom proved by oath of James GRUBB
DESCRIPTION	7y old
DATE	12 Aug 1856
RECORD #	2330
PAGE	205

NAME	FIELDS, Mary Ellen (child of Amanda FIELDS)
PROOF	freedom proved by oath of James GRUBB
DESCRIPTION	between 2y & 3y old
DATE	12 Aug 1856
RECORD #	2330
PAGE	205

NAME	FIELDS, Sarah Elizabeth (child of Amanda FIELDS)
PROOF	freedom proved by oath of James GRUBB
DESCRIPTION	6m old
DATE	12 Aug 1856
RECORD #	2330
PAGE	205

NAME	HEATER, Henry
PROOF	freedom proved by oath of Isaac EATON
DESCRIPTION	in his 41st year, 5' 6¾" tall, very dark color, small scar on his nose
DATE	8 Sep 1856
RECORD #	2331
PAGE	205

NAME	HEATER, Susan (wife of Henry HEATER)
PROOF	freedom proved by oath of Isaac EATON
DESCRIPTION	abt 33y old, 5' 2½" tall, dark copper color, without any perceptible scar
DATE	8 Sep 1856
RECORD #	2332
PAGE	206

NAME	HEATER, Jonathan (child of Susan HEATER)
PROOF	freedom proved by oath of Isaac EATON
DESCRIPTION	abt 7y old
DATE	8 Sep 1856
RECORD #	2332
PAGE	206

NAME	HEATER, Mahlon Kirkbright (child of Susan HEATER)
PROOF	freedom proved by oath of Isaac EATON
DESCRIPTION	abt 5y old
DATE	8 Sep 1856
RECORD #	2332
PAGE	206

NAME	HEATER, Samuel (child of Susan HEATER)
PROOF	freedom proved by oath of Isaac EATON
DESCRIPTION	abt 3y old
DATE	8 Sep 1856
RECORD #	2332
PAGE	206

NAME	HEATER, Susannah (child of Susan HEATER)
PROOF	freedom proved by oath of Isaac EATON
DESCRIPTION	abt 1y old
DATE	8 Sep 1856
RECORD #	2332
PAGE	206

NAME	DEVINGER, James Henry (son of Julia DEVINGER)
PROOF	freedom proved by affirmation of William WILLIAMS & Dr. Richd. H. EDWARDS
DESCRIPTION	in 4th year, without any scars or marks
DATE	8 Sep 1856
RECORD #	2333
PAGE	206

NAME	HULL, Catharine Ann (wife of James HULL, formerly Catharine THROGSMORTON, daughter of Catharine DEVONSHIRE)
PROOF	freedom proved by oath of Joshua PUSEY
DESCRIPTION	abt 28y old, 6' 1", copper color, without any perceptible scars
DATE	8 Sep 1856
RECORD #	2334
PAGE	206

NAME	WHITING, John Emanuel (alias BEANER)
PROOF	freedom proved by oath of Danl. T. CRAWFORD & John JONES
DESCRIPTION	in his 28th year, 6' tall, brown color, scar on back of left hand also on wrist of same hand, crippled in his left knee
DATE	8 Sep 1856
RECORD #	2335
PAGE	207

NAME ALEXANDER, Charlotta
PROOF freedom proved by oath of Logan SMITH
DESCRIPTION in her 24th year, 5' 3" tall, brown color, scar on the forehead and some spots on the right wrist caused by the bite of a copperhead snake
DATE 8 Sep 1856
RECORD # 2336
PAGE 207

NAME DAVIS, Catharine (alias Catharine ALLEN)
PROOF freedom proved by oath of Johnson T. PALMER
DESCRIPTION abt 19y old, 5' 5" tall, very light mulatto color nearly white with long hair, no scars
DATE 8 Sep 1856
RECORD # 2337
PAGE 207

NAME DAVIS, Harriet Cecilia (daughter of Catharine DAVIS)
PROOF freedom proved by oath of Johnson T. PALMER
DESCRIPTION infant
DATE 8 Sep 1856
RECORD # 2337
PAGE 207

NAME ALEXANDER, Thomas
PROOF freedom proved by oath of Geo. K. FOX
DESCRIPTION abt 28y old, 5' 4½" tall, dark complexion, very plain scar on right cheek bond and a scar just above the knuckles of the two forefingers on the left hand, his under jaw projects
DATE 9 Sep 1856
RECORD # 2338
PAGE 208

NAME CARTWRIGHT, Necodemus
PROOF freedom proved by oath of Benj. F. TAYLOR
DESCRIPTION in his 43rd year, 6' 2" tall, black color, scar on right side of the neck, scar near the corner of left eye, scar near the edge of right eye brow, two marks below the right eye
DATE 13 Oct 1856
RECORD # 2339
PAGE 208

Loudoun County, Virginia Register of Free Negroes 1844-1861

NAME	DAVIS, Jane
PROOF	freedom proved by oath of Henry S. TAYLOR
DESCRIPTION	in her 23rd year, 5' 6" tall, bright color with a scar on the left cheek
DATE	13 Oct 1856
RECORD #	2340
PAGE	209

NAME	CARTWRIGHT, Anna
PROOF	freedom proved by oath of Benj. F. TAYLOR
DESCRIPTION	in her 34th year, black color, scar just below the right eye, scar on forefinger of the left hand
DATE	13 Oct 1856
RECORD #	2341
PAGE	209

NAME	CARTWRIGHT, Margaret (child of Anna CARTWRIGHT)
PROOF	freedom proved by oath of Benj. F. TAYLOR
DESCRIPTION	15y old, 5' 2½" tall, bright colour, scar on right side of neck
DATE	13 Oct 1856
RECORD #	2341
PAGE	209

NAME	CARTWRIGHT, James William (child of Anna CARTWRIGHT)
PROOF	freedom proved by oath of Benj. F. TAYLOR
DESCRIPTION	9y old, black color
DATE	13 Oct 1856
RECORD #	2341
PAGE	209

NAME	CARTWRIGHT, Leanna (child of Anna CARTWRIGHT)
PROOF	freedom proved by oath of Benj. F. TAYLOR
DESCRIPTION	6y old, black color
DATE	13 Oct 1856
RECORD #	2341
PAGE	209

NAME	CARTWRIGHT, George Henry (child of Anna CARTWRIGHT)
PROOF	freedom proved by oath of Benj. F. TAYLOR
DESCRIPTION	4y old, black color
DATE	13 Oct 1856
RECORD #	2341
PAGE	209

NAME	CARTWRIGHT, Mahala (child of Anna CARTWRIGHT)
PROOF	freedom proved by oath of Benj. F. TAYLOR
DESCRIPTION	2y old, black color
DATE	13 Oct 1856
RECORD #	2341
PAGE	209

NAME	MOXLEY, Catharine
PROOF	freedom proved by oath of S. G. DONOHOE
DESCRIPTION	25y old, 5' 1" tall, bright color
DATE	13 Oct 1856
RECORD #	2342
PAGE	210

NAME	MOXLEY, George William (child of Catharine MOXLEY)
PROOF	freedom proved by oath of S. G. DONOHOE
DESCRIPTION	10y old, brown color, scar at the corner of the left eye brow
DATE	13 Oct 1856
RECORD #	2342
PAGE	210

NAME	MOXLEY, David James (child of Catharine MOXLEY)
PROOF	freedom proved by oath of S. G. DONOHOE
DESCRIPTION	7y old, brown color, small scar on the forehead
DATE	13 Oct 1856
RECORD #	2342
PAGE	210

NAME	JENNINS, Nancy
PROOF	freedom proved by oath of S. G. DONOHOE
DESCRIPTION	33y old, 5' 3" tall, bright color, small mole on the forefinger of each hand
DATE	13 Oct 1856
RECORD #	2343
PAGE	210

NAME	GRAYSON, Chas.
PROOF	registered in Stafford Co. by oath of David CARR
DESCRIPTION	between 50y & 60y old, 5' 6" tall, brown color
DATE	13 Oct 1856
RECORD #	2344
PAGE	210

NAME	PHILIPS, Alfred
PROOF	freedom proved by oath of Nathan GREGG
DESCRIPTION	abt 50y old, 5' 8" tall, mulatto color, very large scar on his right arm extending from his wrist to his elbow caused by a burn
DATE	13 Oct 1856
RECORD #	2345 [renewed from No. 1124]
PAGE	211

NAME	ROBINSON, Nancy
PROOF	freedom proved by oath of Wm. HOUGH
DESCRIPTION	45y old, 5' 4" tall, bright mulatto color
DATE	13 Oct 1856
RECORD #	2346
PAGE	211

NAME	ROBINSON, John Thomas (child of Nancy ROBINSON)
PROOF	freedom proved by oath of Wm. HOUGH
DESCRIPTION	13y old, brown color
DATE	13 Oct 1856
RECORD #	2346
PAGE	211

NAME	ROBINSON, Robert (child of Nancy ROBINSON)
PROOF	freedom proved by oath of Wm. HOUGH
DESCRIPTION	10y old, bright color
DATE	13 Oct 1856
RECORD #	2346
PAGE	211

NAME	ROBINSON, Noble (child of Nancy ROBINSON)
PROOF	freedom proved by oath of Wm. HOUGH
DESCRIPTION	8y old, bright color, scar on the corner of the left eye & also on the forehead
DATE	13 Oct 1856
RECORD #	2346
PAGE	211

NAME	ROBINSON, Henry (child of Nancy ROBINSON)
PROOF	freedom proved by oath of Wm. HOUGH
DESCRIPTION	6y old, brown color
DATE	13 Oct 1856
RECORD #	2346
PAGE	211

NAME	ROBERSON, Wm. [not ROBINSON] (son of Nancy ROBINSON)
PROOF	freedom proved by oath of Wm. T. HOUGH
DESCRIPTION	25y old, 5' 10" tall, bright color, mole in his left eye
DATE	13 Oct 1856
RECORD #	2347
PAGE	212

NAME	ROBINSON, Virginia (alias BOYD, daughter of Nancy ROBINSON)
PROOF	freedom proved by oath of Wm. T. HOUGH
DESCRIPTION	24y old, 5' 1" tall, bright color, several moulds on her face
DATE	13 Oct 1856
RECORD #	2348
PAGE	212

NAME	ROBINSON, Silas (son of Nancy ROBINSON)
PROOF	freedom proved by oath of Wm. T. HOUGH
DESCRIPTION	21y old, 5' 8" tall, bright color
DATE	13 Oct 1856
RECORD #	2349
PAGE	212

NAME	JONES, Mary Frances (daughter of Nancy ROBINSON)
PROOF	freedom proved by oath of Wm. T. HOUGH
DESCRIPTION	23y old, 5' 4" tall, brown color
DATE	13 Oct 1856
RECORD #	2350
PAGE	213

NAME	JONES, John Wm. (child of Mary Frances JONES)
PROOF	freedom proved by oath of Wm. T. HOUGH
DESCRIPTION	4y old, bright color
DATE	13 Oct 1856
RECORD #	2350
PAGE	213

NAME	JONES, Sarah Alice (child of Mary Frances JONES)
PROOF	freedom proved by oath of Wm. T. HOUGH
DESCRIPTION	3y old, bright color
DATE	13 Oct 1856
RECORD #	2350
PAGE	213

Loudoun County, Virginia Register of Free Negroes 1844-1861

NAME JONES, George (child of Mary Frances JONES)
PROOF freedom proved by oath of Wm. T. HOUGH
DESCRIPTION 1y old, bright color
DATE 13 Oct 1856
RECORD # 2350
PAGE 213

NAME LEWIS, Lucinda (daughter of Lucy LEWIS)
PROOF freedom proved by oath of Wm. T. HOUGH
DESCRIPTION 29y old, 5' tall, brown color
DATE 13 Oct 1856
RECORD # 2351
PAGE 213

NAME LEWIS, James Henry (child of Lucinda LEWIS)
PROOF freedom proved by oath of Wm. T. HOUGH
DESCRIPTION 10y old, black color with a scar on his left cheek
DATE 13 Oct 1856
RECORD # 2351
PAGE 213

NAME LEWIS, George Washington (child of Lucinda LEWIS)
PROOF freedom proved by oath of Wm. T. HOUGH
DESCRIPTION 8y old, black color, scar on right leg above the ankle
DATE 13 Oct 1856
RECORD # 2351
PAGE 213

NAME LEWIS, Sarah Frances (child of Lucinda LEWIS)
PROOF freedom proved by oath of Wm. T. HOUGH
DESCRIPTION 6y old, brown color, a burn at the corner of the right eye
DATE 13 Oct 1856
RECORD # 2351
PAGE 213

NAME LEWIS, William Thomas (child of Lucinda LEWIS)
PROOF freedom proved by oath of Wm. T. HOUGH
DESCRIPTION 2y old, black color
DATE 13 Oct 1856
RECORD # 2351
PAGE 213

NAME	TURNER, Geo. Henry
PROOF	emancipated by will of Elizabeth BEATTY as proved by oath of R. C. LITTLETON
DESCRIPTION	22y old, 5' 9" tall, copper color, small scar on left shoulder
DATE	13 Oct 1856
RECORD #	2352
PAGE	214

NAME	MINOR, Danl. Webster
PROOF	freedom proved by oath of Charles F. ANDERSON
DESCRIPTION	21y old, 5' 9" tall, brown color, scar under the right jaw and one on left knee
DATE	13 Oct 1856
RECORD #	2353
PAGE	214

NAME	JOHNSON, Amanda
PROOF	freedom proved by oath of Joshua PUSEY
DESCRIPTION	28y old, 5' 8" tall, bright color, scar on knuckle of one of the fingers of the right hand
DATE	13 Oct 1856
RECORD #	2354
PAGE	214

NAME	JOHNSON, John Henry (child of Amanda JOHNSON)
PROOF	freedom proved by oath of Joshua PUSEY
DESCRIPTION	13y old, brown color, scar on left cheek and one on the forehead
DATE	13 Oct 1856
RECORD #	2354
PAGE	214

NAME	JOHNSON, William Fenton (child of Amanda JOHNSON)
PROOF	freedom proved by oath of Joshua PUSEY
DESCRIPTION	8y old, bright color, scar on the forehead
DATE	13 Oct 1856
RECORD #	2354
PAGE	214

NAME	JOHNSON, George Aaron (child of Amanda JOHNSON)
PROOF	freedom proved by oath of Joshua PUSEY
DESCRIPTION	6y old, brown color, scar on the left hand
DATE	13 Oct 1856
RECORD #	2354
PAGE	214

NAME	JOHNSON, Harriet Ann (child of Amanda JOHNSON)
PROOF	freedom proved by oath of Joshua PUSEY
DESCRIPTION	4y old, brown color
DATE	13 Oct 1856
RECORD #	2354
PAGE	214

NAME	JOHNSON, Daniel (child of Amanda JOHNSON)
PROOF	freedom proved by oath of Joshua PUSEY
DESCRIPTION	1y old, brown color
DATE	13 Oct 1856
RECORD #	2354
PAGE	214

NAME	SINKFIELD, Elizabeth
PROOF	freedom proved by oath of Ashford WEADON
DESCRIPTION	22y old, 5' 1" tall, brown color, blind in left eye, scar at corner of right eye and above the eye
DATE	13 Oct 1856
RECORD #	2355
PAGE	215

NAME	SINKFIELD, Mary Ann
PROOF	freedom proved by oath of Ashford WEADON
DESCRIPTION	1y old
DATE	13 Oct 1856
RECORD #	2355
PAGE	215

NAME	RICHARDSON, William
PROOF	freedom proved by oath of Jacob T. WINE
DESCRIPTION	39y old, 5' 9" tall, black colour, two scars leading from the corner of the right eye nearly an inch long each
DATE	13 Oct 1856
RECORD #	2356
PAGE	216

NAME	THOMPSON, David Wm.
PROOF	freedom proved by oath of Saml. PURSEL
DESCRIPTION	19y old, 6' tall, brown colour, scar on one of the fingers of the right hand
DATE	13 Oct 1856
RECORD #	2357
PAGE	216

NAME   JONES, Lucius
PROOF   freedom proved by oath of Elam H. VEALE
DESCRIPTION 33y old, 5' 3½" tall, bright mulatto with a scar in the right eye brow and a small mole just below the right eye
DATE   14 Oct 1856
RECORD #   2358 [renewed from No. 1336]
PAGE   216

NAME   FLEET, William (alias Fleet BALES)
PROOF   emancipated by will of Laurinda V. GRIFFIN of record in Fauquier Co. as proved by oath of Thos. P. KNOX
DESCRIPTION 37y old, 5' 11" tall, bright mulatto color, scar on the right side of his face, near the mouth and a large scar on the left side of his face
DATE   14 Oct 1856
RECORD #   2359
PAGE   217

NAME   BURKE, William R. (son of Sophia BURKE)
PROOF   registered this day
DESCRIPTION 25y old, 5' 10½" tall, black wooly hair, long face, small features, small scar just below the nose, also a small one just below the left jaw bone
DATE   10 Nov 1856
RECORD #   2360
PAGE   217

NAME   MEGINNIS, Charlotte A.
PROOF   free born as proved by oath of Geo. K. FOX
DESCRIPTION abt 27y old, 5' 5" tall, bright colour, mole on her right cheek
DATE   10 Nov 1856
RECORD #   2361
PAGE   217

NAME   MEGINNIS, Harriet Ann (daughter of Charlotte A. MEGINNIS)
PROOF   mother free born, freedom proved by oath of Geo. K. FOX
DESCRIPTION 11y old, bright colour, scar on the left eye brow
DATE   10 Nov 1856
RECORD #   2361
PAGE   217

Loudoun County, Virginia Register of Free Negroes 1844-1861

NAME	MEGINNIS, Rachel Ann (daughter of Charlotte A. MEGINNIS)
PROOF	mother free born, freedom proved by oath of Geo. K. FOX
DESCRIPTION	10y old, bright colour, scar on the right arm
DATE	10 Nov 1856
RECORD #	2361
PAGE	217

NAME	DAVIS, Hannah Ann (daughter of Matilda STINGER)
PROOF	freedom proved by oath of Elijah HOLMES
DESCRIPTION	abt 25y old, 5' 4" tall, black colour, scar on left side of neck
DATE	9 Nov 1856
RECORD #	2362 [renewed from No. 1641]
PAGE	218

NAME	THOMAS, Jane Ann (alias BRADY)
PROOF	freedom proved by oath of John MEAD
DESCRIPTION	abt 27y old, 5' 2" tall, brown colour, scar at the corner of right eye brow and one on forefinger of left hand
DATE	9 Nov 1856
RECORD #	2363
PAGE	218

NAME	THOMAS, Mahlon (child of Jane Ann THOMAS)
PROOF	freedom proved by oath of John MEAD
DESCRIPTION	5y old, brown color
DATE	9 Nov 1856
RECORD #	2363
PAGE	218

NAME	THOMAS, Amos Wm. (child of Jane Ann THOMAS)
PROOF	freedom proved by oath of John MEAD
DESCRIPTION	4y old, bright color
DATE	9 Nov 1856
RECORD #	2363
PAGE	218

NAME	THOMAS, Chandler (child of Jane Ann THOMAS)
PROOF	freedom proved by oath of John MEAD
DESCRIPTION	3y old, bright color
DATE	9 Nov 1856
RECORD #	2363
PAGE	218

NAME	HURLEY, Rewben [crossed out entry above this gives as HARLEY]
PROOF	registered in Culpeper County 19 Mar 1851
DESCRIPTION	abt 50y old, 5' 7" tall, mulatto colour, very small scar on left eye brow
DATE	12 Jan 1857
RECORD #	2364
PAGE	219

NAME	GANT, Bill
PROOF	freedom proved by oath of W. N. BERKELEY
DESCRIPTION	abt 42y old, 5' 6½" tall, dark brown, scar on upper of forehead on a line of the corner of left eye, a scar on the upper part of the nose
DATE	13 Jan 1857
RECORD #	2365
PAGE	219

NAME	THOMPSON, Rose
PROOF	freedom proved by oath of W. N. BERKELEY
DESCRIPTION	abt 38y old, 5' 3" tall, black colour, has but one eye, has a burn on the right cheek
DATE	13 Jan 1857
RECORD #	2366
PAGE	220

NAME	THOMPSON, Mary (daughter of Rose THOMPSON)
PROOF	freedom proved by oath of W. N. BERKELEY
DESCRIPTION	abt 18y old, 5' 6" tall, brown color
DATE	13 Jan 1857
RECORD #	2367
PAGE	220

NAME	JACKSON, Tom
PROOF	freedom proved by oath of W. N. BERKELEY
DESCRIPTION	abt 26y old, 5' 10" tall, mulatto complexion, scar on his forehead about half way between the left eye brow & hair, a long scar on the right finger running from the upper joint downward & between that finger & the next
DATE	13 Jan 1857
RECORD #	2368
PAGE	220

NAME	JACKSON, George Alexander
PROOF	freedom proved by oath of W. N. BERKELEY
DESCRIPTION	abt 28y old, 5' 10" tall, mulatto complexion, some black specks on face, recent mark in centre of forehead & a scar across right knee
DATE	13 Jan 1857
RECORD #	2369
PAGE	221

NAME	JACKSON, Mahala (wife of George JACKSON)
PROOF	freedom proved by oath of W. N. BERKELEY
DESCRIPTION	abt 29y old, 5' 4" tall, mulatto colour, scar on left side of neck
DATE	13 Jan 1857
RECORD #	2370
PAGE	221

NAME	JACKSON, Permelia (wife of Tom JACKSON, was Permelia HARRIS)
PROOF	freedom proved by oath of W. N. BERKELEY
DESCRIPTION	abt 31y old, 5' 9" tall, bright mulatto color, face freckled
DATE	13 Jan 1857
RECORD #	2371
PAGE	221

NAME	JONES, Leven Harrison
PROOF	freedom proved by oath of W. N. BERKELEY
DESCRIPTION	abt 28y old, 5' 7" tall, bright mulatto color, some moles on the neck and a scar on the upper lip
DATE	13 Jan 1857
RECORD #	2372
PAGE	222

NAME	JONES, Rosa Ann (late Rose THOMAS)
PROOF	freedom proved by oath of W. N. BERKELEY
DESCRIPTION	abt 17y old, 5' 1½" tall, mulatto colour, scar on forehead
DATE	13 Jan 1857
RECORD #	2373
PAGE	222

NAME	GRAYSON, John
PROOF	freedom proved by oath of Jas. N. GULICK
DESCRIPTION	abt 25y old, 5' 9" tall, quite dark complexion, scar on his neck caused by a burn
DATE	13 Jan 1857
RECORD #	2374
PAGE	222

NAME	GRACEN, Daniel
PROOF	freedom proved by Jas. H. GULICK
DESCRIPTION	abt 32y old, 5' 6" tall, dark complexion, scar on the outer side of the left leg
DATE	13 Jan 1857
RECORD #	2375
PAGE	223

NAME	CROSS, Thomas
PROOF	freedom proved by oath of Jas. M. GULICK
DESCRIPTION	abt 28y old, 5' 7" tall, black colour
DATE	13 Jan 1857
RECORD #	2376
PAGE	223

NAME	MANLY, Charles
PROOF	freedom proved by oath of Lloyd LOWE
DESCRIPTION	abt 23y old, 6' tall, mulatto colour, scar on the forehead
DATE	13 Jan 1857
RECORD #	2377
PAGE	223

NAME	MANLY, Sally
PROOF	freedom proved by oath of Lloyd LOWE
DESCRIPTION	abt 22y old, 5' 6" tall, mulatto colour, slightly freckled
DATE	13 Jan 1857
RECORD #	2378
PAGE	224

NAME	MANLEY, Lydia
PROOF	freedom proved by oath of Lloyd LOWE
DESCRIPTION	abt 17y old, 5' 7½" tall, mulatto colour
DATE	13 Jan 1857
RECORD #	2379
PAGE	224

NAME	MANLEY, Raleigh
PROOF	freedom proved by oath of Lloyd LOWE
DESCRIPTION	abt 14y old, brown colour
DATE	13 Jan 1857
RECORD #	2380
PAGE	224

Loudoun County, Virginia Register of Free Negroes 1844-1861

NAME	MANLEY, Ann
PROOF	freedom proved by oath of Lloyd LOWE
DESCRIPTION	abt 28y old, 5' 7" tall, brown colour
DATE	13 Jan 1857
RECORD #	2381
PAGE	224

NAME	MANLEY, Thomas
PROOF	freedom proved by oath of R. H. SUMMERS
DESCRIPTION	abt 36y old, 5' 10" tall, brown colour, scar on the right eye brow, a scar on the right hand
DATE	13 Jan 1857
RECORD #	2382
PAGE	225

NAME	MANLEY, Matilda
PROOF	freedom proved by oath of R. H. SUMMERS
DESCRIPTION	abt 42y old, 5' 8" tall, brown colour
DATE	13 Jan 1857
RECORD #	2383
PAGE	225

NAME	GANT, Mary (daughter of Bella JACKSON)
PROOF	freedom proved by oath of Jonah HOOD
DESCRIPTION	abt 36y old, 5' 4" tall, brown colour, scar on left eye brow
DATE	13 Jan 1857
RECORD #	2384
PAGE	225

NAME	JACKSON, Hortensia (daughter of Mary JACKSON)
PROOF	freedom proved by oath of Jonah HOOD
DESCRIPTION	abt 19y old, 5' 3" tall, brown colour, scar on the forehead
DATE	13 Jan 1857
RECORD #	2385
PAGE	226

NAME	GANT, Henry (son of Chas. GANT)
PROOF	freedom proved by oath of Jonah HOOD
DESCRIPTION	abt 21y old, 5' 3½" tall, brown colour, scar on the forehead
DATE	13 Jan 1857
RECORD #	2386
PAGE	226

NAME   GANT, Chas. (son of Mary GANT)
PROOF   freedom proved by oath of Jonah HOOD
DESCRIPTION   abt 18y old, 5' 6" tall, black colour
DATE   13 Jan 1857
RECORD #   2387
PAGE   226

NAME   GANT, Edmund (son of Mary GANT)
PROOF   freedom proved by oath of Jonah HOOD
DESCRIPTION   abt 14y old, brown colour
DATE   13 Jan 1857
RECORD #   2388
PAGE   226

[page 227 is missing from film, stated as missing at time of filming, but appears it was blank]

NAME   COLEMAN, Isabella (daughter of Eliza JACKSON)
PROOF   freedom proved by oath of Jonah HOOD
DESCRIPTION   abt 22y old, 5' tall, black colour, scar on the forehead
DATE   13 Jan 1857
RECORD #   2389
PAGE   228

NAME   ALLEN, Amanda (daughter of Charlotte ALLEN)
PROOF   freedom proved by oath of Hampton R. BREWER
DESCRIPTION   abt 36y old, 5' 7" tall, brown colour
DATE   13 Jan 1857
RECORD #   2390
PAGE   228

NAME   ALLEN, John (son of Amanda ALLEN)
PROOF   freedom proved by oath of Hampton R. BREWER
DESCRIPTION   abt 14y old, mulatto colour
DATE   13 Jan 1857
RECORD #   2390
PAGE   228

NAME   GASKINS, Jas. (son of Amy GASKINS)
PROOF   freedom proved by oath of Hampton R. BREWER
DESCRIPTION   abt 12y old, black colour
DATE   13 Jan 1857
RECORD #   2391
PAGE   228

Loudoun County, Virginia Register of Free Negroes 1844-1861

NAME	ALLEN, Martha (daughter of Harriet FLETCHER)
PROOF	freedom proved by oath of Hampton R. BREWER
DESCRIPTION	abt 21y old, 5' 1" tall, brown colour, scar on the left side of the jaw
DATE	13 Jan 1857
RECORD #	2392
PAGE	229

NAME	MANLEY, John
PROOF	freedom proved by oath of Sidney L. HODGSON
DESCRIPTION	abt 25y old, 5' 7½" tall, mulatto colour, a little cross eyed
DATE	13 Jan 1857
RECORD #	2393
PAGE	229

NAME	HARRIS, Henry
PROOF	emancipated by deed from Catharine B. GASSAWAY admitted 9 Feb 1857, proved by oath of Chas. B. WILDMAN
DESCRIPTION	abt 30y old, 5' 6" tall, black, scar on the right side of the nose near the eye
DATE	1 Feb 1857
RECORD #	2394
PAGE	229

NAME	ROBINSON, Rebecca Jane
PROOF	freedom proved by oath of Isaac PIGGOTT
DESCRIPTION	abt 23y old, 5' 7½" tall, mulatto colour, scar on the right wrist
DATE	9 Mar 1857
RECORD #	2395
PAGE	230

NAME	ALLEN, Isaiah (son of Amanda ALLEN)
PROOF	freedom proved by oath of Nicholas OSBURN
DESCRIPTION	abt 18y old, 5' 8" tall, brown colour, scar on the forehead
DATE	14 Apr 1857
RECORD #	2396
PAGE	230

NAME	ALEXANDER, John (child of Jane ALEXANDER)
PROOF	free born as proved by oath of Burr P. NOLAND
DESCRIPTION	abt 16y old, light colour freckled with a mole near his right ear, one on the right hand between the second joint of thumb
DATE	14 Apr 1857
RECORD #	2397
PAGE	230

NAME	ALEXANDER, Richardetta (child of Jane ALEXANDER)
PROOF	free born as proved by oath of Burr P. NOLAND
DESCRIPTION	abt 11y old, light mulatto, scar from a burn on the right wrist
DATE	14 Apr 1857
RECORD #	2397
PAGE	230

NAME	ALEXANDER, Geo. T. (child of Jane ALEXANDER)
PROOF	free born as proved by oath of Burr P. NOLAND
DESCRIPTION	abt 8y old, light mulatto with a scar under the left eye brow and a scar on the left forefinger
DATE	14 Apr 1857
RECORD #	2397
PAGE	230

NAME	BRYANT, Lydia Ann
PROOF	free born as proved by oath of Geo. K. FOX
DESCRIPTION	abt 21y old, 5' tall, brown colour, scar on back of left hand and one the chin
DATE	14 Apr 1857
RECORD #	2398
PAGE	231

NAME	BROOKS, Alfred
PROOF	emancipated by a deed admitted by Eleanor GULLATT on 1 Jan 1857 as proved by oath of Jno. H. BROWN
DESCRIPTION	abt 50y old, 5' 9½" tall, black colour
DATE	12 May 1857
RECORD #	2399
PAGE	231

NAME	LUCAS, John H.
PROOF	freedom proved by oath of Thomas NICHOLS
DESCRIPTION	abt 44y old, 5' 9" tall, bright complexion, large scar on the tip of the right elbow
DATE	9 Jun 1857
RECORD #	2400
PAGE	232

NAME	RUST, Patsy (wife of John Thos. RUST)
PROOF	emancipated by Isaac G. NICHOLS
DESCRIPTION	abt 30y old, 5' 1" tall, brown colour, scar on end of the second finger of the right hand
DATE	9 Jun 1857
RECORD #	2401
PAGE	232

Loudoun County, Virginia Register of Free Negroes 1844-1861

NAME   RUST, Ann Maria (child of Patsy RUST)
PROOF   emancipated by Isaac G. NICHOLS
DESCRIPTION   abt 6y old, brown colour
DATE   9 Jun 1857
RECORD #   2401
PAGE   232

NAME   RUST, Sarah Elizabeth (child of Patsy RUST)
PROOF   emancipated by Isaac G. NICHOLS
DESCRIPTION   abt 3y old, brown colour
DATE   9 Jun 1857
RECORD #   2401
PAGE   232

NAME   RUST, Martha Jane (child of Patsy RUST)
PROOF   emancipated by Isaac G. NICHOLS
DESCRIPTION   abt 1y old, brown colour
DATE   9 Jun 1857
RECORD #   2401
PAGE   232

NAME   RUST, George William (child of Patsy RUST)
PROOF   emancipated by Isaac G. NICHOLS
DESCRIPTION   2m old, brown colour
DATE   9 Jun 1857
RECORD #   2401
PAGE   232

NAME   HOOE, Jim (or HOVE)
PROOF   emancipated by will of Mrs. Margaret MEDLEY as proved by oath of Beverley HUTCHISON
DESCRIPTION   abt 30y old, 5' 8" tall, black colour, scar on left side of nose & scar on thumb of right hand
DATE   13 Jul 1857
RECORD #   2402
PAGE   233

NAME   HOOE, Mary (or HOVE)
PROOF   emancipated by will of Mrs. Margaret MEDLEY as proved by oath of Beverley HUTCHISON
DESCRIPTION   abt 59y old, 5' tall, brown colour
DATE   13 Jul 1857
RECORD #   2403
PAGE   233

NAME	THOMPSON, Samuel
PROOF	freedom proved by oath of Bernard TAYLOR
DESCRIPTION	abt 21y old, 5' 11" tall, brown colour, scar on right wrist and scar on left leg
DATE	13 Jul 1857
RECORD #	2404
PAGE	233

NAME	CARTER, Alcinda
PROOF	emancipated by will of John STATLER dec'd as proved by oath of Noble S. BRADEN
DESCRIPTION	abt 32y old, 5' 5" tall, brown colour, scar on forefinger of left hand
DATE	14 Sep 1857
RECORD #	2405
PAGE	234

NAME	CARTER, Susannah
PROOF	emancipated by will of John STATLER dec'd as proved by oath of Noble S. BRADEN
DESCRIPTION	abt 12y old, brown colour
DATE	14 Sep 1857
RECORD #	2406
PAGE	234

NAME	DAVIS, Lewis
PROOF	freedom proved by oath of Thomas PHILIPS
DESCRIPTION	28y old, 6' 1" tall, black colour, scar on back of left hand
DATE	14 Sep 1857
RECORD #	2407
PAGE	234

NAME	DAVIS, Samuel
PROOF	freedom proved by oath of Thomas PHILIPS
DESCRIPTION	abt 20y old, 5' 6½" tall, black colour, scar on back of left hand
DATE	14 Sep 1857
RECORD #	2408
PAGE	235

NAME	DAVIS, Jefferson
PROOF	freedom proved by oath of Thomas PHILIPS
DESCRIPTION	abt 22y old, 5' 10" tall, black colour, scars on 2nd & 3rd fingers of the left hand
DATE	14 Sep 1857
RECORD #	2409
PAGE	235

Loudoun County, Virginia Register of Free Negroes 1844-1861

NAME	CRAVEN, John H. (son of Elisa CRAVEN)
PROOF	freedom proved by oath of T. PHILIPS
DESCRIPTION	8y old, mulatto colour
DATE	14 Sep 1857
RECORD #	2410
PAGE	235

NAME	ALEXANDER, Harriet
PROOF	free born as proved by oath of William B. NOLAND
DESCRIPTION	abt 18y old, 5' tall, bright mulatto color, scar on left wrist
DATE	14 Sep 1857
RECORD #	2411
PAGE	236

NAME	WINTERS, George
PROOF	free born as proved by oath of Jas. McDONALD
DESCRIPTION	abt 19y old, 5' 5" tall, brown colour, scar on left side near eye
DATE	15 Sep 1857
RECORD #	2412
PAGE	236

NAME	MANDLEY, Malinda
PROOF	free born as proved by oath of R. H. SUMMERS
DESCRIPTION	abt 40y old, 5' 4" tall, black colour, mole on forefinger of left hand, one on the back of right hand, scar on the same hand and a scar on the forefinger of the same
DATE	15 Sep 1857
RECORD #	2413
PAGE	236

NAME	MANDLEY, Caroline
PROOF	free born as proved by oath of R. H. SUMMERS
DESCRIPTION	abt 33y old, 5' 7" tall, black colour, scar on left breast and mole on nose
DATE	15 Sep 1857
RECORD #	2414
PAGE	237

NAME	MAN[D]LEY, John
PROOF	free born as proved by oath of Nimrod CROSS
DESCRIPTION	abt 20y old, 5' 4" tall, black colour, scar on nuckle of the middle finger of right hand, a scar on left arm
DATE	15 Sep 1857
RECORD #	2415
PAGE	237

NAME	MANDLEY, Eliza
PROOF	free born as proved by oath of Nimrod CROSS
DESCRIPTION	abt 19y old, 5' 4" tall, black colour, scar on wrist of left hand
DATE	15 Sep 1857
RECORD #	2416
PAGE	237

NAME	ALLEN, Mary Ann
PROOF	freedom proved by oath of Wm. T. J. CRAIG
DESCRIPTION	37y old, 5' 3" tall, bright colour, least finger of the right hand is crooked
DATE	15 Sep 1857
RECORD #	2417
PAGE	238

NAME	ALLEN, Arabella (child of Mary Ann ALLEN)
PROOF	freedom proved by oath of Wm. T. J. CRAIG
DESCRIPTION	abt 17y old, 5' 2" tall, brown colour, mole on her forehead
DATE	15 Sep 1857
RECORD #	2417
PAGE	238

NAME	ALLEN, Stewart Thornton (child of Mary Ann ALLEN)
PROOF	freedom proved by oath of Wm. T. J. CRAIG
DESCRIPTION	abt 14y old, brown colour, scar on right knee
DATE	15 Sep 1857
RECORD #	2417
PAGE	238

NAME	ALLEN, Samuel Smith (child of Mary Ann ALLEN)
PROOF	freedom proved by oath of Wm. T. J. CRAIG
DESCRIPTION	12y old, brown colour
DATE	15 Sep 1857
RECORD #	2417
PAGE	238

NAME	ALLEN, Jas. Spencer (child of Mary Ann ALLEN)
PROOF	freedom proved by oath of Wm. T. J. CRAIG
DESCRIPTION	8y old, brown colour
DATE	15 Sep 1857
RECORD #	2417
PAGE	238

Loudoun County, Virginia Register of Free Negroes 1844-1861

NAME	ALLEN, Harriet Levenia (child of Mary Ann ALLEN)
PROOF	freedom proved by oath of Wm. T. J. CRAIG
DESCRIPTION	10y old, brown colour
DATE	15 Sep 1857
RECORD #	2417
PAGE	238

NAME	FITZHUGH, Tazewell
PROOF	free born as proved by oath of Peyton W. CHAMBLIN
DESCRIPTION	abt 24y old, 5' 2" tall, black colour, scar on nose & one scar on left hand
DATE	15 Sep 1857
RECORD #	2418
PAGE	238

NAME	ASHTON, Julia Ellen
PROOF	free born as proved by oath of Wm. T. J. CRAIG
DESCRIPTION	abt 19y old, 5' 4" tall, mulatto colour, scar on forehead
DATE	15 Sep 1857
RECORD #	2419
PAGE	239

NAME	ASHTON, Victoria Mildrish
PROOF	free born as proved by oath of Wm. T. J. CRAIG
DESCRIPTION	abt 16y old, 5' 1" tall, mulatto colour, scar on left side of face near the ear
DATE	15 Sep 1857
RECORD #	2420
PAGE	239

NAME	ALLEN, Spencer
PROOF	free born as proved by oath of Wm. T. J. CRAIG
DESCRIPTION	abt 56y old, 5' 6" tall, black colour, the least finger of his left hand is crooked
DATE	15 Sep 1857
RECORD #	2421
PAGE	239

NAME	LEWIS, Priscilla
PROOF	free born as proved by oath of Jonas SCHOOLEY
DESCRIPTION	abt 46y old, 5' 3" tall, dark complexion, small scar on left brow and large scar on right arm below the elbow caused by a burn
DATE	15 Sep 1857
RECORD #	2422
PAGE	240

NAME	LEWIS, John W. (child of Priscilla LEWIS)
PROOF	free born as proved by oath of Jonas SCHOOLEY
DESCRIPTION	abt 12y old, brown colour
DATE	15 Sep 1857
RECORD #	2422
PAGE	240

NAME	LEWIS, Columbus (child of Priscilla LEWIS)
PROOF	free born as proved by oath of Jonas SCHOOLEY
DESCRIPTION	10y old, brown colour
DATE	15 Sep 1857
RECORD #	2422
PAGE	240

NAME	LEWIS, Franklin Peirce (child of Priscilla LEWIS)
PROOF	free born as proved by oath of Jonas SCHOOLEY
DESCRIPTION	abt 3y old, brown colour
DATE	15 Sep 1857
RECORD #	2422
PAGE	240

NAME	LEWIS, Laura Jane (child of Priscilla LEWIS)
PROOF	free born as proved by oath of Jonas SCHOOLEY
DESCRIPTION	abt 10m old, brown colour
DATE	15 Sep 1857
RECORD #	2422
PAGE	240

NAME	LEWIS, Mary Louisa
PROOF	free born as proved by oath of Jonas P. SCHOOLEY
DESCRIPTION	abt 17y old, 5' 2" tall, brown colour, scar on left arm
DATE	17 Sep 1857
RECORD #	2423
PAGE	240

NAME	MANDLEY, Chas.
PROOF	free born as proved by oath of Benjn. B. BEARD
DESCRIPTION	abt 29y, 5' 6" tall, brown colour, scar on forehead and one on right cheek
DATE	15 Sep 1857
RECORD #	2424
PAGE	241

Loudoun County, Virginia Register of Free Negroes 1844-1861

NAME MANDLEY, Ellen
PROOF free born as proved by oath of Benj. B. BEARD
DESCRIPTION abt 42y old, 5' 7" tall, black colour
DATE 15 Sep 1857
RECORD # 2425
PAGE 241

NAME MANDLEY, Louisa
PROOF free born as proved by oath of Benj. B. BEARD
DESCRIPTION abt 13y old, 5' 2" tall, brown colour, scar near corner of left eye
DATE 15 Sep 1857
RECORD # 2426
PAGE 241

NAME MANDLEY, Elizabeth
PROOF free born as proved by oath of Benj. B. BEARD
DESCRIPTION 22y old, 5' 5" tall, brown colour, mole under her jaw
DATE 15 Sep 1857
RECORD # 2427
PAGE 242

NAME MANDLEY, Mary
PROOF free born as proved by oath of Benj. B. BEARD
DESCRIPTION abt 21y old, 5' 4" tall, bright mulatto, scar on end of her third finger on right hand
DATE 15 Sep 1857
RECORD # 2428
PAGE 242

NAME ROBINSON, Sampson
PROOF emancipated by deed from S. J. LINDSEY dated 11 Aug 1857
DESCRIPTION abt 60y old, 5' 5" tall, dark brown, right hand crippled and left also crippled and lame
DATE 15 Sep 1857
RECORD # 2429
PAGE 242

NAME ROBINSON, Jane
PROOF emancipated by deed from S. M. JANNEY dated 30 Jan 1857
DESCRIPTION 40y old, 5' tall, brown colour, scar on right cheek and lame in her left foot
DATE 15 Sep 1857
RECORD # 2430
PAGE 243

NAME	MORGAN, Charles Henry
PROOF	free born as proved by oath of Geo. K. FOX
DESCRIPTION	abt 22y old, 5' 8½" tall, bright mulatto, scar in left temple
DATE	15 Sep 1857
RECORD #	2431
PAGE	243

NAME	ALLEN, Mary M.
PROOF	free born as proved by oath of Margaret HUMPHREY
DESCRIPTION	abt 20y old, 5' 3" tall, mulatto colour, burn on 3d finger of left hand
DATE	13 Oct 1857
RECORD #	2432
PAGE	243

NAME	MASON, George Henry
PROOF	emancipated by will of Jane POTTS recorded in 1856 as proved by oath of George BACKHOUSE
DESCRIPTION	abt 30y old, 5' 4" tall, brown colour, scar on forehead, scar on right hand
DATE	13 Oct 1857
RECORD #	2433
PAGE	244

NAME	PEARSON, James
PROOF	emancipated by will of George ABEL dec'd and granted permission to reside in state
DESCRIPTION	abt 30y old, 5' 8" tall, bright mulatto, scar above right eye brow, last finger of right hand is crooked at the middle joint
DATE	13 Oct 1857
RECORD #	2434
PAGE	244

NAME	BOYD, Nancy Catharine (child of Mary Catharine BOYD)
PROOF	free born as proved by oath of Wm. H. RUSSELL
DESCRIPTION	abt 12y old, brown colour, scar on left cheek
DATE	13 Oct 1857
RECORD #	2435
PAGE	245

NAME	BOYD, Alfred Nathaniel (child of Mary Catharine BOYD)
PROOF	free born as proved by oath of Wm. H. RUSSELL
DESCRIPTION	abt 9y old, brown colour, scar on right hand
DATE	13 Oct 1857
RECORD #	2435
PAGE	245

Loudoun County, Virginia Register of Free Negroes 1844-1861

NAME	ADAMS, Sally (daughter of Hannah JOHNSON)
PROOF	emancipated by will of David LACEY about 1825 as proved by oath of Wm. H. RUSSELL
DESCRIPTION	abt 50y old, brown colour, scar on left arm, no permission granted to reside in this state
DATE	13 Oct 1857
RECORD #	2436
PAGE	245

NAME	ADAMS, Francis Ann (daughter of Hannah JOHNSON)
PROOF	emancipated by will of David LACEY as proved by oath of Wm. H. RUSSELL
DESCRIPTION	abt 12y old, brown colour, no permission to reside in this state
DATE	12 Oct 1857
RECORD #	2437
PAGE	245

NAME	ADAMS, Phebe Ann
PROOF	free born as proved by oath of Wm. H. RUSSELL
DESCRIPTION	abt 16y old, mulatto colour, scar on left cheek near the ear, lump on right arm
DATE	13 Oct 1857
RECORD #	2438
PAGE	246

NAME	BRADY, Samuel
PROOF	free born as proved by oath of Wm. Henry TAYLOR
DESCRIPTION	abt 22y old, 5' 4½" tall, brown colour, no scars
DATE	14 Dec 1857
RECORD #	2439
PAGE	246

NAME	GUY, Maria
PROOF	emancipated by will of Ann SAUNDERS
DESCRIPTION	21y old, 5' 5" tall, brown colour
DATE	14 Dec 1857
RECORD #	2440
PAGE	246

NAME	GUY, Mary Virginia (daughter of Maria GUY)
PROOF	emancipated by will of Ann SAUNDERS
DESCRIPTION	5y old, brown colour
DATE	14 Dec 1857
RECORD #	2440
PAGE	246

NAME   GUY, Hannah Ann (daughter of Maria GUY)
PROOF   emancipated by will of Ann SAUNDERS
DESCRIPTION abt 3y old, brown colour
DATE   14 Dec 1857
RECORD #   2440
PAGE   246

NAME   JACKSON, Sarah
PROOF   free born as proved by oath of Thomas MUNDAY
DESCRIPTION abt 21y old, 5' 3" tall, brown colour, small scar on right hand
DATE   15 Dec 1857
RECORD #   2441
PAGE   247

NAME   TRIPLETT, John
PROOF   free born proved by producing papers from Pendleton Co. VA
DESCRIPTION 38y old, 5' 8¼" tall, black colour, round scar on right check from a burn, no other apparent marks
DATE   15 Dec 1857
RECORD #   2442
PAGE   247

NAME   AMBROSE, Sina
PROOF   emancipated by deed from George RICHARDS as proved by oath of Geo. K. FOX Sr.
DESCRIPTION abt 58y old, 5' 3" tall, brown colour, scar on back of left hand, scar on back of right hand
DATE   9 Feb 1858
RECORD #   2443
PAGE   248

NAME   BRYANT, George
PROOF   free born as proved by oath of Geo. K FOX Sr.
DESCRIPTION abt 20y old, 5' 3½" tall, dark colour, scar on forehead
DATE   9 Feb 1858
RECORD #   2444
PAGE   248

NAME   RUST, Thornton (son of Betsey RUST)
PROOF   free born as proved by oath of Isaac EATON
DESCRIPTION abt 21y old, 5' 11" tall, bright mulatto, small scar on right cheek, one on right arm
DATE   9 Feb 1858
RECORD #   2445
PAGE   248

Loudoun County, Virginia Register of Free Negroes 1844-1861

NAME	RUST, Mary Virginia (daughter of Betsey RUST)
PROOF	free born as proved by oath of Isaac EASTON
DESCRIPTION	abt 14y old, 5' 2½" tall, brown colour, scar on one of the fingers of left hand, one on right arm
DATE	9 Feb 1858
RECORD #	2446
PAGE	249

NAME	RUST, Marshall Pendleton (son of Betsey RUST)
PROOF	free born as proved by oath of Isaac EASTON
DESCRIPTION	11y old, brown colour
DATE	9 Feb 1858
RECORD #	2447
PAGE	249

NAME	RUST, Emma Jane (daughter of Betsey RUST)
PROOF	free born as proved by oath of Isaac EASTON
DESCRIPTION	8y old, brown colour, scar on left hand
DATE	9 Feb 1858
RECORD #	2447
PAGE	249

NAME	RUST, Ann Elizabeth (daughter of Frances RUST)
PROOF	free born as proved by oath of Isaac EATON
DESCRIPTION	abt 4y old, bright mulatto colour
DATE	9 Feb 1858
RECORD #	2448
PAGE	249

NAME	BURK, John Thomas (son of Elizabeth BURK)
PROOF	free born as proved by oath of Isaac EATON
DESCRIPTION	abt 2y old, brown colour
DATE	9 Feb 1858
RECORD #	2449
PAGE	250

NAME	BURK, Sarah Elizabeth (daughter of Elizabeth BURK)
PROOF	free born as proved by oath of Isaac EATON
DESCRIPTION	abt 9m old, brown colour
DATE	9 Feb 1858
RECORD #	2449
PAGE	250

NAME   CLEMMONS, Hezekiah
PROOF   free born as proved by oath of Wesley JENKINS
DESCRIPTION   abt 55y old, 5' 1" tall, bright mulatto colour
DATE   9 Feb 1858
RECORD #   2450
PAGE   250

NAME   BAILY, William
PROOF   emancipated by will of Nancy NEALE dec'd as proved by oath of Thos. H. CLAGETT
DESCRIPTION   abt 45y old, 5' 11" tall, dark brown colour
DATE   9 Mar 1858
RECORD #   2251 [misnumbered]
PAGE   250

NAME   DAVIS, Dennis
PROOF   free born as proved by oath of Wm. WILLIAMS
DESCRIPTION   abt 23y old, 5' tall, brown colour, scar on left foot
DATE   13 Apr 1858
RECORD #   2252
PAGE   251

NAME   GAINES, Issabella
PROOF   freedom proved by oath of George K. FOX
DESCRIPTION   abt 55y old, 5' 4½" tall, dark complexion, scar on throat, two moles below the right eye
DATE   14 Apr 1858
RECORD #   2253
PAGE   251

NAME   GODFREY, William
PROOF   free born [as stated in paper from Pr. Wm. Co. has been crossed out]
DESCRIPTION   abt 34y, 5' 9½" tall, bright mulatto, small scar on right arm caused by burn
DATE   11 May 1858
RECORD #   2254
PAGE   [251]

NAME   MASON, Henry
PROOF   free born as proved by oath of Wm. B. NOLAND
DESCRIPTION   abt 27y old, 5' 8" tall, mulatto colour, fingers on left hand is burnt
DATE   11 May 1858
RECORD #   2255
PAGE   [252]

NAME	GRAYSON, Eliza
PROOF	free born as proved by oath of Jos. L. HAWLING
DESCRIPTION	abt 53y old, 5' 3" tall, dark complexion, scar on middle finger of right hand
DATE	12 May 1858
RECORD #	2256
PAGE	[252]

NAME	GRAYSON, Joseph (son of Eliza GRAYSON)
PROOF	free born as proved by oath of Jos. L. HAWLING
DESCRIPTION	abt 18y old, black colour, scar on upper lip, one on back of right hand
DATE	12 May 1858
RECORD #	2256
PAGE	[252]

NAME	GRAYSON, Washington (son of Eliza GRAYSON)
PROOF	free born as proved by oath of Jos. L. HAWLING
DESCRIPTION	abt 13y old, copper colour, small mole under the left eye
DATE	12 May 1858
RECORD #	2256
PAGE	[252]

NAME	MORGAN, Alfred
PROOF	free born as proved by oath of Henry FAWLEY
DESCRIPTION	abt 51y old, 5' 9" tall, mulatto colour, forefingers of right hand is stiff and the little finger of the left has been mashed off
DATE	16 Jun 1858
RECORD #	2257
PAGE	[253]

NAME	MASON, Julius
PROOF	emancipated by Ezekiel POTTS per will of Jane POTTS dec'd
DESCRIPTION	abt 60y old, 5' 4" tall, black colour, scar on back of right hand and cripple in the right shoulder
DATE	16 Jun 1858
RECORD #	2258
PAGE	[253]

NAME	MASON, John E.
PROOF	emancipated by Ezekiel POTTS per will of Jane POTTS dec'd
DESCRIPTION	13y old, brown colour, scar on forehead
DATE	16 Jun 1858
RECORD #	2259
PAGE	[253]

NAME   MASON, Wm. F.
PROOF   emancipated by Ezekiel POTTS per will of Jane POTTS dec'd
DESCRIPTION abt 9y old, brown colour
DATE   16 Jun 1858
RECORD #   2260
PAGE   [254]

NAME   DADE, Henrietta
PROOF   freedom proved by oath of Dr. T. LEITH
DESCRIPTION abt 43y old, 5' 3" tall, dark complexion, small scar on first
            finger of left hand between first & second joint of finger
DATE   16 Jun 1858
RECORD #   2261
PAGE   [254]

NAME   DADE, William (child of Henrietta DADE)
PROOF   freedom proved by oath of Dr. T. LEITH
DESCRIPTION 18y old, bright colour, scar on joint of first finger of right hand
            and one on forehead
DATE   16 Jun 1858
RECORD #   2261
PAGE   [254]

NAME   DADE, Cornelius (child of Henrietta DADE)
PROOF   freedom proved by oath of Dr. T. LEITH
DESCRIPTION 16y old, bright colour, scar in eyebrow over right eye
DATE   16 Jun 1858
RECORD #   2261
PAGE   [254]

NAME   DADE, Marietta (child of Henrietta DADE)
PROOF   freedom proved by oath of Dr. T. LEITH
DESCRIPTION abt 11y old, bright mulatto colour
DATE   16 Jun 1858
RECORD #   2261
PAGE   [254]

NAME   DADE, Louisa (child of Henrietta DADE)
PROOF   freedom proved by oath of Dr. T. LEITH
DESCRIPTION abt 9y old, bright mulatto colour, a burn on the head
DATE   16 Jun 1858
RECORD #   2261
PAGE   [254]

Loudoun County, Virginia Register of Free Negroes 1844-1861

NAME	DADE, Robert (child of Henrietta DADE)
PROOF	freedom proved by oath of Dr. T. LEITH
DESCRIPTION	abt 6y old, dark complexion, scar between eyes
DATE	14 Sep 1858
RECORD #	2261
PAGE	[254]

NAME	JOHNSON, Samuel (son of Sally JOHNSON)
PROOF	free born as proved by oath of Jas. W. NIXON
DESCRIPTION	abt 28y old, 5' 7" tall, black colour, one scar in the corner of each eye brow
DATE	13 Oct 1858
RECORD #	2262
PAGE	[255]

NAME	JACKSON, John J. (son of John & Sally JACKSON)
PROOF	free born as proved by oath of Jno. L. CHAMBLIN
DESCRIPTION	abt 20y old, 5' 6" tall, brown colour, scar on forehead near hair
DATE	13 Oct 1858
RECORD #	2263
PAGE	[255]

NAME	TURNER, Margaret (wife of Geo. H. TURNER, daughter of Betsey POLAND)
PROOF	free born as proved by oath of Jno. L. CHAMBLIN
DESCRIPTION	abt 24y old, 5' 3" tall, mulatto colour
DATE	9 Nov 1858
RECORD #	2264
PAGE	[256]

NAME	POLAND, Mary (daughter of Betsey POLAND)
PROOF	free born as proved by oath of Jno. L. CHAMBLIN
DESCRIPTION	abt 18y old, 5' 6" tall, bright mulatto colour, scar on back of right hand
DATE	9 Nov 1858
RECORD #	2265
PAGE	[256]

NAME	HALL, Maria
PROOF	emancipated by deed from Elzekiel POTTS recorded 10 Nov 1858
DESCRIPTION	abt 43y old, 5' 2" tall, black colour, scar on forehead, her little finger on right hand is crooked
DATE	10 Nov 1858
RECORD #	2266
PAGE	[256]

NAME	BROWN, Mason (son of Sarah BROWN)
PROOF	free born as proved by oath of Richard TAVENNER
DESCRIPTION	abt 17y old, brown colour
DATE	11 Nov 1858
RECORD #	2267
PAGE	[257]

NAME	BROWN, Frank (son of Sarah BROWN)
PROOF	free born as proved by oath of Richard TAVENNER
DESCRIPTION	abt 14y old, black color, scar on right wrist
DATE	11 Nov 1858
RECORD #	2267
PAGE	[257]

NAME	RIVERS, Joseph
PROOF	emancipated by will of Margaret DOUGLAS recorded Liber 2, page 160 as proved by Charles B. TEBBS
DESCRIPTION	abt 34y old, 6' 1½" tall, black colour, scar on back of left hand
DATE	14 Dec 1858
RECORD #	2268
PAGE	[257]

NAME	THOMAS, Laura Elizabeth (daughter of Negro Elizabeth)
PROOF	emancipated by Wm. CARR
DESCRIPTION	abt 22y old, 5' 1½" tall, brown colour, scar on back of left hand
DATE	15 Dec 1858
RECORD #	2269
PAGE	[257]

NAME	THOMAS, Lewis Newman (son of Laura Elizabeth THOMAS)
PROOF	freedom proved by oath of Wm. F. BARRETT
DESCRIPTION	2y old, brown colour
DATE	15 Dec 1858
RECORD #	2269
PAGE	[257]

NAME	THOMAS, Ida Ann Florida (daughter of Laura Elizabeth THOMAS)
PROOF	freedom proved by oath of Wm. F. BARRETT
DESCRIPTION	abt 1y old, brown colour
DATE	15 Dec 1858
RECORD #	2269
PAGE	[257]

Loudoun County, Virginia Register of Free Negroes 1844-1861

NAME	FORD, John R. (son of Kitty FORD)
PROOF	free born as proved by oath of Joseph W. HOLMES
DESCRIPTION	abt 16y old, 5' 8" tall, brown colour, scar on joint of the thumb of left hand
DATE	15 Dec 1858
RECORD #	2270
PAGE	[258]

NAME	FORD, Kitty
PROOF	free born as proved by oath of Joseph W. HOLMES
DESCRIPTION	abt 46y old, 5' 4" tall, brown colour, scar on right hand near the middle of the hand, scar on the middle finger of left hand
DATE	15 Dec 1858
RECORD #	2271
PAGE	[258]

NAME	FORD, Alice (daughter of Kitty FORD)
PROOF	free born as proved by oath of Joseph W. HOLMES
DESCRIPTION	abt 15y old, brown colour, scar on left arm
DATE	15 Dec 1858
RECORD #	2271
PAGE	[258]

NAME	FORD, Albert (son of Kitty FORD)
PROOF	free born as proved by oath of Joseph W. HOLMES
DESCRIPTION	abt 11y old, brown colour
DATE	15 Dec 1858
RECORD #	2271
PAGE	[258]

NAME	FORD, Patsey (daughter of Kitty FORD)
PROOF	free born as proved by oath of Joseph W. HOLMES
DESCRIPTION	abt 8y old, brown colour
DATE	15 Dec 1858
RECORD #	2271
PAGE	[258]

NAME	McINTOSH, James
PROOF	manumitted by deed of Janet HENDERSON recorded Fauquier Co. 24 Aug 1835 and proved by oath of Fenton M. HENDERSON
DESCRIPTION	abt 35y old, 5' 6" tall, dark mulatto colour, scar on forehead
DATE	16 Feb 1859
RECORD #	2272
PAGE	[259]

NAME	THORNTON, Charles
PROOF	free born as proved by oath of David HIXSON
DESCRIPTION	abt 45y old, 5' 5" tall, dark brown colour, scar on forehead, also one on chin
DATE	16 Feb 1859
RECORD #	2273
PAGE	[259]

NAME	McDANIEL, Lee
PROOF	free born as proved by oath of Alfred WRIGHT
DESCRIPTION	abt 37y old, 5' 9" tall, dark brown colour, scar caused by a burn on thumb of right hand
DATE	16 Feb 1859
RECORD #	2274
PAGE	[260]

NAME	CARTER, Margaret Elizabeth (of Malinda CARTER)
PROOF	free born as proved by oath of James WALKER
DESCRIPTION	abt 6y old, brown colour
DATE	16 Feb 1859
RECORD #	2275
PAGE	[260]

NAME	CARTER, Charles William (son of Malinda CARTER)
PROOF	free born as proved by oath of James WALKER
DESCRIPTION	4y old, brown colour
DATE	16 Feb 1859
RECORD #	2275
PAGE	[260]

NAME	WATSON, Martha
PROOF	free born as proved by oath of H. H. RHODES
DESCRIPTION	abt 6y old, bright mulatto colour
DATE	16 Feb 1859
RECORD #	2276
PAGE	[260]

NAME	VALENTINE, Hamilton
PROOF	emancipated by will of Malinda MAHONEY
DESCRIPTION	abt 28y old, 6' ½", black colour, scar in middle of forehead, has a split right thumb, also six fingers on each hand, scar on 3rd finger of the left hand
DATE	12 Apr 1859
RECORD #	2277
PAGE	[261]

Loudoun County, Virginia Register of Free Negroes 1844-1861

NAME   WATSON, Emily
PROOF   free born as proved by oath of James SINCLAIR
DESCRIPTION abt 19y old, 5' 4½" tall, light brown colour, no scars to be seen
DATE   [12 Apr 1859]
RECORD #   2278
PAGE   [261]

NAME   THORNTON, Emily
PROOF   free born as proved by oath of Henry A. BALL
DESCRIPTION abt 35y old, 5' 2" tall, dark brown colour, scar on back of left hand
DATE   [12 Apr 1859]
RECORD #   2279
PAGE   [261]

NAME   THORNTON, Mary Ellen (daughter of Emily THORNTON)
PROOF   free born as proved by oath of Henry A. BALL
DESCRIPTION abt 8y old, light brown colour, no scars to be seen
DATE   [12 Apr 1859]
RECORD #   2279
PAGE   [261]

NAME   ALLEN, Elizabeth
PROOF   free born as proved by oath of Joseph HOLMES
DESCRIPTION abt 23y old, 5' 3½" tall, light mulatto colour, no scars
DATE   11 May 1859
RECORD #   2280
PAGE   [262]

NAME   ALLEN, Maria (daughter of Elizabeth ALLEN)
PROOF   free born as proved by oath of Joseph HOLMES
DESCRIPTION abt 3y old, light mulatto colour
DATE   11 May 1859
RECORD #   2280
PAGE   [262]

NAME   ALLEN, Juliet (daughter of Elizabeth ALLEN)
PROOF   free born as proved by oath of Joseph HOLMES
DESCRIPTION abt 17m old, dark mulatto colour
DATE   11 May 1859
RECORD #   2280
PAGE   [262]

NAME   FORD, Clara
PROOF   free born as proved by oath of Joseph HOLMES
DESCRIPTION abt 21y old, 5' ½?" tall, dark mulatto colour, no scars
DATE   11 May 1859
RECORD #   2281
PAGE   [262]

NAME   FORD, Martha Ann (daughter of Clara FORD)
PROOF   free born as proved by oath of Joseph HOLMES
DESCRIPTION abt 6m old, very light mulatto
DATE   11 May 1859
RECORD #   2281
PAGE   [262]

NAME   DOUGLAS, Joseph
PROOF   emancipated by will of Nicholas ROPP dec'd as proved by oaths of Samuel ROPP & John McCLENAN
DESCRIPTION abt 40y old, 5' 9½" tall, yellow colour, scar caused by a burn on right wrist
DATE   12 Sep 1859
RECORD #   2282
PAGE   [263]

NAME   TALIFARIO, Jane
PROOF   emancipated by will of Mahlon BALDWIN dec'd as proved by oath of John T. ROSS
DESCRIPTION abt 44y old, 5' 1" tall, bright mulatto, scar on right elbow
DATE   [12 Sep 1859]
RECORD #   2283
PAGE   [263]

NAME   TALIFARIO, Gilmore (son of Jane TALIFARIO)
PROOF   emancipated by will of Mahlon BALDWIN dec'd as proved by oath of John T. ROSS
DESCRIPTION abt 8y old, bright mulatto colour
DATE   [12 Sep 1859]
RECORD #   2283
PAGE   [263]

NAME   BURKE, John
PROOF   free born as proved by oath of Jno. H. SIMPSON, formerly registered in Stafford Co., produced free papers
DESCRIPTION abt 30y, 5' 8½" tall, black colour, small scar on right hand
DATE   12 Sep 1859
RECORD #   2284
PAGE   [264]

Loudoun County, Virginia Register of Free Negroes 1844-1861   203

NAME	GRAYSON, Jane (alias Jane BURKE)
PROOF	formerly registered in Stafford Co. & produced free papers, freedom proved by oath of Jno. H. SIMPSON
DESCRIPTION	abt 34y old, 5' tall, black colour, scar on lid of left eye
DATE	12 Sep 1859
RECORD #	2285
PAGE	[264]

NAME	BURKE, Ann S. (daughter of Jane GRAYSON)
PROOF	free born as proved by oath of Jno. H. SIMPSON
DESCRIPTION	12y old, brown
DATE	12 Sep 1859
RECORD #	2285
PAGE	[264]

NAME	BURKE, John O. (son of Jane GRAYSON)
PROOF	free born as proved by oath of Jno. H. SIMPSON
DESCRIPTION	abt 8y old, brown colour, scar on right breast
DATE	12 Sep 1859
RECORD #	2285
PAGE	[264]

NAME	BURKE, Malinda A. (daughter of Jane GRAYSON)
PROOF	free born as proved by oath of Jno. H. SIMPSON
DESCRIPTION	abt 6y old, brown colour
DATE	12 Sep 1859
RECORD #	2285
PAGE	[264]

NAME	BURKE, Eliza T. (daughter of Jane GRAYSON)
PROOF	free born as proved by oath of Jno. H. SIMPSON
DESCRIPTION	abt 3y old, brown colour
DATE	12 Sep 1859
RECORD #	2285
PAGE	[264]

NAME	BURKE, Powhatan M. (child of Jane GRAYSON)
PROOF	free born as proved by oath of Jno. H. SIMPSON
DESCRIPTION	abt 9m old, brown colour
DATE	12 Sep 1859
RECORD #	2285
PAGE	[264]

NAME	GUY, Virginia
PROOF	emancipated by will of Ann SAUNDERS as proved by oath of Geo. K. FOX
DESCRIPTION	abt 28y old, 5' 1" tall, dark brown colour, no scars
DATE	13 Sep 1859
RECORD #	2246 [misnumbered]
PAGE	[265]

NAME	WHEELER, Hester
PROOF	emancipated by deed from Leven POWELL dated 20 Nov 1798?, as proved by oath of Saml. M. BOSS
DESCRIPTION	abt 71y old, 5' 1" tall, black colour, scar on ankle caused by a cancer, also one over the left eye
DATE	13 Sep 1859
RECORD #	2247
PAGE	[265]

NAME	BALL, Joseph (son of Alpheus BALL)
PROOF	free born as proved by oath of William P. THOMAS
DESCRIPTION	abt 28y old, 5' 10" tall, brown colour, scar on forehead over right eye, also a finger on left hand cut off
DATE	12 Sep 1859
RECORD #	2248
PAGE	[266]

NAME	HOWARD, John
PROOF	free born as proved by oath of W. S. BRADEN, formerly register in Stafford Co. and produced free papers
DESCRIPTION	abt 27y old, 5' 11" tall, brown colour, small scar on left leg just below the knee, scar on third finger of right hand
DATE	10 Oct 1859
RECORD #	2249
PAGE	[266]

NAME	HOWARD, Julia Ann Virginia (wife of John HOWARD)
PROOF	registered in Stafford Co. & produced free papers
DESCRIPTION	abt 20y old, 5' 5" tall, mulatto colour, two scars on left side of left leg just below the knee abt ½" apart
DATE	10 Oct 1859
RECORD #	2250
PAGE	[266]

NAME	HOWARD, Noah Alexander (child of Julia Ann Virginia HOWARD)
PROOF	free born as proved by oath of N. S. BRADEN
DESCRIPTION	abt 9y old, mulatto colour, scar on back of left hand
DATE	10 Oct 1859
RECORD #	2250
PAGE	[266]

NAME	HOWARD, Mary Frances (child of Julia Ann Virginia HOWARD)
PROOF	free born as proved by oath of N. S. BRADEN
DESCRIPTION	abt 6y old, brown colour, scar on right arm just below elbow
DATE	10 Oct 1859
RECORD #	2250
PAGE	[266]

NAME	HOWARD, John William (child of Julia Ann Virginia HOWARD)
PROOF	free born as proved by oath of N. S. BRADEN
DESCRIPTION	abt 4y old, brown colour, scar on left side of face near ear caused by burn
DATE	10 Oct 1859
RECORD #	2250
PAGE	[266]

NAME	HOWARD, Algernon (child of Julia Ann Virginia HOWARD)
PROOF	free born as proved by oath of N. S. BRADEN
DESCRIPTION	abt 2y old, brown colour
DATE	10 Oct 1859
RECORD #	2250
PAGE	[266]

NAME	HOWARD, Permelia (child of Julia Ann Virginia HOWARD)
PROOF	free born as proved by oath of N. S. BRADEN
DESCRIPTION	abt 7m old, bright mulatto colour
DATE	10 Oct 1859
RECORD #	2250
PAGE	[266]

NAME	HOLLIDAY, David
PROOF	free born as proved by oath of Dr. Theo'e LEITH
DESCRIPTION	abt 24y old, 5' 10½" tall, light brown colour, no scars
DATE	15 Nov 1859
RECORD #	2251
PAGE	[267]

NAME	BALL, John (son of Allison & Nancy BALL)
PROOF	free born as proved by oath of John L. CHAMBLIN
DESCRIPTION	22y old, 5' 10½" tall, light brown colour, scar near centre of the forehead, scar on or above the chin, dark spot on left cheek
DATE	9 Jan 1860
RECORD #	2252
PAGE	[268]

NAME	MANLEY, Samuel
PROOF	free born as proved by oath of Alexander McFARLAND
DESCRIPTION	abt 27y old, 5' 6½" tall, dark brown colour, scar on left leg below knee, scar on left eye brow
DATE	12 Mar 1860
RECORD #	2253
PAGE	[268]

NAME	WATSON, Wilson (son of William & Emily WATSON)
PROOF	free born as proved by oath of George K. FOX
DESCRIPTION	23y old, 5' 11" tall, brown colour, scar on end of the second finger of left hand, mole on left wrist
DATE	10 Apr 1860
RECORD #	2254
PAGE	[268]

NAME	TIMBERS, Ann (formerly Ann BIRD who was formerly Ann STAUNTON)
PROOF	free born as proved by oath of Mrs. Catharine WILT
DESCRIPTION	abt 37y old, 5' 3" tall, mulatto colour, mole on right side of neck
DATE	14 May 1860
RECORD #	2255
PAGE	[269]

NAME	BIRD, Jonathan A. (son of Ann TIMBERS)
PROOF	free born as proved by oath of Mrs. Catharine WILT
DESCRIPTION	abt 11y old, bright mulatto colour, mole on right cheek, scar on forehead near hair
DATE	14 May 1860
RECORD #	2255
PAGE	[269]

NAME	BIRD, Saml. E. W. (son of Ann TIMBERS)
PROOF	free born as proved by oath of Mrs. Catharine WILT
DESCRIPTION	abt 9y old, brown colour, scar on forehead, two moles on back of left hand
DATE	14 May 1860
RECORD #	2255
PAGE	[269]

NAME	BIRD, Benjn. O. (son of Ann TIMBERS)
PROOF	free born as proved by oath of Mrs. Catharine WILT
DESCRIPTION	abt 7y old, bright mulatto colour, no scars
DATE	14 May 1860
RECORD #	2255
PAGE	[269]

NAME	TIMBERS, Lydia Ellen (daughter of Ann TIMBERS)
PROOF	free born as proved by oath of Mrs. Catharine WILT
DESCRIPTION	abt 4y old, bright mulatto colour, scar on forehead
DATE	14 May 1860
RECORD #	2255
PAGE	[269]

NAME	TIMBERS, James Wm.
PROOF	free born as proved by oath of Emanuel WALTMAN
DESCRIPTION	abt 28y old, 5' 6" tall, bright mulatto Colour, scar on right side of face near eyebrow & 2 or 3 on right cheek
DATE	14 May 1860
RECORD #	2256
PAGE	[269]

NAME	BIRD, Sarah J. F. (daughter of Ann TIMBERS alias BIRD alias STAUNTON)
PROOF	free born as proved by oath of Mrs. Catharine WILT
DESCRIPTION	abt 14y old, 5' 4" tall, very light colour, small scar on left cheek
DATE	14 May 1860
RECORD #	2257
PAGE	[270]

NAME	CARROLL, Ann Maria
PROOF	freedom proved by oath of Michael & Thomas SANBOWER
DESCRIPTION	abt 27y old, 5' 2½" tall, dark brown colour, scar on forefinger of right hand
DATE	12 Jun 1860
RECORD #	2258
PAGE	[270]

NAME   CARROLL, George Washington (son of Ann Maria
                CARROLL)
PROOF   freedom proved by oath of Michael & Thomas SANBOWER
DESCRIPTION   abt 9m old, dark brown color
DATE   12 Jun 1860
RECORD #   2258
PAGE   [270]

NAME   FLETCHER, Benjamin Franklin
PROOF   free born as proved by oath of Wm. HOLMES
DESCRIPTION   abt 23y old, 5' 11" tall, light mulatto colour
DATE   14 Aug 1860
RECORD #   2259
PAGE   [271]

NAME   GUY, Lucinda
PROOF   emancipated by will of Ann SAUNDERS as proved by oath of
                Wilson C. SAUNDERS
DESCRIPTION   abt 23y old, 5' 1" tall, brown colour, burn on left wrist
DATE   14 Aug 1860
RECORD #   2260
PAGE   [271]

NAME   GUY, Joseph (son of Lucinda GUY)
PROOF   emancipated by will of Ann SAUNDERS as proved by oath of
                Wilson C. SAUNDERS
DESCRIPTION   abt 5y old, brown colour, scar on right cheek
DATE   14 Aug 1860
RECORD #   2260
PAGE   [271]

NAME   BURK, Charles Richard (son of Sophia BURK)
PROOF   free born as proved by free papers (No. 611) from Stafford Co.
DESCRIPTION   abt 20y old, 5' 9" tall, brown colour, scar on back of left hand,
                scar on first & second finger on right hand, mole in corner of
                mouth
DATE   14 Aug 1860
RECORD #   2261
PAGE   [271]

Loudoun County, Virginia Register of Free Negroes 1844-1861

NAME	HULL, James
PROOF	free born as proved by oath of Wm. WILLIAMS
DESCRIPTION	abt 38y old, 5' 8" tall, bright mulatto, scar on left arm between elbow & shoulder
DATE	10 Sep 1860
RECORD #	2262
PAGE	[272]

NAME	GOWEN, Martha Ann
PROOF	free born as proved by oath of Hezekiah KIDWELL
DESCRIPTION	abt 35y old, 5' 4" tall, dark brown colour, scar on left eye brow, scar on back of right hand
DATE	10 Sep 1860
RECORD #	2263
PAGE	[272]

NAME	GOWEN, Caleb (child of Martha Ann GOWEN)
PROOF	free born as proved by oath of Hezekiah KIDWELL
DESCRIPTION	abt 10y old, dark brown colour
DATE	10 Sep 1860
RECORD #	2263
PAGE	[272]

NAME	GOWEN, Charles (child of Martha Ann GOWEN)
PROOF	free born as proved by oath of Hezekiah KIDWELL
DESCRIPTION	abt 8y old, dark brown colour
DATE	10 Sep 1860
RECORD #	2263
PAGE	[272]

NAME	GOWEN, Joseph Connard (child of Martha Ann GOWEN)
PROOF	free born as proved by oath of Hezekiah KIDWELL
DESCRIPTION	abt 6y old, dark brown colour, scar on back of left hand
DATE	10 Sep 1860
RECORD #	2263
PAGE	[272]

NAME	GOWEN, Anna Augusta (child of Martha Ann GOWEN)
PROOF	free born as proved by oath of Hezekiah KIDWELL
DESCRIPTION	abt 5y old, dark brown colour
DATE	10 Sep 1860
RECORD #	2263
PAGE	[272]

NAME   GOWEN, John Wm. (child of Martha Ann GOWEN)
PROOF   free born as proved by oath of Hezekiah KIDWELL
DESCRIPTION   abt 4y old, dark brown colour
DATE   10 Sep 1860
RECORD #   2263
PAGE   [272]

NAME   GOWEN, Susan V. (child of Martha Ann GOWEN)
PROOF   free born as proved by oath of Hezekiah KIDWELL
DESCRIPTION   abt 2y old, dark brown colour
DATE   10 Sep 1860
RECORD #   2263
PAGE   [272]

NAME   GOWEN, Amanda E. (daughter of Martha GOWEN)
PROOF   free born as proved by oath of Hezekiah KIDWELL
DESCRIPTION   abt 20y old, dark brown colour, left forefinger has been mashed
DATE   10 Sep 1860
RECORD #   2264
PAGE   [273]

NAME   TALBOTT, Christina (daughter of Nancy TALBOTT)
PROOF   free born as proved by oath of Wm. HOLMES
DESCRIPTION   abt 35y old, 5' tall, brown colour, scar in middle of left hand, scar near end of middle finger
DATE   9 Oct 1860
RECORD #   2265
PAGE   [273]

NAME   LEWIS, George
PROOF   emancipated by deed from William HOLMES this day
DESCRIPTION   abt 37y old, 5' 6" tall, black colour, scar on chin
DATE   13 Nov 1860
RECORD #   2266
PAGE   [274]

NAME   BRADY, Susan (daughter of Willis BRADY)
PROOF   free born as proven by oath of Joseph PANCOAST
DESCRIPTION   abt 21y old, 5' 1½" tall, light brown colour, scar on right side of face caused by burn
DATE   14 Nov 1860
RECORD #   2267
PAGE   [274]

NAME	THOMAS, William
PROOF	free born as proved by oath of Joshua SMITH
DESCRIPTION	abt 14y old, 5' ½" tall, light brown
DATE	10 Dec 1860
RECORD #	2268
PAGE	[274]

NAME	JONES, John W.
PROOF	free born as proved by oath of John L. CHAMBLIN
DESCRIPTION	abt 30y old, 5' 9" tall, brown colour
DATE	11 Dec 1860
RECORD #	2269
PAGE	[275]

NAME	BANK, Presley Francis
PROOF	emancipated by will of James HILL dec'd as proved by oath of Jared CHAMBLIN
DESCRIPTION	abt 32y old, 5' 8½" tall, brown colour, small scar on forehead
DATE	15 Jan 1861
RECORD #	2270
PAGE	[275]

NAME	BANK, Richard Henry
PROOF	emancipated by will of James HILL dec'd as proved by oath of Jared CHAMBLIN
DESCRIPTION	abt 31y old, 5' 8", brown colour, scar in corner of left eye
DATE	15 Jan 1861
RECORD #	2271
PAGE	[275]

NAME	BANK, Harriet Ann
PROOF	emancipated by will of James HILL dec'd as proved by oath of Jared CHAMBLIN
DESCRIPTION	abt 28y old, 5' 6½" tall, brown colour
DATE	15 Jan 1861
RECORD #	2272
PAGE	[276]

NAME	BANK, George
PROOF	emancipated by will of James HILL dec'd as proved by oath of Jared CHAMBLIN
DESCRIPTION	abt 25y old, 5' 10½", brown colour, small scar on the back of left hand, one in his forehead
DATE	15 Jan 1861
RECORD #	2273
PAGE	[276]

NAME	DUVALL, James W. H. (son of Wilson & Harriet DUVALL)
PROOF	free born as proved by oath of C. F. FADELEY
DESCRIPTION	abt 24y old, 5' 11" tall, dark brown colour, scar on forehead above right eye
DATE	11 Feb 1861
RECORD #	2274
PAGE	[277]

NAME	SANDS, Elizabeth (alias DOUGLAS)
PROOF	emancipated by deed from Joseph CONARD Admr of Mary CONARD dec'd dated 17 Jan 1861
DESCRIPTION	abt 52y old, 5' 4" tall, dark brown colour, large scar or mark on inside of left arm above wrist
DATE	11 Feb 1861
RECORD #	2275
PAGE	[277]

NAME	ROBINSON, Henry
PROOF	emancipated by will of Cupid ROBINSON as proved by oath of Wm. D. HAVENNER
DESCRIPTION	abt 30y old, 5' 8½" tall, brown colour, scar on forehead over the left eye
DATE	12 Feb 1861
RECORD #	2276
PAGE	[278]

NAME	ROBINSON, Joseph
PROOF	emancipated by will of Cupid ROBINSON as proved by oath of Wm. D. HAVENNER
DESCRIPTION	abt 27y old, 5' 8½" tall, brown colour, only three fingers n right hand, thumb & forefinger gone
DATE	12 Feb 1861
RECORD #	2277
PAGE	[278]

NAME	ROBINSON, Henry
PROOF	emancipated by will of Robert GRAY dec'd as proved by oath of Wm. H. GRAY
DESCRIPTION	abt 21y old, 5' ½" tall, dark mulatto colour
DATE	11 Mar 1861
RECORD #	2278
PAGE	[279]

NAME	PERRY, Jefferson
PROOF	free born as proved by oath of R. C. LITTLETON
DESCRIPTION	abt 30y old, 5' 9" tall, copper colour, scar on little finger of left hand
DATE	12 Mar 1861
RECORD #	2279
PAGE	[279]

NAME	PERRY, John
PROOF	free born as proved by oath of R. C. LITTLETON
DESCRIPTION	abt 47y old, 5' 5" tall, copper colour, scar on left side of neck & one on right knee
DATE	12 Mar 1861
RECORD #	2280
PAGE	[279]

NAME	NICKENS, Thomas
PROOF	free born as proved by oath of R. C. LITTLETON
DESCRIPTION	abt 24y old, 5' 7" tall, dark brown colour, scar on left side of his breast, one side of his face much darker than the other
DATE	12 Mar 1861
RECORD #	2281
PAGE	[280]

Index

A

ABEL
  George, 61, 190
ADAMS
  Albert, 45
  Amanda, 21, 54
  Charles, 23, 146
  Francis Ann, 191
  Hannah Elizabeth, 66
  Harriet Ann, 21
  Phebe Ann, 191
  Sally, 191
  Sally Ann, 21
  Virginia Ann, 21
  William, 45
ADDISON
  Henrietta, 51
  Milly, 50, 51
  Richard, 51
  Sally Janney, 51
ALEXANDER
  Charlotta, 166
  George T., 182
  Harriet, 185
  Henry, 95
  James, 6
  Jane, 181, 182
  Jane E., 74
  John, 181
  Jonathan H., 74
  Mary M., 74
  Richardetta, 182
  Samuel Thomas, 75
  Thomas, 82, 166
  William F., 74
ALLEN
  Alex, 135
  Amanda, 135, 180, 181
  Arabella, 186
  Betsy, 134
  Catharine, 135, 166
  Charlotte, 180
  Elizabeth, 201
  Harriet Levenia, 187
  Isaiah, 181
  James "Jim", 26
  James Spencer, 186
  John, 180
  Juliet, 201
  Leroy, 124
  Maria, 201
  Martha, 181
  Mary, 134
  Mary Allen, 135
  Mary Ann, 186, 187
  Mary M., 190
  Narcissa, 134
  Samuel Smith, 186
  Spencer, 187
  Stewart Thornton, 186
  Uginta, 134
  William, 134
AMBROSE
  Sina, 192
  Sinah, 10
ANDERSON
  Abraham, 18
  Charles F., 155, 156, 172
  Eliza Ann, 20
  Mary Ann, 20
  Sarah, 20
  Wilson, 19
ARNETT
  Nancy, 163
ASHTON
  Julia Ellen, 187
  Victoria Mildrish, 187
ATHEY
  John M., 115

B

BACKHOUSE
  George, 190
BAILY
  William, 194
BALDWIN
  Mahlon, 202
BALES
  Fleet, 174
BALL
  Allison, 206
  Alpheus, 204
  Eliza, 91
  Henry A., 201
  James Allison, 82, 91
  John, 206
  Joseph, 204
  Nancy, 206
  Richard Henry Thomas, 91
  William, 104
BANK
  George, 211
  Harriet Ann, 211
  Presley Francis, 211
  Richard Henry, 211
BANKS
  Eli, 110
BARNES
  Dyer, 6
  Samuel, 6
BARRETT
  William F., 198
BAYLEY
  Robert, 12
BEANER
  John Emanuel, 165
BEANS
  Isaiah B., 93
BEARD
  Benjamin B., 188, 189
BEATTY
  Elizabeth, 172
BEATY
  Elizabeth G., 94
BEAVERS
  John, 13, 89, 115, 116
  Washington, 113
BELL
  Squire, 89, 92
BENER
  George William, 116
  Mary A., 116
BERKELEY

Loudoun County, Virginia Register of Free Negroes 1844-1861   215
Index

W. N., 176, 177
BESICKS
  Jesse, 37
  Priscilla, 129
BEVER
  George William, 116
  Mary A., 116
BEVERLY
  James B., 112
BIGBY
  Frances, 92
BIGSBY
  Peter, 149
BINNS
  Elizabeth D., 36
  John A., 41, 60
  Kitty, 55
  Sally, 71
BIRD
  Ann, 206, 207
  Benjamin O., 207
  Caroline, 85
  Cecelia, 86
  Henrietta, 85, 86
  James, 85, 86
  Jonathan A., 206
  Samuel E. W., 207
  Sarah J. F., 207
BIRDSALL
  Benjamin, 61, 83
  David, 36
BIRKE
  James William, 74
  Lewis, 75
  Mary Ann, 73
  Mary Jane, 73, 74
  Richard Henry, 74
BISICKS
  Priscilla, 49
  Rowena, 49
BOSS
  Samuel M., 204
BOWLES
  James, 40, 68, 83, 84
BOYD
  Alfred Nathaniel, 190
  James, 119

Mary, 43
Mary Catharine, 190
Nancy Catharine, 190
Virginia, 170
BRADEN
  N. S., 205
  Noble S., 26, 66, 80, 110, 184
  W. S., 204
BRADEY
  Frances, 162
BRADY
  Jane Ann, 62, 175
  Peyton, 9
  Samuel, 191
  Susan, 210
  Willis, 210
BREWEN
  Hampton R., 134, 135
BREWER
  Hampton R., 180, 181
BRICE
  John, 134
BROOKS
  Alfred, 182
  Betty, 64
  David, 163
  James, 138
  Susan, 93
  Susan A., 142
BROWN
  David, 55, 56
  Frank, 198
  John H., 182
  Mason, 198
  Sarah, 198
  William, 145
BRYANT
  Eliza, 67
  George, 192
  James, 67
  Lydia Ann, 67, 182
  Martha, 67
  Moses, 67
  Susan, 67
BUCKINGHAM

Robert H., 87
Thomas Henry, 87
BURK
  Charles Richard, 208
  Elizabeth, 193
  John Thomas, 193
  Louisa, 108
  Martha Jane, 90
  Sarah Elizabeth, 193
  Sophia, 208
BURKE
  Ann S., 203
  Elias William, 127
  Eliza T., 203
  Enos, 90, 127, 128
  James Wesley, 128
  Jane, 127, 203
  John, 202
  John O., 203
  Malinda A., 203
  Mary Cornelia, 127
  Powhatan M., 203
  Richard, 110
  Sophia, 174
  Susan Mahala, 127
  William R., 174
BUSH
  Alsey Ann, 86
  Alsy Ann, 4
  Amy Eleanor, 4
  Amy Elenor, 86
  Duana, 4
  Duanna, 86
  Mary, 43
  Nelson W., 4, 120

C

CANADY
  Nelly, 40
CANNADY
  Elizabeth, 136
  James, 137
CARR
  David, 9, 101, 137, 158, 168
  George, 116, 117
  George W., 116

216 Loudoun County, Virginia Register of Free Negroes 1844-1861
Index

James H., 116
John, 138
Peggy Allen, 117
Phenias, 117
Rebecca, 114, 116, 117
Washington M., 111, 137
William, 12, 32, 47, 198
CARROLL
  Ann Maria, 207, 208
  George Washington, 208
CARTER
  Alcinda, 97, 184
  Andrew Jackson, 36
  Charles William, 200
  Elizabeth, 31
  Elizabeth O., 128
  Harriet Ann, 96
  Helon, 40
  Jinny, 40
  John, 96
  Joseph, 96, 97
  Malinda, 100, 110, 200
  Margaret Elizabeth, 200
  Martha Ann, 96, 97
  Mary Jane, 28
  Robert Isaac, 100
  Samuel, 26
  Susannah, 184
  William H., 96
CARTWRIGHT
  Ann Mahala, 10
  Anna, 167, 168
  George Henry, 167
  James William, 167
  Leanna, 167
  Letitia, 10
  Mahala, 168
  Margaret, 167
  Necodemus, 166
  Philip, 9, 10
  Warren, 9
  Zacchariah, 8

CHAMBERS
  Albina, 69
  Alven, 69
  Burr Thomas, 70
  John Henry, 69
  Letty, 83
  Nancy, 69, 70
CHAMBLIN
  James, 211
  Jared, 211
  John L., 197, 206, 211
  Peyton W., 187
CLAGETT
  Fanny, 12
  Thomas H., 194
CLAGGETT
  Daniel, 140
  Fanny, 140
  Mary E., 140
CLEMMONS
  Hezekiah, 194
CLENDENING
  Samuel, 4
CLINE
  Alfred, 162, 163
CLOWES
  Joseph, 43, 139
COATES
  Daniel, 157
COLBERT
  Amanda, 86
  Armistead, 86
  Leonard, 52
COLEMAN
  Isabella, 180
  Robert, 95
CONARD
  Joseph, 212
  Mary, 212
CONNER
  Lucinda, 45
CONTEE
  Amanda Elizabeth, 5
  George, 5, 54
  Mason, 5
  Sally, 5
COOK
  Josiah, 146

Mary, 146
Mary Jane, 146
Robert, 146
COOPER
  Rachel, 25
CORAM
  Benjamin, 41
COSS
  Elizabeth, 37
COX
  Eleanor, 70
  George W., 71
CRAIG
  James, 23
  William T. J., 186, 187
CRAVEN
  Allison, 137
  Amanda, 22, 23
  Elisa, 185
  Giles, 138
  Joel, 69, 70
  John H., 185
  John Henry, 23
CRAWFORD
  Daniel T., 157, 165
CRIDLER
  John, 51
CRIM
  John, 74, 75
  John H., 84
CROSS
  Betty, 64, 92, 93
  Charles, 114, 145
  Charles William, 110
  James, 115
  James Maddison, 153
  Jesse, 154
  John, 15
  Joseph, 26
  Nancy, 64
  Nimrod, 185, 186
  Polly, 145
  Priscilla, 49, 129
  Priscilla Elizabeth, 153
  Rowena, 49

Loudoun County, Virginia Register of Free Negroes 1844-1861

Index

Sarah, 114, 115, 145
Thomas, 178
Thomas William, 81
Victoria, 154
CUMMINGS
  W. E., 124
  William E., 124, 125, 126
  Wm. E., 125
CURTIS
  Ann Elizabeth, 155
  Hannah Maranda, 155
  Mary Catharine, 155
  Mary Martha, 155
  Priscilla, 107

D

DADE
  Cornelius, 196
  Henrietta, 50, 196, 197
  Louisa, 196
  Marietta, 196
  McGill, 138
  Robert, 197
  William, 196
DAGG
  Susan G., 7
DAVIS
  Catharine, 166
  Charles, 72, 102
  Courtney, 102
  Dennis, 29, 146, 194
  Duana, 61
  Eliza Ann, 147
  Elizabeth, 85
  Hannah Ann, 72, 175
  Harriet Cecilia, 166
  Jane, 72, 167
  Jefferson, 84, 184
  John, 103
  John Samuel Thomas, 85

Letitia, 28
Lewis, 184
Maria, 28, 29, 146
Marsalena, 29
Mary A., 102
Mary Elizabeth, 85
Ralph, 85
Reamless, 147
Samuel, 184
Thomas, 5, 129
Washington, 66
William, 106, 107
William Cynthia, 85
DAVISON
  Dr., 121
DENHAM
  Amos, 133
DENSMORE
  William, 135
DEVAWL
  Charles, 139
DEVINGER
  James Henry, 165
  Julia, 165
DEVONSHIRE
  Catharine, 165
DIGGS
  John, 104
  Robert, 82, 104
  Sarah, 104
  William, 104
DIMMY
  Mary Ann, 16
  Samuel, 16
DIMY
  Elizabeth, 91
  Marcus, 90, 91
  Nimrod, 90
  Turney, 90
DIXSON
  Elizabeth, 126
DONOHOE
  S. G., 168
DORRELL
  Margaret, 33, 34, 35, 47, 53, 59, 60
  Thomas S., 108, 126, 127
  Thoms S., 108
DORSEY

Mary, 146
DOUGLAS
  Archibald N., 131
  Elizabeth, 212
  Joseph, 202
  Margaret, 198
  Peggy, 24, 36
DOUGLASS
  Ann, 78
DRISH
  William D., 55
DUNCAN
  Susan, 26
DUVAL
  Duana Jane, 3
  Melvina, 3
  Orpha, 2, 3
  Sarah Elizabeth, 3
DUVALL
  Harriet, 212
  James W. H., 212
  Wilson, 212
DYER
  Samuel, 6

E

EATON
  Isaac, 92, 93, 164, 165, 192, 193
  J., 154
EDWARDS
  Richard H., 165
  Thomas W., 8, 122, 123

F

FADELEY
  C. F., 212
  Charles F., 10
FADELY
  Charles F., 124
FAWLEY
  Henry, 195
FENTON
  Greenberry, 64
FIELDS
  Aaron, 98
  Amanda, 163, 164

Catharine, 99
Charles, 163
Clary, 130
Ellen William, 97
George, 99
George William, 97, 163
Hannah, 99
James, 13, 98
Jane, 99
John, 99
John William, 164
Kitty, 8
Louisa, 97, 99
Louisa, 97
Martha, 98
Mary Ellen, 164
Sally, 98
Sarah Elizabeth, 164
Susan, 97, 98, 99
Winny, 98
FITZHUGH
 Tazewell, 187
FLEET
 William, 174
FLETCHER
 Archilus, 106
 Benjamin Fletcher, 208
 Harriet, 181
 John William, 119
 Mary, 106, 145, 158
 William, 145
FLORENCE
 Betty, 44
 Harrison, 44
 Louisa, 44
 Sarah, 44
 Smith, 44
FORD
 Albert, 199
 Alice, 199
 Clara, 202
 John R., 199
 Kitty, 199
 Martha Ann, 202
 Patsey, 199
 Rosana, 86
FOX

Catharine E., 40
Geo K., 140
Geo. K., 152
George K., 8, 138, 152, 153, 166, 174, 175, 182, 190, 192, 194, 204, 206
Hester, 43
William, 106
FRANK
 Benj. T., 110
FRAZIER
 Mary M., 96
FRED
 Thomas, 143
FRY
 Daniel, 114
FRYE
 Margaret, 8
FULTON
 Margaret, 70, 71
 William, 45, 111
FURR
 Catharine, 1
 Elzey, 121
 Frances Ann, 121
 Harriet Ann, 121
 Mary Ann, 1
 Robert, 121
 William G., 37, 38
 William Henry, 121

G

GAINES
 Ann Elizabeth, 152
 Armstead, 153
 Edwin, 153
 Eliza, 107
 Issabella, 194
 Jane, 107
 Josephine, 153
 Kitty, 107
 Mary Elizabeth, 152
 Nelly Ann, 152
GAINS
 Issabella, 114
GALES
 Lucinda, 105

GANT
 Alexander, 161
 Amanda Jane, 149
 Ann, 14
 Ann Maria, 35, 84
 Bill, 176
 Charles, 115, 179, 180
 Charles Elwood, 149
 Cornelia E., 123
 Daniel, 19
 Edmund, 180
 Elizabeth, 148, 149
 Eve, 21
 Fenton, 19
 Frances Amelia, 148
 George, 18, 23
 Henry, 179
 Isaac, 20
 John Thomas, 148
 John William, 19
 Julia Ann, 148
 Keziah, 80
 Lloyd, 20
 Lucy, 78
 Martha Ellen, 149
 Mary, 179, 180
 Mary E. J., 84
 Mary Elizabeth, 148
 Mary Francis, 22
 Milly, 78
 Nancy Catharine, 148
 Nelson Talbert, 17
 Rachel Ann, 78
 Robert Thorn, 78
 Sarah Love, 149
 Susan Ann, 22
 Talbert, 35
 William, 14, 80
 Winefred Jane, 22
GANTT
 Alcinda, 79
 Annie, 80
 George Henry, 79
 Kezziah, 79, 80
 Lucy, 79
 Philip, 79

Loudoun County, Virginia Register of Free Negroes 1844-1861

Index

Thomas, 79
GARRISON
  James, 48, 68, 110, 118, 162
GASKIN
  Elisa, 143
  Harrison, 143
  Joseph, 143
  Margaret, 143
  Nelson, 143
  William F., 143
GASKINS
  Amy, 180
  Areana, 65
  James, 180
  Judy, 65
  Moses, 65
GASSAWAY
  Catharine B., 181
GIBBINS
  Jane, 129
GIBBONS
  Jane, 49
GIBSON
  Joseph, 112, 113, 139, 140
GILBERT
  Ann, 122, 123
  Margaret, 25
  Phebe, 66
GILES
  Samuel, 157
GLASGOW
  Catharine, 48, 95
  Henry, 124
GODFREY
  William, 194
GOINGS
  Lewis, 48, 142
  Mary, 48
  Mary Catharine, 48
GOODIN
  Robert F., 58, 59
GORAM
  Elizabeth, 57, 59
  George Washington, 57
  James T., 57
  John Henry, 59
GORDAN

Harry, 9
GORE
  Tilghman, 84
GOVER
  Henry T., 66
GOWAN
  Amanda E., 77
  Martha Ann, 77
  Thomas H.
    Maddison, 77
GOWEN
  Amanda E., 210
  Anna Augusta, 209
  Caleb, 209
  Charles, 209
  John William, 210
  Joseph Connard, 209
  Martha, 210
  Martha Ann, 77, 132, 209, 210
  Susan V., 210
  Thomas H., 132
GRACEN
  Daniel, 178
GRAY
  Robert, 212
  William H., 212
GRAYSON
  Amy, 33
  Benson, 158
  Bushrod, 113
  Charles, 168
  Charles F., 158
  Daniel, 113
  Eliza, 195
  Georgiana, 158
  James A., 113
  Jane, 203
  Jesse, 33, 34, 53
  John, 177
  Joseph, 195
  Lee, 34
  Marshall W., 158
  Martha, 113, 158
  Martha Elizabeth, 65
  Martha Jane, 90
  Matilda, 33, 34
  Parfarla, 158

  Washington, 195
  Wesley, 34
  William, 34
GREEN
  Betty, 4
  Lucy, 51
  Westwood, 52
GREENFIELD
  James, 63
GREGG
  Nathan, 169
GRIFFIN
  Laurinda V., 174
GRIFFITH
  John W., 75, 76
GRIMES
  Jonathan, 109
GRUBB
  James, 163, 164
GUIDER
  Adolphus, 113
  Eli, 112
  Joseph, 43
  Lydia, 43
  Lydia Alice, 112
  Mary, 112, 113
  Peter, 43
  Richard, 124
  Thomas, 124
GULICK
  James H., 178
  James M., 178
  James N., 177
GULLATT
  Eleanor, 182
GUY
  Hannah Ann, 192
  Harriet, 119
  Joseph, 119, 208
  Lucinda, 208
  Maria, 191, 192
  Mary Virginia, 191
  Virginia, 204

H

HALES
  Warner, 114
HALL
  Edward, 89

Loudoun County, Virginia Register of Free Negroes 1844-1861
Index

Eliza, 89
Maria, 197
Mary Ann, 89
Nat., 89
HAMILTON
 Charles B., 40
 Eli J., 75
 John, 63
HAMMATT
 Edward, 62
HAMMERLY
 John W., 115
 Manly, 116
HARLEY
 Rewben, 176
HARPER
 Charlotte, 58
 Elizabeth, 24
 Enoch, 24, 42
 Frances Ann, 42
 Ignatius, 42
 Sally Ann, 32
 Samuel, 24
HARRIS
 J. S., 140
 James, 38
 Henry, 181
 Permelia, 177
HAVENNER
 William D., 212
HAWLING
 Isaac W., 51, 52
 John, 51, 52
 Joseph L., 195
 Joseph Lewis, 52
HAZLIP
 Thomas, 66
HEAD
 George, 1, 82, 130
HEATER
 George Henry, 30
 Henry, 164
 Jonathan, 164
 Mahlon Kirkbright, 165
 Nancy, 30
 Samuel, 165
 Susan, 164, 165
 Susannah, 165
HENDERSON

Fenton M., 199
Janet, 199
HENRY
 Maria, 38
HEPBURN
 William, 28
HICKS
 R. G., 46
HILL
 James, 211
HILLIARD
 Joseph, 37, 64, 104
HIXSON
 D., 96
 David, 42, 114, 120, 200
HODGSON
 Sidney L., 181
HOGAN
 Ann Maria, 123
 Cornelia E., 123
 Craven A., 123
 James Henry, 124
 Patrick, 123, 124
 Sarah V., 123
HOLD
 Miriam, 1, 2
HOLE
 Miriam, 2, 7
HOLLIDAY
 David, 205
 Harvey, 111
 Kitty, 40
HOLLY
 Martha, 158
 Martha Elizabeth, 65
HOLMES
 Elijah, 175
 Fenton, 27
 Hunton, 27
 Joseph, 201, 202
 Joseph W., 199
 William, 208, 210
HOOD
 Jonah, 85, 179, 180
HOOE
 Jim, 183
 Mary, 183
HOPKINS

Elizabeth, 55
HOUGH
 Amasa, 28, 134
 Elizabeth, 77
 Joseph, 17
 Joseph S., 5, 6, 31
 Mary, 78
 William, 49, 97, 98, 99, 169
 William T., 170, 171
HOVE
 Jim, 183
 Mary, 183
HOWARD
 Algernon, 205
 Armistead, 31
 John, 204
 John William, 205
 Julia Ann Virginia, 204, 205
 Mary Frances, 205
 Noah Alexander, 205
 Permelia, 205
HUDLAND
 Sarah, 47
HUGHES
 Elias, 88, 89
 William, 84
HUGHS
 Willis, 12
HULL
 Catharine Ann, 165
 James, 165, 209
 James William, 61
HULLS
 Catharine, 31
 Elizabeth, 17
 Mary, 62
HUMPHREY
 Margaret, 190
 Thomas G., 111
 Thomas L., 37, 92, 118
 Thomas M., 95
HUNT
 Lewis, 129, 130
 William, 80, 114, 138

Index

HURLEY
  Rewben, 176
HUTCHISON
  B., 118
  Beverley, 183
  Sampson, 48

I

ISETT
  John, 60, 114
ISH
  John, 9, 10
  Robert A., 161

J

JACKSON
  America Mahala, 77
  America Mahalah T., 132, 133
  Andrew, 122
  Ann, 122, 123
  Annanias, 17, 105, 106
  Bella, 6, 179
  Charles William, 2
  Clarissa, 137
  Ebenezer, 37
  Edmond, 129, 130
  Eliza, 180
  George, 1, 135, 177
  George A., 133
  George Alexander, 65, 177
  George W., 123
  Hannah Ann, 94
  Henry, 2
  Hester Ann, 2
  Hezekiah, 63
  Hortensia, 179
  Huldah, 94
  Isabella, 1, 114
  Isaiah, 13
  James William, 7
  Jeremiah, 109
  Jerry, 162
  John, 104, 197
  John J., 197
  John T., 133
  Joseph, 107
  Kern, 135
  Kitty, 94
  Lewis, 18
  Lewis C., 122, 123
  Lewis Coaten, 52
  Mahala, 177
  Martha, 105, 106
  Martha Ellen, 106
  Martha J., 122
  Mary, 28, 94, 179
  Mary Ellen, 2, 60
  Milly E., 129
  Obediah Dixon, 129
  Permelia, 177
  Phebe Ann, 105
  Pleasant A., 122
  Robert, 63
  Sally, 197
  Sarah, 1, 2, 114, 129, 130, 192
  Sarah Pleasant, 105
  Teresa, 7
  Teressa, 7
  Thomas, 64
  Thomas Henry, 7
  Tom, 176, 177
  Townsend, 105
  William B., 49
  William Price, 132
JACOBS
  Peter, 84
JANNEY
  Abel, 55, 56
  Albert H., 68, 69
  Daniel, 90, 95
  Eli, 17, 19, 139
  Elisha, 148, 149
  Ely, 18, 19, 20, 21, 22
  John, 61, 78
  Jonas, 17
  Mayo C. W., 76
  Nathan, 112, 113
  Nathan H., 159, 160, 161
  S. M., 189
  Samuel, 84
JENKINS
  Wesley, 194
JENNINGS
  Ann Elizabeth, 101
  Elias Edward, 101
  John, 101
  John Henry, 101
  Lewis Fenton, 101
  Mary Ann, 101
  Mary Ellen, 101
  Samuel William, 101
JENNINS
  Nancy, 168
JEWIT
  Jane, 28
JINKINS
  Mahala, 58
JINNINGS
  Lewis, 38
JOHNSON
  Amanda, 135, 136, 172, 173
  Daniel, 173
  Fenton, 135
  Francis, 114
  George, 12
  George Aaron, 135, 172
  Hannah, 191
  Harriet Ann, 136, 173
  Jacob, 107
  John, 138
  John Henry, 172
  Malinda, 23
  Sally, 197
  Samuel, 9, 197
  Samuel Benjamin, 120
  Sarah Ann, 108
  William Fenton, 172
JONES
  Adeline, 137
  Asbury, 91
  Benjamin Franklin, 126
  Beverly, 26
  Charles Henry, 125
  George, 171
  George William, 91

Loudoun County, Virginia Register of Free Negroes 1844-1861
Index

James Maddison, 153
James Wesley, 125
Jane, 80, 124, 140
Jesse, 154
John, 165
John W., 211
John William, 170
Joseph Parkison, 91
Leander, 69
Leven Harrison, 177
Levin Harrison, 53
Lewin F., 157
Lucius, 174
Margaret Ann, 92
Martha Ellen, 125
Mary, 140
Mary Ann, 30, 69
Mary Frances, 170, 171
Nelson, 37, 118
Philip, 91, 92
Priscilla, 153
Riley, 38
Rosa Ann, 177
Samuel Washington, 125
Sarah, 91, 92, 125
Sarah Alice, 170
Sarah Virginia, 30
Victoria, 154
William Henry, 53, 80

K

KEENE
  George, 23, 24
  Newton, 8
  William, 96
KENEDY
  Jonathan, 109
KENNEDY
  Nancy, 143
  Nelly, 143
KIDWELL
  Hezekiah, 209, 210
  Kezekiah, 209
KILGOUR

James M., 129
KLINE
  Mordecai C., 26
KNOX
  Thomas P., 174

L

LACEY
  David, 41, 45, 56, 128, 191
LACY
  David, 126
LANE
  Cecelia, 36
  Cecelia, 36
  Charles William, 53
  Eliza, 36
  Rachel, 53
LAWSON
  Elizabeth Ann, 50
  Mahala, 50
LEE
  A. D., 128
  Amanda, 88
  Amanda Ellen, 109
  Armistead, 89
  Arther, 88
  Hamiton, 84
  Hannah, 88
  Harriet, 87, 88, 89
  Helen, 108, 109
  Henry Clay, 109
  James Armistead, 109
  John William, 108
  Lydia Ann, 109
  Martha, 88
  Mary, 88
  Wesley, 87
LEITH
  T., 157, 196, 197
  Theodore, 205
LESLIE
  John, 102
LEWIS
  Ann, 96
  Columbus, 188
  Franklin Peirce, 188
  George, 210

George Washington, 171
  James Henry, 171
  John W., 188
  Joseph, 26, 67
  Laura Jane, 188
  Lucinda, 171
  Lucy, 171
  Mary Louisa, 188
  Priscilla, 187, 188
  Sarah Frances, 171
  William Thomas, 171
LINDSEY
  S. J., 189
LITTLETON
  F., 138
  Fielding, 138
  R. C., 172, 213
LLOYD
  Ann, 73, 74
LOOKWOOD
  Robert, 47
LOVE
  Fenton M., 44, 96, 97
  Mary K.?, 44
  Susan A., 48
LOVETT
  David, 23
LOWE
  Lloyd, 178, 179
LUCAS
  Anthony, 84, 118
  Bersheba, 102
  Charles W., 59
  Charles William, 50
  Delila, 84
  Eliza R., 59
  Fanny, 75, 76
  James, 102
  James F., 58
  Jane S., 58
  Job. William, 63
  John H., 182
  Margaret E., 59
  Maria, 58, 59
  Noah, 102
  Sarah, 102
LUCKETT

Index

Ludwell, 157
LUCUS
  Lewis, 142
  Mary Ann, 142
  Melissa Ann, 157
  Sarah Elizabeth, 132
LYONS
  Leander, 96

M

MADDISON
  Frances, 92
  Levi, 92
MAGINIS
  Charlotte Ann, 81
MAGRAK
  Margaret, 43
MAGRAUGH
  Peggy, 100
MAHONEY
  Bushrod, 156
  Catharine, 156
  Charles Henry, 156
  Eliza C., 155, 156
  John, 157
  Malinda, 200
  Mary, 13
  Nelly, 143
  Richard John?, 156
  Wesley, 156
  William, 156
MAHONY
  Catharine E., 54
  Eliza Ann, 40
  Eliza J., 54
  Elizabeth, 54
MANDLEY
  Bill, 12
  Caroline, 185
  Charles, 188
  Eliza, 186
  Elizabeth, 189
  Ellen, 189
  John, 185
  Louisa, 189
  Malinda, 185
  Mary, 189
  William, 12

MANLEY
  Ann, 179
  John, 181
  Lydia, 178
  Matilda, 179
  Raleigh, 178
  Samuel, 206
  Thomas, 179
  William Henry, 128
MANLY
  Charles, 178
  Enoch, 48, 118
  Frances, 92
  Gabriel, 119
  Nancy, 163
  Sally, 178
MARLOW
  Thomas J., 120
MARSHALL
  William B., 162
MASON
  Ama, 49
  Amy, 133
  Charles William, 61
  Cosmelia, 130
  Eliza French, 133
  Ellen Douglas, 133
  Fanny, 46
  George Henry, 190
  Hannah, 46, 130, 131
  Henry, 194
  James William, 131
  Jesse, 32
  John E., 195
  John Henry, 31
  John W., 131
  Julius, 195
  Lee, 121
  Margaret Elizabeth, 62
  Mary, 62, 133
  Mary Catharine, 62
  Samuel, 130
  William F., 196
McCABE
  James E., 146
  John, 79
  John H., 16
McCARTY

  Charles William, 162
  Elizabeth, 162
  Louisa Ellen, 163
  Mary Jane, 162
  Rachel, 92, 162, 163
  Susannabel, 162
McCLENAN
  John, 202
McCORMICK
  Sarah, 7
McDANIEL
  Bernard, 27
  Casa Ann, 27
  Elizabeth, 27, 57, 58
  Ellen, 100
  James William, 117
  Lee, 200
  Mary Elizabeth, 27
  Stephen, 27
  Theodore, 27
  Travis Henry, 57, 58
McDONAH
  James, 114, 115
McDONALD
  James, 185
McDONAUGH
  James, 32
McDONOUGH
  James, 126, 145
McFARLAND
  Alexander, 206
  Joseph, 155
McGEE
  Meranda, 8
  Sophia, 8
McILHANY
  James, 31, 51, 93, 102
McINTOSH
  James, 199
McPHERSON
  Armistead, 6
  Charles William Cross, 48
  Ellen, 48
  Eli Banks, 48

Henry, 116
Peter, 115
Sophia, 122
MEAD
  Aquilla, 67, 76
  John, 26, 175
  Joseph, 121
  Manly, 67
MEDLEY
  Margaret, 183
MEGINNIS
  Charlotte A., 174, 175
  Harriet Ann, 174
  Rachel Ann, 175
MILBOURN
  David, 117
MILLER
  Daniel, 54
MINOR
  Daniel Webster, 172
  Lewis, 135
  Nathan, 63
  Sarah Ann, 63
  William Henry, 35
MOCK
  George W., 94
  Jacob, 94
MOLDON
  Sarah, 54
MONDAY
  Daniel, 34
MOORE
  John, 53, 63, 64, 65, 137
MORALLEE
  Michael, 6
MORGAN
  Alfred, 195
  Andrew, 34
  Archelus, 147
  Charles Henry, 34, 190
  Delila, 34, 35
  Drusilla, 147
  James William, 147
  Jane, 107
  Mary, 147
  Mary Catharine, 35

Rachel, 34
William Wright, 35
MOXLEY
  Catharine, 168
  David James, 168
  George, 95
  George William, 168
  Sarah Ann, 114
MUDD
  Fletcher, 35
MUDDARE
  Delila Frances, 75
  Emily Jane, 75
  Fanny, 75
  James Henry, 76
  John William, 75
MUNDAY
  Thomas, 192
MURRAY
  James Wesley, 110
  John C., 25, 41
MYERS
  Emily Ann, 1
  Israel, 155

N

NEALE
  Nancy, 194
NEWMAN
  Martha, 61
NICHOLS
  Isaac G., 182, 183
  John, 26
  Joseph, 108, 125, 127, 128
  Joshua, 62
  Stacy M., 163
  Thomas, 17, 18, 19, 20, 21, 22, 35, 50, 105, 106, 118, 130, 131, 144, 147, 182
  Thomas J., 121, 149
NICKENS
  James H., 138
  Thomas, 213
NIXON
  James W., 197

Joel L., 163
NIXSON
  John, 17, 18, 19, 20, 21, 22
NOAKS
  Malinda, 110
NOKES
  Malinda, 47
  Nancy, 47
NOLAND
  Burr P., 181, 182
  Sarah C., 81
  W. B., 157
  William B., 185, 194
NORRIS
  Betty, 120
  Wilson, 80

O

ONEALE
  John, 143
OSBURN
  A. F., 163
  Craven, 25
  Logan, 81
  Nicholas, 181

P

PAINE
  William Jefferson, 14
PALMER
  Abraham, 56
  Ann Elizabeth, 100
  Bushrod, 56
  Daniel, 95
  Eliza, 55, 56
  Flavius, 56
  Frank, 55
  George, 159
  Jane, 100
  John, 100
  Johnson T., 166
  John William, 100
  Lee, 139
  Philip H., 100
  Samuel, 100

Loudoun County, Virginia Register of Free Negroes 1844-1861
Index

Townsend, 139
William Henry, 55
PANCOAST
 John S., 118
 Joseph, 210
PARMER
 Allen, 160
 George, 159
 Israel, 137
 Jesse, 159
 Jonah, 160
 Joseph, 160
 Levi, 160
 Percilla, 159, 160
 Ruth Hannah, 160
PAXSON
 Griffith W., 16, 17
PAYNE
 James Edward, 15
 James Henry, 113
 Joseph A., 108
 Nancy, 113
 Robert, 145
 Samuel Dade, 120
PEARSON
 James, 61, 190
PERRY
 Jefferson, 157, 213
 John, 213
 Ralph, 43
 Verlinda, 87, 88, 89
PEYTON
 William, 25
PHILIPS
 Alfred, 169
 T., 185
 Thomas, 184
PHILLIPS
 Harriet, 49, 78
 Landon, 120
 Thomas, 28
PIERCE
 Margaret, 14
 Martha, 144
PIGGOT
 Burr, 13
PIGGOTT
 Isaac, 181
PLASTER
 Michael, 30

POLAND
 Betsey, 197
 Julia Ann, 163
 Mary, 197
POTTS
 Elzekiel, 197
 Ezekiel, 195, 196
 Jane, 190, 195, 196
POWELL
 Charles L., 82
 Leven, 204
 William, 46
PRICE
 Samuel, 40
PURCEL
 Samuel, 102, 103
PURCELL
 Jonah, 122
PURSEL
 Enos, 58
 Margaret, 58
 Samuel, 15, 16, 35, 173
PURSELL
 Samuel, 103
PURSEY
 Joshua, 135
PUSEY
 Joshua, 13, 14, 30, 55, 57, 100, 109, 119, 136, 137, 143, 165, 172, 173

R

RAMSEY
 Charlotte, 76
 Charlotte Ann, 76
 Colvin, 51
 Delilah Jane, 76
 Theodore Fry, 76
 William Wilson, 76
RANDOLPH
 Adolphus, 76
 Hannah, 30
 Martha, 67
 Sarah E., 86, 118
 Turner, 67
RANOLPH

Rosanna, 22
REED
 Alcinda, 73
 George Henry, 73
RHODES
 H. H., 200
RICHARDS
 George, 192
 Leven, 152
RICHARDSON
 Corida?, 145
 Hannah, 16
 Hannah Ann, 17, 144, 145
 Helen E., 145
 Jamima, 16
 William, 16, 173
RIDOUT
 Aaron Moses, 103
 Courtney Ann, 103
 Georgianna, 103
 James Aaron, 83
 John William, 83
 Martha, 93
 Mary Catharine, 83
 Mary Louisa, 103
 Sarah Wineford, 103
 Sarah Winefred, 93
 Susan Jane, 83
 William, 102
RIPPEN
 Mary, 135
 Mary A., 132, 133
RITICOR
 John, 85
RIVERS
 Cecelia, 36
 Daniel, 131
 Dinah, 93
 Jacob, 93
 James Robert Rudolph, 93
 Joseph, 198
 Mary Jane, 28
 Sarah, 132
 Stephen, 66
 Susan, 24
ROBERSON
 William, 170

Index

ROBERTSON
  Alfred Fitzallen, 68
  John, 69
  John Jefferson, 68
  John M., 117
  Maranda, 69
  Margaret, 68
  Maria, 69
  Samuel, 69
  Susannah, 75
ROBINSON
  Alice T., 140
  Counsel C., 139
  Cupid, 212
  Hamilton, 161
  Henry, 169, 212
  Isaac, 161
  Isaiah, 161
  Jane, 189
  John Thomas, 169
  Joseph, 212
  Kitty Ann, 161
  Leanna, 161
  Nancy, 169, 170
  Noble, 169
  Rebecca Jane, 181
  Robert, 169
  Sampson, 189
  Silas, 170
  Susannah, 140
  Virginia, 170
  William, 170
ROGERS
  Thomas, 43, 56, 57, 66, 81, 105, 111, 120, 126
ROOKWOOD
  Robert, 38, 39
ROPP
  Nicholas, 202
  Samuel, 202
ROSE
  John, 63
ROSS
  John T., 202
RUSSEL
  Charley Ann, 35
  Ethelip, 106
  Jane E., 35
RUSSELL
  Elizabeth, 158
  Ethelip, 106
  William, 35, 144, 145
  William H., 190, 191
RUST
  Ann Elizabeth, 193
  Ann Maria, 183
  Betsey, 154, 192, 193
  Betsy, 92, 93
  Emma Jane, 193
  Frances, 193
  George William, 154, 183
  John Thomas, 92
  Lucinda Catharine, 154
  Lydia E., 93
  Marshall Pendleton, 193
  Martha, 154
  Martha Jane, 183
  Mary Virginia, 193
  Patsy, 182, 183
  Samuel Manley, 155
  Sarah Elizabeth, 183
  Thomas, 182
  Thornton, 192
RUTTER
  Matilda, 72, 73
RYAN
  Catharine, 86
RYON
  Alfred, 120
  Ann, 80

S

SANBOWER
  Michael, 207, 208
  Thomas, 207, 208
SANDERS
  Ann, 40
  Thomas, 23
  W. C., 119
  Wilson C., 40
SANDS
  Elizabeth, 212
  Jonah, 136
SAUNDERS
  Ann, 191, 192, 204, 208
  Curtis R., 25, 52, 66
  Gunnell, 33
  James, 84
  P., 67, 82, 86, 121
  Presley, 8, 30, 31, 33, 42, 61, 104
  Presly, 105
  Thomas R., 71
  Wilson C., 208
SCHOOLEY
  Jonas, 187, 188
  Jonas P., 188
  William, 46
SELF
  Ann Virginia, 46
  Duskin, 46
SELVEY
  Esther, 10, 11
  Francis, 11
  Harriett, 11
  John, 11
  Margaret, 11
  Martha, 11
  Martha Ann, 10
SENATE
  Eliza, 128
  Elmina, 128
  Oscar, 128
  William, 128
SHAFER
  Sally, 5
SHARPER
  Daniel, 15
  Samuel, 15
  Susan, 26
SHIPMAN
  Susan, 1
SHORES
  Mary, 117
SHREVE
  Charles, 22, 23
SIMMS
  Betsy, 139
  Charita, 139

Loudoun County, Virginia Register of Free Negroes 1844-1861
Index

SIMPSON
  Francis, 50
  French, 36, 46
  John, 72
  John H., 202, 203
SINCLAIR
  James, 22, 50, 51, 105, 140, 201
  John, 14, 79, 80
  Joseph, 78
  Leanner, 41
SINKFIELD
  Elizabeth, 173
  Mary Ann, 173
  Samuel Francis, 37
  Thomas William, 37
SKINNER
  Armistead, 70
  Eleanor, 70
  George, 71
  Harriet, 57, 70, 71
  Harriet Ann, 70
  Harrison, 71
  Isaac, 70
  Mary Elizabeth, 70
  Sarah, 71
  Usher, 6
SMALE
  John, 32, 41, 43, 115
SMITH
  Corian, 159
  John, 9, 159
  Joshua, 211
  Logan, 166
  Mary Frances, 159
  Percilla, 159
  Rozilla, 152
  Seth, 14, 15, 63, 81, 82, 91, 109, 110, 117, 122, 129, 131, 132, 137
  Solomon, 87
SPEAKS
  Richard, 84
STATLER
  John, 184
STAUNTON
  Ann, 7, 206, 207

STEER
  Jonah, 8
STEPTOE
  Dorinda, 105
  Frederick, 33
STEWARD
  John, 128
  John E., 68
  Maria, 6
STEWART
  Alfred, 124
  Elizabeth, 46
  Esther, 46
  Fenton, 137
  Hester, 24
  Jane, 124
  John, 24
STINGER
  Enos, 73
  George, 72
  John, 73
  Matilda, 72, 73, 175
  Samuel, 73
  Thomas, 72
STONEBURNER
  Christian, 105
STROTHER
  Catharine, 111
  Charlotte, 111
  Elisha T., 111
  John W., 111
  Mary, 111
  William, 45, 111
SULLIVAN
  Elizabeth, 66
  John L., 28, 29
  William B., 16
SUMMERS
  R. H., 179, 185
  Richard H., 28, 32, 107
SUTTON
  William, 58
SWART
  John, 12
  Robert P., 119
SWARTS
  Jane, 42
SWEENY
  Edward, 51

Leuisa, 51

T

TALBERT
  Ely, 18
TALBOTT
  Christina, 210
  Nancy, 210
TALIFARIO
  Gilmore, 202
  Jane, 202
TATE
  William, 30, 65, 91, 92
TAVENNER
  Richard, 198
TAYLOR
  Ann, 8, 28
  Benjamin F., 139, 166, 167, 168
  Bernard, 52, 116, 117, 137, 141, 142, 149, 150, 151, 152, 184
  H. S., 128
  Henry S., 167
  Margaret, 28
  Oliver, 119
  William Henry, 191
  Yardley, 145
TEBBS
  A. S., 107
  Charles B., 24, 198
  M. H. D., 132
THOMAS
  Amos William, 175
  Chandler, 62, 175
  Dotia Ann, 47
  Edward, 41
  Elisa, 144
  Elizabeth, 42
  Enoch, 25, 129
  Frances, 38
  Frances Ann, 42
  Francis, 39, 85
  Gustavus, 39
  Henry, 39
  Ida Ann Florida, 198

Index

James, 95, 108, 109
James William, 74
Jane Ann, 175
John, 39
John N., 144
Josiah, 39
Laura Elizabeth, 198
Lewis Newman, 198
Mahlon, 175
Mary Ann, 73
Mary Elizabeth, 85
Mary Jane, 73, 74, 77
Newman, 25
Richard Henry, 74, 82
Rose, 177
Ross, 36
Sally Ann, 32
Samuel, 112, 144
Susan, 47
Thadeus, 47
William, 24, 39, 68, 211
William H., 144
William P., 204
THOMPSON
Alfred, 151
Alice, 141
Archibald Washington, 142
Archy, 52
Ardella Ringold, 151
Asa Moore, 142
Carlisle, 150
Cordelia, 152
David William, 173
Delia, 10, 149, 150, 151
Edward, 63
Elizabeth Ann, 112
Frances Ann, 150
Franky, 42
Frederick, 116
George Albert, 83
George Henry, 150

George William Annamore, 151
Georgeanna, 151
J. E., 141
James, 14, 90, 91, 137
James Eskridge, 9
James William, 150
John Eskridge, 150
John H., 144
John Harrison, 142
Louisa, 151
Margaret, 81
Mary, 176
Mary Catharine, 142
Mary Jane, 81, 141, 142
Nathan, 141
Rebecca Dallas, 152
Rose, 176
Samuel, 184
Samuel Francis, 150
Sarah, 141
Sarah Elizabeth, 151
Semore, 141
Susannah, 141
Townsend, 118
William, 142
William H., 42
THORNTON
Alfred Dangerfield, 131
Ann, 131
Ann R., 58
Bushrod Washington Muse, 131
Cariann, 14
Cary Ann, 30
Charles, 200
Eliza, 55, 56
Emily, 201
Franklin, 55
James Douglas, 132
Lavina, 30
Maria, 58
Mary Ellen, 201
Nancy, 131

Philip, 82
Welby Debuts, 132
THROCKMORTON
Samuel, 40
THROGSMORTON
Catharine, 165
THYAR
Mary, 27
TILLETT
Jane, 72, 73
TIMBERS
Ann, 206, 207
Ann Maria, 60
Betsy, 33, 60
James William, 122, 207
Lydia Ellen, 207
Margaret, 60
Margaretta, 60
Maria, 59, 60
Mariah, 59
Matilda, 33
Rutha, 33, 59
Samuel Benjamin, 60
TIMMS
Jesse, 24
TRAMMELL
Joseph, 108
TRIPLETT
John, 192
TURLEY
Matilda, 38
TURNER
George H., 197
George Henry, 172
Margaret, 197

V

VALENTINE
Hamilton, 200
VANDEVANTER
Isaac, 111, 137, 138
John, 139
Mary, 26
VEALE
Elam H., 174
VENEY
Eliza Ann, 29

Loudoun County, Virginia Register of Free Negroes 1844-1861

Index

James Moten, 29
Joseph, 29
Maria, 29
Mary Bell, 29

W

WALKER
  Garret, 108
  Garrett, 120
  James, 200
  James M., 146, 147
  Nathan, 61
WALTMAN
  Emanuel, 207
WASHINGTON
  Augustus, 106
WATERS
  Eliza, 42
WATSON
  Emily, 201, 206
  Martha, 200
  Sally, 140
  William, 206
  William "Billy", 49
  Wilson, 206
WATT
  Duana, 2, 3, 4
  Duanna, 32, 86
WEADON
  Ashford, 118, 173
  John, 91
WEAVER
  Jonathan, 54
WENNER
  Jonathan, 5
WHEELER
  Anna, 11
  Hester, 78, 204
  Mary, 11, 78
WHITACRE
  Amos, 83
WHITE
  Thomas, 47
WHITING
  John Emanuel, 165
WILDMAN
  Charles B., 181
WILLIAMS
  Amanda, 2, 3
  Eliza, 13
  Francis Ann, 3
  Harriet, 94
  John, 99
  Kitty, 8
  William, 54, 165, 194, 209
WILT
  Catharine, 206, 207
WINE
  Jacob T., 173
WINTERS
  Andrew, 105
  Charles W., 126
  Charles William, 115
  Dennis, 56, 126
  Eliza, 41
  Emily, 115
  George, 57, 185
  George H., 126
  Grace, 41, 56
  Henry C., 120
  Hester, 24
  James, 118
  James E., 126
  Jane, 115
  John, 6, 45
  Mary, 126, 127
  Mary Ellen, 60, 68, 115
  Nancy, 64
  Samuel F., 127
  Sarah, 2, 127, 130
  Thomas, 81
  William, 2
WITTINGHAM
  Dilcey Ann, 136
  Mary Alice, 136
  Preccella Jane, 136
  Rodney, 136
WOOD
  Ann Maria, 68
  Sarah Ellen, 68
  Townsend, 68
WOODARD
  George, 153, 154
WORTHINGTON
  Joseph, 25
  Landon, 78
  Landon W., 10, 11
WRIGHT
  Alfred, 4, 200
  Amelia, 57
  Archibald, 32
  Betty, 4, 80
  Delila, 47
  Delilah, 53
  George Benjamin, 32
  Harriet, 31
  James Fenton, 80
  James William, 80
  Jane Eveline, 43
  Maria, 7
  Nancy, 32, 41, 43, 163
  Oscar, 57
  Rozannah, 41
  Sarah Francis, 53

Y

YOUNG
  Doctor Franklin, 24
  Henson, 94
  Leven Burr, 24
  Margaret, 23
  William, 22

Other Heritage Books by Patricia B. Duncan:

1850 Fairfax County and Loudoun County, Virginia Slave Schedule

1850 Fauquier County, Virginia Slave Schedule

1860 Loudoun County, Virginia Slave Schedule

Clarke County, Virginia Death Register, 1853-1896, with Birth Records, 1855-1856, Entered on Death Register

Clarke County, Virginia Marriages, 1836-1886

Clarke County, Virginia Marriages, 1887-1925

Clarke County, Virginia Will Book Abstracts: Books A-I (1836-1904) and 1A-3C (1841-1913)

Fairfax County, Virginia Birth Register, 1853-1879

Fairfax County, Virginia Birth Register, 1880-1896

Fauquier County, Virginia, Birth Register, 1853-1880

Fauquier County, Virginia, Birth Register, 1881-1896

Fauquier County, Virginia, Marriage Register, 1854-1882

Fauquier County, Virginia, Marriage Register, 1883-1906

Fauquier County, Virginia Death Register, 1853-1896

Hunterdon County, New Jersey 1895 State Census, Part I: Alexandria-Junction

Hunterdon County, New Jersey 1895 State Census, Part II: Kingwood-West Amwell

Genealogical Abstracts from The Lambertville Press, *Lambertville, New Jersey: 4 November 1858 (Vol. 1, Number 1) to 30 October 1861 (Vol. 3, Number 155)*

Genealogical Abstracts from The Democratic Mirror *and* The Mirror, *1857-1879, Loudoun County, Virginia*

Genealogical Abstracts from The Mirror, *1880-1890, Loudoun County, Virginia*

Genealogical Abstracts from The Mirror, *1891-1899, Loudoun County, Virginia*

Genealogical Abstracts from The Mirror, *1900-1919, Loudoun County, Virginia*

Genealogical Abstracts from The Telephone, *1881-1888, Loudoun County, Virginia*

Genealogical Abstracts from The Telephone, *1889-1896, Loudoun County, Virginia*

Jefferson County, [West] Virginia Death Register, 1853-1880

Jefferson County, West Virginia Death Register, 1881-1903

Jefferson County, Virginia 1802-1813 Personal Property Tax Lists

Jefferson County, Virginia 1814-1824 Personal Property Tax Lists

Jefferson County, Virginia 1825-1841 Personal Property Tax Lists

1810-1840 Loudoun County, Virginia Federal Population Census Index

1860 Loudoun County, Virginia Federal Population Census Index

1870 Loudoun County, Virginia Federal Population Census Index

Abstracts from Loudoun County, Virginia Guardian Accounts: Books A-H, 1759-1904

Abstracts of Loudoun County, Virginia Register of Free Negroes, 1844-1861

Index to Loudoun County, Virginia Land Deed Books A-Z, 1757-1800

Index to Loudoun County, Virginia Land Deed Books 2A-2M, 1800-1810

Index to Loudoun County, Virginia Land Deed Books 2N-2U, 1811-1817

Index to Loudoun County, Virginia Land Deed Books 2V-3D, 1817-1822

Index to Loudoun County, Virginia Land Deed Books 3E-3M, 1822-1826

Index to Loudoun County, Virginia Land Deed Books 3N-3V, 1826-1831

Index to Loudoun County, Virginia Land Deed Books 3W-4D, 1831-1835

Index to Loudoun County, Virginia Land Deed Books 4E-4N, 1835-1840

Index to Loudoun County, Virginia Land Deed Books 4O-4V, 1840-1846

Loudoun County, Virginia Birth Register, 1853-1879

Loudoun County, Virginia Birth Register, 1880-1896

Loudoun County, Virginia Clerks Probate Records Book 1 (1904-1921) and Book 2 (1922-1938)

(With Elizabeth R. Frain) *Loudoun County, Virginia Marriages after 1850, Volume 1, 1851-1880*

Loudoun County, Virginia Partially Proven Deeds

Loudoun County, Virginia 1800-1810 Personal Property Taxes

Loudoun County, Virginia 1826-1834 Personal Property Taxes

Loudoun County, Virginia Will Book Abstracts, Books A-Z, Dec. 1757-Jun. 1841

Loudoun County, Virginia Will Book Abstracts, Books 2A-3C, Jun. 1841-Dec. 1879 and Superior Court Books A and B, 1810-1888

Loudoun County, Virginia Will Book Index, 1757-1946

Genealogical Abstracts from The Brunswick Herald, *Brunswick, Maryland: Mar. 6 1891-Dec. 28 1894*

Genealogical Abstracts from The Brunswick Herald, *Brunswick, Maryland: Jan. 4 1895-Dec. 30 1898*

Genealogical Abstracts from The Brunswick Herald, *Brunswick, Maryland: Jan. 6 1899-Dec. 26 1902*

Genealogical Abstracts from The Brunswick Herald, *Brunswick, Maryland: Jan. 2 1903-June 29 1906*

Genealogical Abstracts from The Brunswick Herald, *Brunswick, Maryland: July 6 1906-Feb. 25 1910*

CD: *Loudoun County, Virginia Personal Property Tax List, 1782-1850*

www.ingramcontent.com/pod-product-compliance
Lightning Source LLC
Chambersburg PA
CBHW050140170426
43197CB00011B/1911